Democracy and Government in European Trade Unions

Democracy and Government in European Trade Unions

ANTHONY CAREW

London   George Allen & Unwin Ltd
Ruskin House   Museum Street

ISBN 0 04 331066 4 hardback
      0 04 331067 2 paperback

Composition in 10 point Times Roman type,
by Linocomp Ltd, Marcham, Oxon
Printed in Great Britain by
Biddles Ltd, Guildford, Surrey

*To W. J. Smith
former President of the Canadian Brotherhood
of Railway, Transport and General Workers
who first led me to see the real
meaning of trade union democracy*

Contents

Acknowledgements

The research for this book was largely financed by the European Educational Research Trust and was conducted at the University of Sussex Centre for Contemporary European Studies.

For their assistance in helping to arrange contacts with European trade unionists I am indebted to Hugh Scanlon, Ray Buckton, Jack Peel, Charles Ford, Günter Köpke, Jan Kulakowski, O. G. de Vries Reilingh, Brigitte Masquet and Sylvan Baeck.

The following union officials generously gave me their time in answering innumerable detailed questions: Jean Bieliaeff, Jean Trioux, Francis Beuzet, Roger Briesche, Louis Bodin, Antoine Barbero, Enzo Pontarollo, Jean Chenoy, Frank Goethals, Pierre Potums, Louis Melis, Gérard Heiremans, Clem Pauwels, Willy Thys, Henk Vos, Bert van Hattem, Tom Wennekes, S. H. Schroer, C. Smit, Clive Iddon, Wolfgang Stender, the late Fritz Opel, Steffen Møller, E. Sørensen, Erik Karlsson, Bengt Bergstrom, Erik Berglund, Ivan Lind, Sigurd Kvilikval, Henry Wold and Harry O. Hanson.

Various drafts of the book were read by Victor Rabinovitch, Walter Kendall, Ian Bullock, Richard Fletcher, Jonathan Williams, David Edelstein and Stephen Yeo, and many of their valuable comments have been incorporated into the text. Successive drafts have been typed by Peggy Painc and Pat Cripps. However, final responsibility for the views expressed and any factual errors in the text is mine alone.

Abbreviations

International Organisations

ETUC European Trade Union Confederation
IMF International Metalworkers' Federation
ITGLWF International Textile, Garment and Leather Workers' Federation

Britain

ASLEF Associated Society of Locomotive Engineers and Firemen
AUEW Amalgamated Union of Engineering Workers
CIR Commission on Industrial Relations
GMWU General and Municipal Workers' Union
NUBSO National Union of Boot and Shoe Operatives
NUDB National Union of Dyers and Bleachers
NUHKW National Union of Hosiery and Knitwear Workers
NUM National Union of Mineworkers
NUR National Union of Railwaymen
NUTGW National Union of Tailors and Garment Workers
TASSA Transport and Salaried Staffs Association
T&GWU Transport and General Workers' Union
TUC Trades Union Congress
USDAW Union of Shop, Distributive and Allied Workers

France

CGT Confédération Générale du Travail
CFDT Confédération Française Démocratique du Travail
CGT–FO Confédération Générale du Travail-Force Ouvrière

Italy

CGIL Confederazione Generale Italiana del Lavoro
CISL Confederazione Italiana dei Sindacati Lavoratori
UIL Unione Italiana del Lavoro

Belgium

FGTB Fédération Générale du Travail de Belgique
CSC Confédération des Syndicats Chrétiens
CGSLB Centrale Générale des Syndicats Libéraux de Belgique

Holland

NVV Nederlands Verbond van Vakverenigingen
NKV Nederlands Katholiek Vakverbond
CNV Christelijk Nationaal Vakverbond in Nederland

Germany
- DGB   Deutscher Gewerkschaftsbund
- DAG   Deutsche Angestellten Gewerkschaft
- DBB   Deutsche Beamtenbund

Denmark
- LO   Landsorganisationen i Danmark

Sweden
- SAF   Svenska Arbetsgivaresöreningen
- LO   Landsorganisationen i Sverige
- TCO   Tjanstemannens Centralorganisation
- SACO   Sveriges Akadamers Centralorganisation

Norway
- LO   Landsorganisasjonen i Norge

1

Introduction

This book has two aims: first to describe trade union structure and government in Europe, and second to examine internal democracy in European unions. Hopefully this information will help fill a gap in our understanding of how continental unions work, and at the same time provide a yardstick with which students and practitioners of industrial relations can compare systems in other countries. The idea for the book arose out of a number of talks on contemporary European trade unionism given to shop steward groups in different parts of the country, and also from a series of seminars involving British trade unionists at all levels of the movement organised by the Centre for Contemporary European Studies and held in Brussels during 1972 and 1973. In the course of these it became apparent that there was a need for a text that attempted to describe the internal government of European unions. The information was collected from union rule books, questionnaires sent to different unions, and by visits to the various headquarters, in the course of which detailed discussions were held with national officials.

The intention has been to approach the question of union government from a practical standpoint, dealing with basic questions of organisation and administration, with particular reference to the way they affect ordinary union members. This should be of assistance to active trade unionists and to students of the labour movement who wish to discover how the workings of these organisations really affect their members.

The international dimension of trade unionism has taken on a new significance in the wake of the growth of multi-national companies and the rising importance of international economic blocs such as the EEC. Socialist, communist and Christian trade union groups are now coming closer together than they have been for a generation. These developments make it that much more urgent to introduce trade unionists to the particular characteristics and styles of operation of different union organisations. The growth of international union co-ordinating bodies has forced union officials to make contacts abroad, often with people whose existence they were unaware of until recently. But a clear understanding of how their counterpart organisations work still escapes many union officials, while the rank and file members are almost completely in the dark.

The existing literature on the European labour movement contains many gaps. Some of the more authoritative post-war surveys of national labour movements are now very dated, especially in view of the widespread changes that have taken place in the field of industrial relations since the late 1960s. In any event descriptions of national labour movements often do not go beyond an outline of the characteristics of the central confederation. And while it is true that in a number of European countries the central union body plays a more prominent part in day-to-day industrial relations than, say, the British TUC or the American Federation of Labour (AFL-CIO), it is nevertheless a fact that most union members see themselves first and foremost as members of a particular national union, or even of a local workshop group, rather than of the central confederation to which their union affiliates.

There are a number of other areas where existing knowledge badly needs supplementing. Not only do we need to know more about trade unionism in individual countries, but that aspect of trade unionism that gives continental unions in general their specifically 'European' flavour also requires detailed examination.[1] Labour movements are the products of the particular historical, political and cultural experiences that operate in given national contexts, but they are also influenced by factors that cut across national boundaries. Wartime experience of foreign occupation had a great effect on trade unionism in most of the countries examined. Cold-war politics have deeply influenced the nature of trade unionism in France and Italy. Religious influences have left their mark on unions in several countries. And while language differences have separated some national movements from one another, similarities in this area have led to a certain amount of cross-fertilisation in the case of Scandinavian unions, French and Belgian unions, and the labour movements of Germany and Holland as well as Germany and Austria. In this sense the European labour movement cannot be seen as simply an aggregation of national labour movements.[2] The international dimension must also be taken into account. And it is perhaps as well to observe that the influences linking the British and North American movements have been stronger than the ties between British and continental unions. In this study we will be trying to identify specifically 'European' characteristics in the internal government of unions as well as features that are peculiar to particular countries or industries.

Another aspect that requires examination is the international labour movement in its institutionalised form. Apart from the world-wide union federations, the International Confederation of Free Trade Unions (ICFTU) and the communist-controlled World Federation of Trade Unions (WFTU), international union co-operation has recently manifested itself in Europe in the European Trade Union Confederation (ETUC) and the various semi-autonomous trade groups operating under its umbrella. More important still, international trade union secretariats for particular industries are now beginning serious-ly to co-ordinate the collective bargaining activities of workers in multi-national companies throughout the world. The ordinary union member's awareness of, or interest in, the international trade union movement itself is still quite limited, especially in the case of bodies such as the ETUC which groups together the various national TUCs. The international lobbying function for which the ETUC is best fitted is some way removed from the daily interests of most trade unionists. On the other hand, the development of international trade secretariats such as the International Metalworkers' Federation and the International Textile, Garment and Leather Workers' Federation, re-presents an attempt to establish a countervailing force to multi-national companies at the level where decisions affecting employment conditions are actually made and can be negotiated. More than any other international union bodies, these secretariats tend to operate on a plane directly relevant to the needs of ordinary trade unionists, and their importance will almost certainly grow in the coming years.

The intention here is not to study international developments as such, nor to present a series of monographs on national labour movements. It is within particular industries that international trade unionism begins to have direct meaning for union members at the grass roots level. This suggests that it would be helpful to conduct our analysis of trade unionism on an industry by industry basis, so that union members of organisations which are forced more and more to establish international contacts will have some understand-ing of their counterpart unions in different countries. An additional reason for an industrial comparison is the fact that unions in the same industry tend to have more in common with one another, despite their location in different countries, than with unions from different industries within the same country. It is remarkable how a particular 'style' of union is found throughout Europe in unions with similar jurisdictions. Historical, technological, social and economic factors related to the development of an industry often operate in a similar manner in different countries and help condition the unions in that industry.

This is evident in the organisations dealt with in this study – metal-

working, railway and textile unions. Textile trade unions are often among the oldest unions in a country, reflecting the importance of the industry in the early stages of the Industrial Revolution. Members tend to be concentrated in older industrial towns which have been bypassed by recent industrial developments. A tendency towards conservatism among members is a product not only of the contraction of the industry but also of the fact that members are often ex-agricultural workers, in many cases women, and in some countries where confessional unionism exists, more likely to be under the influence of the Church. Metalworking unions, on the other hand, tend to be the largest and most radical organisations throughout Europe. Continuing technological change and the attendant disruption of working conditions have combined to place metalworkers in the van of the class struggle. The industry is also sufficiently diverse that as older sectors such as shipbuilding decline in importance, they are replaced in the front line of the industrial battlefield by new sectors based on the latest technology.[3] By contrast, a common characteristic of railway trade unionists in many European countries is the fact that they are civil servants. In some cases full collective bargaining rights have been won only recently, and some railway workers are still prevented from taking industrial action. The combination of these factors has frequently bred a conservative, bureaucratic form of trade unionism.

In most countries these industries account for three of the largest union groups and therefore embrace a substantial section of the labour movement. The differences between them referred to above enable us to look at unions in a variety of environmental settings – in large- and small-scale enterprises, technologically advanced and traditional sectors, expanding and declining areas, and privately owned as well as nationalised industries.

While no attempt is made to cover all aspects of union government, this study deals with a number of key features which help to convey the 'tone' of unionism in particular organisations. Among the questions considered are: the overall structure of the labour movement; the relationship of individual unions to the national confederation or TUC; the financial structure of the movement; the relationship between rival union confederations in cases where dual unionism exists; and political and religious affiliations of the unions. In terms of the actual government of individual unions, particular attention is paid to the working of the legislative process (conference); the role of union executives and general councils; and the position of full-time union officials. We also examine the nature of union representation at the crucial plant level, as well as the element of democracy in the collective bargaining process.

To some extent the study is concerned with the question of efficiency in union administration. But, of course, descriptions of how unions are administered inevitably invite discussion of the practice of internal union democracy. Our approach to this subject is that the fullest development of union democracy is necessary if members are to be adequately represented. But more than that, union democracy is a vitally important dimension of democracy in society as a whole. Countries whose trade unions are not fully self-governing can never be healthy democracies. Internal union democracy requires unions to be under the complete control of the members, in the most direct way possible. It involves active participation by the rank and file in all aspects of union life; membership control of the legislative, executive and judicial functions; total freedom of access to information and freedom of communication within the organisation; and leaders regularly elected and immediately accountable to the members. It does not mean unions acting 'responsibly' according to establishment values while being unresponsive to the wishes of the rank and file. And it is not compatible with elitist leaders imposing their views on a quiescent and cowed membership.

The question of union democracy has been the subject of numerous academic studies, and various attempts have been made to devise general theories of union democracy. The starting point for all these is the problem for democracy posed by large-scale organisation. Strongly influenced by the work of Robert Michels,[4] many writers have pointed to an inevitable tendency towards oligarchy, or government by a small number of people, in unions. Michels' 'Iron Law of Oligarchy' has led a number of writers to construct theories of union democracy which concentrate on institutional aspects of the electoral process. Best known of these is S. M. Lipset's work[5] which concludes that, as in parliamentary government, the existence of an institutionalised opposition is the essential condition for the existence of democracy in trade unions. Lipset's theory is based on his analysis of the American International Typographical Union (ITU) with its unique two-party system of government, and the implication of his argument is that the ITU is probably the only democratic union in the world. That is certainly not the case. The right to organise opposition to union leaders is fundamental for union democracy,[6] but this need not involve an institutionalised party system, and various other writers have pointed, quite rightly, to the inappropriateness of the parliamentary analogy in discussions of trade union government. As John Hughes says,

'trade union government involves an electoral situation and underlying social relations simpler than, and in some way, significantly different from, those of our political democracy. This can be seen in the continuing and active "direct" democratic participation of members (not confined to representatives) or in the greater scope in a trade union for the existence of, or emergence of, a common interest.'[7]

Lipset's preoccupation with the electoral process is echoed, though in a more acceptable and refined form, by David Edelstein whose theory of union democracy stresses the importance not only of union members having a formal right to oppose the leadership, but of their actually exercising that right.[8] And with a different emphasis Roderick Martin has argued that the toleration of factions by union leaders is a sufficient condition for democracy.[9]

In contrast to this general line of argument, other writers have played down the importance of institutional safeguards for democracy. V. L. Allen argued that so long as the closed shop is absent and trade unionists possess the ultimate sanction of being able to 'vote with their feet' and terminate their membership of a union, then a sufficient degree of democracy is assured.[10] The related idea that dual unionism can be an important factor in union democracy has been suggested by Walter Galenson.[11] However, Allen is not so much concerned with the practice of internal democracy as with the need for unions to succeed in their primary aim of adequately representing their members in external dealings with employers and governments. This argument is taken further by the French writer, Sabine Erbes-Seguin, whose analysis of union democracy completely ignores all institutional aspects of formal democracy and seeks to relate the level of democracy in an organisation to the consciousness of its active members as expressed in their aims and actions.[12] This disregard for formal democratic structures is unfortunate since an important dimension of democracy is surely the educational process that the system entails. Trade unions must be seen as important training grounds for democrats. However, at the same time, the process of union government ought not to be treated as something separate and apart from the organisation's outside activities. Indeed, in their attempt to grapple with the problem of union democracy, the Welsh miners associated with 'The Miners' Next Step' were very conscious of the close relationship between union structure and union policy,[13] and G. D. H. Cole's analysis of trade unionism in *The World of Labour* saw the question of internal democracy in very practical terms of how strikes and wage demands could best be directed.[14] This suggests that any analysis of the process of internal government should extend to, or be tested against, an appraisal of how unions approach the problem of collective bargaining.

Internal union democracy has many sides and the various attempts to sum it up in terms of a single key factor are not adequate, though each approach helps to shed light on a different facet of the problem. Perhaps the best way of viewing the question is in terms of the analysis developed by Beatrice and Sydney Webb in their classic study of trade union government, *Industrial Democracy*.[15] A number of the above approaches, especially those emphasising the element of parliamentarism, conceive of democracy as a system in which members play a passive role, only occasionally being called on to approve the actions taken by the leaders. But as the Webbs demonstrated, an earlier and much more vital concept of democracy in trade unionism based itself on the active participation of the membership at large. As the size of organisations grew and made the practice of 'primitive democracy' impossible, a variety of devices such as the referendum, the rotation of office and mass meetings were introduced to retain as much power for the rank and file as possible. Large sections of the labour movement preferred the 'delegate' mandated by the base rather than the 'representative' with full freedom to speak for all, as a way of accommodating the need for indirect government. And as the above quotation from Hughes suggests, the idea of delegatory democracy has always remained strong in the trade union movement. In general, British rank and file trade unionists have desired to venture as little away from direct democracy as possible, in spite of strong trends in the opposite direction in practice.

It is against this background of the traditional commitment to 'active democracy' that the discussion of union government needs to be conducted. Over the years trade unionists have developed a variety of institutional practices designed to counteract the tendency to oligarchic rule, and where formal structures have failed to guarantee democracy, informal practices have been used with considerable effect to ensure that rank and file members maintained some control over their own destiny. Thus parallel trade unionism in the form of unofficial shop steward organisation and unofficial strike action has been resorted to at times when inflexible and unresponsive formal systems of government have failed to achieve what the members wanted.[16] To Michels' 'Iron Law of Oligarchy' J. A. Banks has counterposed the idea of an Iron Law of Democracy operating through a variety of formal and informal channels.[17]

It would certainly seem to be more realistic to regard union democracy as a range of possible positions on a spectrum, with different unions achieving different levels of internal democracy. Full oligarchic control only exists at one extreme, and in most unions the power of leadership is balanced to a greater or lesser extent by the power of different groups of members. The problem of union size is not insurmountable : systems of internal representation can be, and have been, used to facilitate greater participation by the membership. The question of office-holding and the electoral process is important, but consideration of democracy must go beyond this and look at the decision-making process, the safeguards for members' individual and collective rights, and checks on authority generally. Moreover, the emphasis must not simply be on whether members have the right to ratify leadership actions but on whether conditions are such that their participation is actively encouraged. In this respect questions such as the control of communications, the adequate dissemination of information, and the right of groups of members in different sections of the union to forge direct contacts with one another, are important. Beyond this, aspects of informal democracy have to be taken into account, especially the role of shop stewards at workshop level in areas not governed by formal procedures. And finally, it is necessary to look at external union activities, particularly collective bargaining, and to treat it not simply as a means by which members obtain economic gains, but as a process requiring democratic participation by the rank and file and through which trade unionists are able to encroach on areas traditionally regarded as the managerial preserve.

A comprehensive analysis of all these elements and their complex interrelationship is beyond the scope of this book. However, in describing the structure of the various union movements, we will consider some factors that are of basic importance for internal democracy: the working of union conferences; the operation of the on-going executive decision-making function; and the hierarchy of full-time union officials, with particular reference to their status and accountability to the membership. No overall measure of democracy is possible, and none is attempted here. But by adding to the above factors a description of how workers are represented at the plant level, and how the decision-making process works in connection with collective bargaining, it should be possible to obtain a 'feel' for the type of trade unionism that is practised in various countries. And it should be possible to convey a reasonable first impression of whether or not a particular union structure is likely to be responsive to membership demands.

In the final analysis formal institutions cannot guarantee the existence of democracy: the deciding factor will be the attitude of the membership. As Edelstein puts it, 'Union democracy can be achieved only through the continuous, self-conscious struggles of numerous union members'.[18] However, even members with a highly developed consciousness will be constantly handicapped by any system in which elementary formal democracy is absent, and therefore this study starts from the position that the existence of formal democratic institutions is a necessary precondition for the attainment of full democracy.

In dealing with the different aspects of union government the approach adopted has been to treat issues thematically so that cross comparisons can more readily be made. There are separate chapters on workshop organisation, union conference, union executives, fulltime officials and collective bargaining. Those wishing to follow the situation in particular unions, industries or countries can read across chapters. By way of setting the scene for this approach Chapter 2 provides a brief general background to the labour movement in each country, with a number of facts and figures about the specific unions under review. This may be treated as a reference chapter in the course of reading through later sections.

2

The European Labour Movement In General:
Some Facts and Figures

This chapter provides a general outline of the structure and orientation of the labour movement in each of the countries studied. It briefly describes the environment in which the individual metalworking, textile and railway unions have to operate, and the way they relate to the central union confederations, the equivalents of the British Trades Union Congress. Certain basic facts about these unions are also recorded, including their membership size, composition, division by industrial sub-sectors and geographical area, and their financial structure, with special reference to the amounts raised from dues contributions and their distribution among different levels of the union hierarchy. All of this is a necessary background to the discussion of union government and democracy which follows.

FRANCE

BACKGROUND

The French trade union movement is divided on religious and political lines. A Christion union body has existed since 1919, and there have been separate communist and non-communist organisations since the early 1920s, except for three years after 1936 and a brief period from 1945–7. Of the three main groupings, the CGT (Confédération Générale du Travail) is predominantly communist, though with a substantial admixture of socialists. The CGT-FO (Force Ouvrière) is a smaller body which broke away from the CGT in the late 1940s and has a social democratic orientation. And the CFDT (Confédération Française Démocratique du Travail) was originally a Catholic trade union organisation which severed its ties with the Church in 1964 and has increasingly adopted radical socialist policies. In addition to these three confederations there are separate union groupings for supervisory staffs, teachers and those Christian trade unionists who refused to accept the deconfessionalisation of the CFDT.

While political influences are strong in the French labour movement, there are no official organic links between the unions and the various political parties. The CGT is effectively under the control of the Communist Party, even though its rules preserve the myth of independence from all outside bodies. On the other hand the CFDT, which has avoided any involvement in the socialist–communist 'common programme' of the left in recent years, began to establish a closer working relationship with the Socialist Party in the latter part of 1974, and this is potentially one of the most significant developments for the labour movement in the post-war period. In recent years the CFDT has shown itself to be rather more militant than the CGT which, for all its revolutionary rhetoric, is more prepared to adapt itself to the present economic system. Since the mid-1960s the CGT and CFDT have developed a close working relationship. However, relations between these two and FO are frequently hostile, the former regarding FO as being too close to the employers.[1]

MEMBERSHIP

Published membership figures are notoriously unreliable and are sometimes inflated by up to 100 per cent. The divisions in the movement have lessened the attraction of trade union membership for French workers, combined union membership now being considerably less than it was in 1946 when the movement was united. In all probability the largest confederation, CGT, does not have more than 1·5 million members. The CFDT is now the second largest body with some 600,000–700,000 members, and FO probably has no more than 500,000 members. Altogether fewer than 25 per cent of French workers are organised. The CGT's strength tends to be in the basic industries with the heaviest concentration of members in the Paris region and Marseilles in the south. The CFDT's traditional membership base has been in older, declining industries such as mining, textiles and also among white collar workers. But in recent years it has grown strongly in the newer process industries and probably has a greater percentage of its members in these than does the CGT. In fact the CFDT's overall growth in recent years has been quite rapid with membership strongholds in Alsace, the north, and around Lyon and Grenoble.

STRUCTURE

The structure of the various union groupings is similar. Members are organised within the confederations on industrial and geographical lines. Local unions or branches in the same industry group themselves into national federations – one for metalworking, one for textiles, and so on. These are the equivalent of national unions in Britain. At the same time all local branches within a geographical area, of whatever industry, affiliate to the district sub-sections (*unions départmentales*) of the central confederation. The confederal sub-sections are based on France's ninety departments or on the country's larger economic regions. These organisations correspond broadly with the federations of labour found in the North American labour movement and the trades councils of Britain. However, they tend to be relatively more important than their American or British counterparts since they may assume bargaining and administrative functions on behalf of local union branches in cases where these are not strong enough to operate independently. And since the full-time officials of the confederations' district sections are often the appointees of the confederal leadership, this provides the latter with an important channel of influence at lower levels of the movement.

The number of industrial federations differs from confederation to confederation. The CGT has 42, FO has 32 and the CFDT has 29. For the most part the industrial federations are free from confederal interference and are responsible for their own policies, especially in matters of collective bargaining. However, they themselves are not directly represented at the confederation conferences held every three years. These conferences draw their delegations directly from the local union branches. In the CGT each local union with over 1,000 members can be represented at the confederal conference. But the relative infrequency of these gatherings means that detailed policy-decisions are taken elsewhere by bodies not elected at conference. A national committee comprising the general secretaries of the federations and of the confederation's district sections meets twice a year, and this body in turn appoints a smaller administrative committee meeting monthly to oversee the work of the leadership. This indirect system of control leaves power effectively centralised in the hands of the dozen or more full-time secretaries who man the national office (Bureau Conféderal) and are in charge of the day-to-day running of the organisation. FO's structure is basically the same, though the existence of different tendencies within the leadership makes it a far less monolithic body than the CGT. However, in the CFDT recent structural changes allow confederal conferences to influence the execution of policy as well as its formulation since conference now elects one-half of the members of the 44-man body which meets every two months to supervise the leadership.[2]

Although national federations are, theoretically, autonomous, the political orientation of French trade unions and the underdeveloped state of collective bargaining tends to increase the relative power of the confederations. In the CGT in particular the operation of political factionalism means that in practice there is less local autonomy than the federal structure implies, the French Communist Party being in a position to control the general line of policy. In any event, in the post-war years the CGT has become more unified and less of a loose federation, with voting systems that once favoured smaller federations against the large now abandoned. In the CFDT too the introduction in the 'sixties of a central strike fund has increased the confederation's influence among affiliates. In addition the fact that in both the CGT and CFDT most of the industrial federations have their headquarters in the confederation's head office building tends to increase their reliance on the services of the parent body, and some weaker federations depend on the confederations for direct financial support. On the other hand, a small number of industrial federations are big enough to be relatively independent, and this applies particularly to the metalworking unions of the CFDT and CGT and also the latter's railway union. As between the union base and the national federation leadership power is, in theory, extremely decentralised: discipline is loose and the absence of a strong pattern of national collective bargaining has encouraged decentralisation. But in practice the weakness of many local unions enhances the relative influence of national bodies. And the frequent lack of any strong, formal organisation at lower levels within which the democratic process can operate means that democracy sometimes goes by default, with decisions left to the higher levels.

METALWORKING

The metalworking sector includes engineering, car manufacturing, shipbuilding and iron and steel production. Altogether there are over 2·8 million workers, with car manufacturing and electrical engineering accounting for approximately 1 million of them. By far the most important metalworking area is the Paris region with one-quarter of the sector's labour force. Most workers are employed in medium-

and small-scale plants of less than 500 workers. About thirty firms employ more than 10,000 workers and approximately forty employ 5,000 or more.

The CGT metalworking union (Fédération des Travailleurs de la Métallurgie) claims 415,000 members, some 15 per cent of the organisable work force. The membership of the CFDT metalworking union (Fédération Générale de la Métallurgie) is around 125,000, and the FO union probably has less than 100,000 members. In both the CGT and CFDT the metalworking unions are the largest organisations in the confederation. No distinction is made between tradesmen and unskilled workers; there are no accurate figures for male and female membership; and the unions do not maintain separate sections for the different industrial groupings within metalworking, though there are separate sections for technicians.

TEXTILES

The textile industry is the third largest employer of labour in France after the car and construction industries. The main concentration of textile workers is in the north, particularly Lille and Roubaix-Tourcoing, and in the south-east around Lyon. Unionisation is very weak and wages and conditions tend to be poor. The CGT textile union (Fédération des Travailleurs du Textile et des Industries Rattachées) claims to have 60,000 members out of a work force of approximately 400,000. Just over 50 per cent of the members are women. There are no accurate figures for union membership in particular regions or sectors, though approximately 25 per cent of the union's membership is in the knitwear and hosiery industry and some 9,000 members work in the synthetic fibre sector, the best organised part of the textile industry with around 30 per cent union membership.

The CFDT union in textiles (Fédération des Industries de l'Habillement, du Cuir et du Textile) also organises clothing and leather workers, groups which in the CGT have their own union. In all three sectors it has a total membership of only 60,000 and the largest group is to be found in clothing. The clothing industry employs a higher percentage of women than the other two sectors, and the union's female membership represents two-thirds of the total. The CFDT is a lot closer in strength to the CGT in these sectors and may well be the stronger party in some areas. Indeed since the early 1950s textiles has been the one basic industry in which the CGT is not clearly dominant. While the CGT union shows signs of being an enfeebled organisation, the CFDT textile union, under its present general secretary, Roger Toutain, has come to be seen as one of the more militant CFDT affiliates.

RAILWAYS

The nationalised railway industry is one of the best organised in France, and the union members have traditionally been regarded as being among the most militant. The CGT railway union (Fédération Nationale des Travailleurs des Chemins de Fer Français) is among the most powerful organisations within the confederation and is the union of Georges Seguy, the current general secretary of the CGT. The organisation claims a total membership of 205,000 of whom 100,000, it is admitted, are retired railway workers. The inclusion of large numbers of pensioners in membership totals is not an uncommon practice in a number of European unions. The 105,000 employed members constitute some 35 per cent of the railway work force, a high rate of unionisation by French standards. The CFDT rail union (Fédération des Cheminots) is much weaker with a total membership of 40,000, of whom 15,000 are retired. Among the union's members the vast majority are recruited from among white collar and administrative workers, only one-third of them being manual employees.

FINANCE[3]

French trade unionists are renowned for their unwillingness to pay full dues. In the CGT the average member is reckoned to pay dues for only seven or eight months a year. The CFDT unions claim that on average contributions are paid in nine or ten out of every twelve months. In general, those who are in arrears are not expelled, and it is difficult to discover at what point the unions cease to claim the allegiance of someone who has lapsed. This is one reason why official membership figures are so unreliable. The non-payment of a portion of union dues is accepted as normal, and in the CGT metalworkers' union it is officially recognised inasmuch as the rule book stipulates that a branch's voting strength at conference is based on the total number of monthly contributions paid in the previous year divided by ten. In other words, a person who only misses paying two months' contributions in a year is effectively regarded as a fully paid-up member.

There is no uniform level of dues; each local branch or plant section is entitled to fix its own amount, contributions being collected chiefly at the plant. The CGT recommends a monthly contribution of approximately £1 with 14p set aside for the use of the plant section,

18p going to the national union, the district body of the CGT itself receiving 17p, and the balance, some 51p, remaining with the branch. The CGT metalworkers' union monthly dues range between 36p and £1·38 depending on the branch, but the amounts are usually in the lower range of the scale. The CGT textile union dues range from 55p to 65p per month, and this is also about the average for the CGT railway union, though better paid members such as train drivers will pay up to 92p.

The CFDT metalworking union's average dues amount to 92p per month. Half of it is kept at the local level, and the balance is divided evenly between the national union and the confederation, part of the latter share going to the confederal strike fund. In the CFDT railway union dues are higher than most and in 1974 the average level was £1·27 per month.

The relatively low level of some dues and the tendency for members to withhold a substantial proportion often leaves the unions in a difficult financial situation and forces them to rely to some extent on outside help. National unions have to count on voluntary donations from branches, but more important in the post-war years they have come to depend on money received in the form of government grants in aid of training and research. For example, in the CFDT textile union income from dues in 1971 only amounted to 70 per cent of total income, and two-thirds of the balance was made up of government subventions.

ITALY

BACKGROUND

Trade unions in Italy have long been regarded as instrumental creations of political or religious groups. Before the end of the First World War there was a Christian confederation competing with the non-confessional unions. And apart from a brief period of unity in the early post-Second World War years, the movement has been split in three directions. The largest confederation, CGIL (Confederazione Generale Italiana del Lavoro), is basically a communist organisation with a minority of Nenni socialist members. CISL (Confederazione Italiana dei Sindacati Lavoratori) draws its membership primarily from among Christian democrats, and UIL (Unione Italiana del Lavoro) is an alliance of trade unionists with republican and social democratic sympathies.

MEMBERSHIP

Accurate membership figures do not exist, but totals of 1·7 million for CGIL, 1·2 million for CISL and under 400,000 for UIL would seem to be not unrealistic. The agrarian background of large numbers of the Italian labour force has an important bearing on trade unionism and it has been suggested, for example, that more than one-quarter of CISL's membership may be made up of sharecroppers and pensioners.[4] And in the past CGIL has been known to include the families of its members in its total membership figures.

For much of the post-war period the Italian unions were among the most centralised in Western Europe. After the war the bureaucratic, state-controlled unions established by Mussolini were not dismantled but merely taken over by the free unions. The national industrial and local unions only came afterwards and were the artificial creation of the confederations rather than the product of spontaneous growth at the base. The confederations faced the problem of having to organise a mass of ex-agricultural workers with little working-class tradition or particular industrial experience, and general recruitment into broad-based confederations rather than industrial unions was found to be the most suitable method.

The structure of Italian unionism now resembles that of France with members organised on industrial and geographical lines. CGIL has 38 industrial unions, UIL has 48, and CISL has 28 constituent groups. But the geographical organisation of all members of whatever industry within a province tends to be even more important than it is in France, since the industrial unions are generally much weaker than their French counterparts. Typically these provincial units of the confederations, or chambers of labour (*camera del lavaro*), tend to be highly political bodies, their interest in detailed industrial questions being secondary. Officials of the chambers are, as in France, often appointees of the confederation leadership, and perhaps indirectly of a political party. Their job often more closely approximates that of a political organiser than an industrial negotiator, and they are likely to be the leading trade union figure in the district where they operate. At the confederation conferences the industrial unions command two-thirds of the votes compared with the one-third controlled by the provincial chambers. But with few exceptions real power lies with the confederations and their provincial sectors rather than the industrial unions. Only a few of the latter are self-financing, and it is usually the confederation that subsidises them rather than the reverse as is the case in many labour movements. Again at the local level only the strongest industrial unions such as the metalworkers have their own separate branches, and local level organisation and administration is often undertaken on their behalf by the chambers of labour.

Since the late 1960s Italian trade unionism has begun to change radically with important structural alterations following proposals for organic unity between the three confederations. As a first step the confederations have had to loosen their ties with political parties, and union officials have been required to give up political offices. The confederations have moved tentatively towards merger, and in April 1974 the first general assembly of the three confederations was held. But progress has been uneven. The impetus for unification has come from the base, and it is at this level that the trend is most pronounced. At higher levels there is less enthusiasm for the merger, and at the national level in metalworking, where the unions are in the process of forming one organisation, the leadership is still shared by three relatively distinct groups.

METALWORKING

The unified metalworkers' union, FLM (Federazione Lavoratori Metalmeccanici) from which most of our examples will be taken, was created following a decision of the three main metal unions in July 1971. This set the pattern for other mergers which are now in various stages of completion. The union has a unified headquarters operation although the three original unions still manage their own finances, and power at the top is shared by the three former general secretaries. As yet there is no common rulebook. The merger of the three metalworking unions has given a tremendous boost to union recruiting, Italian workers no longer regarding the unions quite so much as the instrumental tools of political parties. Whereas in the early 1960s no more than 40 per cent of the metalworkers were organised, 60–70 per cent are now in the union and as many as 250,000 new members are estimated to have been recruited since the late 1960s. Of the 900,000 or so FLM members, 290,000 are from the former CISL union, 116,000 from the UIL metalworkers, and the CGIL has contributed just under 500,000. There are no figures for membership of the different sectors of metalworking or for female membership. Five out of six of the members are located in the north of Italy, mainly in the iron triangle of Milan, Turin and Genoa.

FINANCE

The system of dues payment in Italy resembles that of France with the provincial level setting its own rates. The overall level also tends to be low. In the unified metalworkers' union the average total dues are of the order of 56p per month. As in France the aim is to have all members pay a standard 1 per cent of monthly wages, but in metalworking, textiles and railways the present level stands at about 0·5 or 0·6 per cent of the wage rate. The division of dues leaves the bulk of the spending power with the provincial organisation of the national union. In most unions 60–80 per cent of total dues are retained at this level. The national union usually receives about 10 per cent or so of the dues, with a further 10–20 per cent being paid to the particular confederation involved.

In the past Italian unions have also experienced financial difficulties as a result of a widespread non-payment of dues. In a 1956 survey it was estimated that only about 40 per cent of dues owing was actually paid, and none of the unions was really self-financing.[5] In the early post-war years at least, all three confederations received substantial amounts of money either from Russia or the CIA.[6] They have also received state subsidies for vocational training and government grants for social welfare services operated by the unions. However, the difficulties connected with the collection of dues have been reduced with the growing use of the check-off since the early 1960s, and a majority of members now pay by this method.

BELGIUM

BACKGROUND

As in France and Italy, trade unions in Belgium are organised on political and religious lines. The FGTB (Fédération Générale du Travail de Belgique) is a socialist organisation which originated as a trade union committee of the Socialist Party, but which, since 1945, has had no formal links with the party at national level. Neither the FGTB nor its constituent unions affiliate to the party, and the combination of political office with an official position in the confederation is not permitted, though officers of FGTB affiliates often combine two jobs in this way. At the regional level trade union groups can belong to joint action committees made up of co-operative and socialist bodies and through these the unions help to finance political activities. The CSC (Confédération des Syndicats Chrétiens) is a Catholic organisation without any formal political ties.

The political and religious divisions in the labour movement are reinforced by regional and language differences. The Catholics are mainly to be found in the west and north where Flemish is spoken, while the socialist stronghold is in the French-speaking area of

Wallonia in the south. Of course the language and regional differences also occur within each confederation and this creates particular problems such as the need to issue all publications in two languages and to balance the leadership with representatives of the two communities. The post-war decline of staple industries in the south, such as mining, and the growth of newer industries in Flanders has been largely responsible for the more rapid growth of the CSC than the FGTB in the past decade or so.

MEMBERSHIP

Membership is more or less evenly divided between these two confederations, the CSC having just over 1 million members and the FGTB slightly less than 900,000. Apart from the two major confederations there is a third, relatively unimportant, body, the CGSLB (Centrale Générale des Syndicats Libéraux de Belgique), affiliated to the Liberal Party with little more than 100,000 members. With some 65 per cent of the labour force organised, Belgium has one of the strongest trade union movements in Europe. Part of the reason for the high rate of unionisation is the fact that the unions act as official agencies for the distribution of social welfare benefits, and at times union membership has actually increased during spells of high unemployment because of this.

STRUCTURE

The Belgian union confederations organise their members on both industrial and geographical lines, though in this system the industrial unions have more influence in the confederations than is the case in either France or Italy. The FGTB has 13 national unions and the CSC has 17. In both confederations there is one national union for white collar workers so that the industrial unions are made up almost entirely of blue collar workers. At the base the individual unions have plant branches which are grouped together at an intermediate stage in regional bodies. In turn these regional groupings of the national unions are affiliated to the regional organisation of the particular confederation. But whereas in France, and more especially in Italy, the regional unit of the confederation often plays an important part in collective bargaining, the Belgian unions are mostly strong enough to manage their own industrial affairs, and the regional confederal body usually confines its activities to routine administration. Nevertheless, in view of the linguistic/regional divisions in the country, the regional level of union organisation is important as a medium for representing the interests of members in the two communities. The FGTB and the CSC are in fact not merely organisations linking national unions, they are also alliances of regional trade union groups. At confederal conferences and general council meetings representation is from the regional sections of the confederation as well as from the national unions, with the former having one-third of the voting power. And at such gatherings in the FGTB, motions must be supported by two-thirds of the overall vote, or 50 per cent of the votes of each of the two language groups, before they are binding.

The distribution of power between the confederations and their constituent unions is not a contentious issue, though with the confederations playing a more prominent role in collective bargaining at the national level the chance of some friction developing between them and the national unions is now greater. FGTB unions enjoy more autonomy than their CSC counterparts whose finances tend to be closely controlled by the confederation. However, a degree of union centralisation in administrative matters would seem to be not unreasonable given the fact that union confederations are still smaller than the largest national unions in Britain.

The FGTB and CSC coexist peacefully and there is considerable co-operation between them although there are no immediate prospects for unification. The FGTB tends to be rather more militant, having adopted a very radical programme on workers' control in 1971. But sections of the CSC have also been influenced by the growing radicalism of parts of the Catholic Church, and on the whole differences between them are not so much over industrial policy as over questions of social morality, the role of the family in society, and so on. The Belgians regard dual unionism as an advantage in as much as if a union loses touch with its members, it runs the risk of them transferring to the rival organisation. In practice, however, there is only a small transfer of membership, estimated by the president of the CSC metalworkers' union to be no more than 2–3 per cent annually. On the other hand the division in the trade unions does have a weakening effect in that members of one confederation feel no obligation to support industrial action taken by members of the other organisation, and in general the crossing of a picket line carries little stigma in Belgium.

METALWORKING

By contrast with the situation in most European union movements, the FGTB metalworkers are not the confederation's largest affiliate, taking second place to the public service union. And it is only in recent years that the CSC metalworkers have overtaken the building workers' union in size of membership. There is much small-scale industry, and with some 3,000 metal manufacturing enterprises the average plant work force is probably under 150. In 1973 the FGTB union (Centrale des Métallurgistes de Belgique) reckoned to have 180,000 members with the CSC metalworkers (Centrale Chrétienne des Métallurgistes de Belgique) claiming 181,000. (By 1975 the CSC metalworkers' union claimed a membership of 213,000.) Both figures are inflated by about 10 per cent, the intention being that the employers should not know the exact membership. Neither union organises white collar workers, and among the manual workers there are no separate union sections based on craft or occupation, though separate national negotiations take place for different occupational groups. In the FGTB metalworkers' union approximately 10,000 members are women whereas the CSC union estimates its female membership as being as high as 25,000.

TEXTILES

This industry is mainly located in Flanders and both major unions have their headquarters in the textile centre of Gent. The unions co-operate very closely. As in metalworking, it is customary for them to publish inflated membership figures. The FGTB union (Centrale des Ouvriers Textiles de Belgique) claims to have 60,000 members. The CSC organises both textile and clothing workers in the same union (Central Chrétienne des Travailleurs du Textile et du Vêtement de Belgique) and claims 47,000 textile workers and 27,000 clothing workers among its total membership of over 120,000. Women account for 90 per cent of the members in the CSC's clothing section, and in both unions there are between 45 and 50 per cent women members in general textiles. Both unions leave the organisation of white collar workers to the specialist unions within their respective confederations.

RAILWAYS

Belgian railway trade unionists, whether socialist or Christian, belong to unions which organise public service employees generally. Between 80 and 90 per cent of railway workers are reckoned to be organised. The FGTB union (Centrale Générale des Services Publics) is the confederation's largest constituent with over 200,000 members, and of these the railwaymen account for just under 40,000. However, 12,000 of this total are pensioned railwaymen paying only half dues. The CSC union (Syndicat Chrétien du Personnel des Chemins de Fer, Postes et Telegraphes) has slightly fewer railway members. Female membership is insignificant in the rail section of both unions. Within the public service unions each sector is autonomous and has its own policy-making and executive bodies for questions concerning only that sector. All the sectors come together to decide overall union policy and to elect the general officers of the organisation.

FINANCE

Compared with France and Italy, union dues are relatively high and regularly paid. The FGTB metalworkers charge a minimum monthly amount of £1·67. Regional bodies can actually set their own contributions above this, and in some places total dues are as high as £1·98. In the FGTB public service union railway workers pay a minimum of £1·36 monthly, rising in some cases to £1·57. And the FGTB textile union dues average out between £1·62 and £1·72 per month. Contributions are collected in different ways. In Flanders it is traditional for confederation collectors to go round to the homes of members. In Wallonia collections are more often made at the place of work. However, on the railways there are facilities for a voluntary check-off of dues and a majority of members avail themselves of this. Dues collection tends to be very thorough, and members who are three or four months in arrears can be expelled.

The division of dues between different levels of the movement varies, depending largely on the amount of services provided for the unions by the confederation. In the FGTB metalworkers 40 per cent goes to the national union, 45 per cent is retained by the regional body of the union for its own administrative purposes and to finance the work of plant sections, and 15 per cent is remitted to the FGTB. In the FGTB textile union, which relies more on assistance from the confederation, 31 per cent of dues goes to the FGTB, the national union receives 66 per cent, and the regions retain only 3 per cent.

In the CSC the financial affairs of individual unions are closely supervised by the confederation. Each year the national unions must send the CSC their proposed budget for the coming twelve months together with a statement of account for the previous year. Dues levels tend to be set at about the same level as in the FGTB in order to maintain a competitive position. In the CSC metalworking union minimum dues are £1·57 per month with the average standing at £1·77. In the CSC textile union the average is about £1·67, and on the railways contributions range from £1·25 to £1·62. The division of dues between different levels of the union tends to be kept secret, though it appears that in the CSC textile union as much as 70 per cent goes to the confederation, while in the CSC railway union the amount is 40 per cent. This high proportion is partly accounted for by the fact that it is the confederation which maintains the strike fund rather than the individual unions.

HOLLAND

BACKGROUND

Holland is another country where the labour movement is divided by religion and politics. In this case there are separate confederations for Catholic workers, NKV (Nederlands Katholiek Vakverbond) and Protestant workers, CNV (Christelijk Nationaal Vakverbond), while the largest confederation, NVV (Nederlands Verbond van Vakvereningingen), is mildly social democratic. The confederations co-exist in relative harmony. At the end of the war there was an attempt at amalgamation and a Joint Council of Trade Union Centres was established. To smooth the way for eventual merger dues payments and rule book provisions were harmonised, and for a number of years there was close co-operation. But in 1954 the Catholic Church forbade its members to belong to the secular union, NVV, and in protest the latter left the Council. The ban was lifted in 1965, by which time co-operation had been resumed through a consultative board. In 1967 this body acquired a full-time secretary, and since then the confederations have operated a joint action programme on economic and social policies. The NVV is in favour of a complete amalgamation of the confederations but so far the confessional bodies have only been prepared to consider a form of federation. In 1973 the NVV and NKV did agree on the principle of a federation though the CNV has been reluctant to participate in anything that might cost it its identity. However, economic pressures arising from the need to provide a range of costly services for a narrowly-based membership may yet force the NKV at least to reconsider establishing closer ties with the NVV.

The political barriers to a full organic merger are not all that formidable. The NVV's political links with the Dutch socialists do not extend to the provision of financial assistance. And although the NVV rules do not prevent union officials from holding political office a number of the affiliated unions forbid this. In the NKV dual political and union office holding is not practised, and there is also a significant tendency to play down the confessional element in trade unionism. The NKV's largest union, the industrial workers union, no longer follows the customary Christian practice of having a cleric on its national executive, and the NKV transport union has ceased altogether to be an exclusively Catholic union. To accommodate this change the NKV now permits affiliation of non-Catholic unions. In general ideological differences between the confederations are not very marked, and as in Belgium the differences tend to involve questions of social morality rather than industrial policy.

MEMBERSHIP

677,000 workers belong to the NVV, 355,000 are in the Catholic NKV, and some 227,000 belong to the Protestant organisation, CNV. This proportional division of membership between the three confederations has remained more or less constant for over a generation now.

STRUCTURE

Dutch unions are highly centralised and in most of the post-war period the confederations have played a dominant role in collective bargaining. In fact centralisation of operations was a deliberate policy of the NVV from its creation in 1906, and in this the unions were reacting against the loose, syndicalist tendencies of the early Dutch unions. Of course union centralisation in a country as small as the Netherlands makes a good deal of sense and was not bound to degenerate into bureaucratic top-heaviness as it has done in the post-war years. To a large extent the power of the confederations has resulted from the post-war reorganisation of the affiliated unions along industrial lines. The original amalgamation proposal involved, as a preliminary, each confederation regrouping its members in fifteen industrial unions. And in the arbitrary process of reallocating members to different industrial unions the confederations greatly enhanced their influence *vis-à-vis* their affiliates.

NVV now has 15 affiliated unions; NKV has 11 industrial unions; and the CNV has 13 constituent bodies.[7] The confederations have a great deal of effective power and there is little scope for the lower levels of the movement to influence policies made at the top. The NVV has recently abolished conference and in its place there is a half-yearly meeting of confederation officials and industrial union leaders. The NKV's conference has no real power, serving only as a forum for discussion between the NKV and the leaders of its affiliates. The confederations keep a close watch on the activities of constituent bodies and expect regular reports on activities. They maintain regional offices with full-time staffs to look after their interests in the various districts. The NVV also reserves the right to approve the rules of its industrial unions. However, during the last decade some of the larger unions have begun to resent the power of the central bodies. During the mid-1960s the NVV metalworkers' union was in dispute with the confederation over its desire to have a greater influence in confederal decision-making. The Netherlands has experienced a major cultural revolution in the last decade and a half during which time many long-established attitudes have been shaken. The long-term effect of this on the structure and operation of trade unions is likely to be profound.

METALWORKING AND TEXTILES

The restructuring of the labour movement has led to the creation within each confederation of a single union for employees in manufacturing. The NVV industrial workers' union (Industriebond) was formed in January 1972. Its main constituent body is the former metalworkers' union, and in addition it organises chemical, paper, food, tobacco, textile, clothing and leather workers. Since 1972 the NKV and CNV have followed suit, establishing their own industrial workers' unions based on four or five pre-existing unions. In each case the industrial workers constitute the largest affiliate of the confederation. The NVV industrial union has a total membership of just under 200,000 of whom 115,000 are metalworkers and 15,000 are in textiles and clothing. The NKV industrial union has 136,000 members, 60,000 of them in metalworking and 15,000 in textiles. The corresponding figures for the CNV are approximately 35,000 metalworkers and 6,000 textile-workers. Unionisation in metalworking is approximately 50 per cent of the total labour force and in textiles the level is around 20 per cent.

The NKV industrial union is strongest in the Catholic south of the Netherlands with the greatest concentration of members in the Limbourg, Eindhoven and Breda districts. The NVV industrial workers' strength is in the major manufacturing towns of the west – Amsterdam, Rotterdam and Utrecht. Just under 40 per cent of its metalworkers are located in these three towns.

The textile industry is mainly located in the eastern part of the country in Enschede, Hengelo and Almelo, and in the NVV industrial union 50 per cent of the textile membership is located in the province of Overijssel which encompasses these towns. Female membership of the union is very low: in the NKV industrial union it amounts to no more than 3,800 out of 136,000. There are no accurate figures for white collar and blue collar membership since the unions are striving to abolish all major status distinctions between them.

RAILWAYS

In both the NVV and NKV railway workers are organised in general transport unions which include road, air and sea transport as well as dock workers. Each sector has its own representational system for questions relating only to that sector. The railway membership in the NVV transport union (Vervoersbond) is 11,000 out of a total of 48,000. The NKV transport union (Vervoersbond) has 9,200 railway members out of a total membership of 24,000. However, these figures again disguise the fact that pensioners are still borne on the unions' books, and in the case of the NKV union only 6,700 of the railwaymen are actually working. An independent railway union, FSV, represents most of the balance of the organised railway workforce, and the total level of unionisation in the industry is 80 per cent. These three unions operate very closely and in 1974 plans were being developed to form a federation of transport unions as a first step towards ultimate merger.

FINANCE

In the NVV industrial workers' union contributions average £1·83 per month. The railway members of the NVV transport union pay 1 per cent of their monthly wages in dues, the amount ranging between £1·68 and £1·98 per month. Some members pay contributions to collectors who visit their homes, but the vast majority have dues deducted at source, and in the NVV industrial union there is a 25 per cent discount if the members agree to the check-off. All NVV unions remit 15 per cent of their dues income to the NVV. In the NVV industrial union about 80 per cent of the contributions remains with the national union, and branches have only limited funds for their own purposes.

The dues in the NKV industrial union are lower than its NVV counterpart charges, amounting to £1·60 per month. However, the NKV railway workers pay the same amount as the NVV transport union members, dues having been equalised in preparation for the creation of a single federation. The division of dues within the movement is much the same as in the NVV. The NKV receives 16 per cent of the income from contributions, 65–75 per cent is retained by the national union, and the remainder goes to the branches.

GERMANY

BACKGROUND

The German labour movement was suppressed by Hitler and had to be rebuilt completely after the war. The reconstruction process was closely supervised by the occupying powers, and in this Britain played a major part. In the early post-war years a proposal to create a totally centralised system, which might have lent itself to authoritarian control, was dropped after strong opposition from the British TUC. But equally, the spontaneous development of radical trade unionism in the British zone in 1945 was halted by the occupying forces on grounds that this was too political. The intention of the German trade unionists was to create a unified structure in which the manifold ideological, religious and craft divisions of the Weimar period would be avoided. The final product succeeded in having a highly streamlined structure with only sixteen national unions comprising the central DGB (Deutscher Gewerkschaftsbund). But the pressures for extreme centralisation were resisted and each of the national unions maintains its complete autonomy.

Unity in the trade union movement had to be bought at the cost of severing all political ties. There is no collective affiliation to the Socialist Party and no direct financing of party activities; support tends to be given in kind. However, this can be quite substantial and it has been estimated that in 1961 18 per cent of DGB expenditure was on political activities.[8]

MEMBERSHIP

With the political connection abolished, a large number of Christian trade unionists were induced to enter the DGB at its foundation in 1949. But total unity has still not been achieved, and outside the DGB with its 7·4 million members are 500,000 salaried workers in the DAG (Deutsche Angestellten-Gewerkschaft), and some 700,000 civil servants in the DBB (Deutscher Beamtenbund). Only one in three German workers are organised and DGB's membership has failed to grow very much over the past two decades.

STRUCTURE

The refusal of the occupying forces to countenance a fully centralised trade union structure in Germany left the sixteen national unions in the DGB with complete autonomy in matters of industrial policy and collective bargaining. Unlike the central confederations in France, Italy, Belgium and Holland, the DGB itself plays no part in these areas. Nevertheless it remains an extremely powerful body with an extensive organisation around the country. It maintains regional offices in the various German states and has a physical presence in some 300 towns and municipalities. These local offices exist to support the national unions with legal, propaganda and other services outside the main area of collective bargaining.

The DGB is governed by a three-yearly federal conference made up of delegates from the local branches of the sixteen affiliated unions. This gathering elects the nine officers who head the DGB. In between conference a federal council comprising the executives of each of the national unions meets quarterly and is responsible for policy, but in reality power is wielded by a smaller executive board consisting of the nine top DGB officials and the presidents of the sixteen national unions.

The German unions are extremely prosperous and rather bureaucratic. The DGB itself owns Germany's fourth largest bank, second largest insurance company and the biggest building society and construction firm in the world. In conjunction with the metalworkers it also runs a travel firm which arranges thousands of package holidays each year. Thus at the highest level union officials also act as directors of massive commercial concerns. The national unions themselves are involved in the administration of social security, and thousands of officials are engaged in this aspect of union operations.

In post-war years the movement has turned its back on radical policies. The system of co-determination which grants workers minority representation on the supervisory boards of most firms, and parity representation in coal and steel companies, has come to symbolise, many believe, the movement's accommodation to the capitalist system. Since 1963 the DGB has ceased to press for the public ownership of major industries, and parity representation on the supervisory boards of private industry is as much as the unions aspire to.

METALWORKING

This group of industries is the largest employer of labour in Germany and the metalworkers' union (IG Metall) accounts for one-third of the DGB membership. With over 2·5 million members this is the largest union in Western Europe. The organisation claims to represent 45 per cent of the organisable workers in the industry. All types of metalworker are included in the union and no distinction is made between craft and non-craft workers, or between members operating in different sectors such as iron and steel, car manufacturing or electrical engineering. White collar workers make up 238,000 of the total membership and there are 227,000 female members. The largest concentration of members is in the state of North Rhine–Westphalia, including the Ruhr, where four of the union's regional bodies account for over 750,000 members. Second in importance is the south-western state of Baden–Wurttemberg where the union's Stuttgart region has over 400,000 members.

TEXTILES

The DGB's textile and clothing union (Gewerkschaft Textil-Bekleidung) has suffered greatly from the overall decline in textiles in the last decade or so and is now the eighth largest union in Germany with

287,000 members. With approximately 900,000 workers in these industries this represents a level of unionisation of some 33 per cent, though union membership in textiles is considerably higher than in clothing. Clothing enterprises tend to be smaller than textile plants, with an average workforce of seventy people – about half the size of the average textile operation. Within the textile sector the woollen industry is a more fertile area for union recruitment than the cotton industry. Seven out of ten members are employed in textiles and 54 per cent of the overall membership is women. Only 19,000 of the members are white collar workers. Nearly one-third of the total membership is located in Baden–Wurttemberg and in the northern-most area of North Rhine–Westphalia, particularly around Munster.

RAILWAYS

The railway union (Gewerkschaft der Eisenbahner Deutschlands) is Germany's fifth largest with 455,000 members. With 71 per cent of the labour force organised, this is one of the most heavily unionised industries. However, in the membership total there are some 123,000 pensioners. German law prevents civil servants from taking industrial action and as there are 132,000 members who fall into this category, including the engine drivers, they constitute a separate section for purposes of wage negotiation. Of the remaining members 166,000 are in manual grades and only 7,000 are salaried staff. As is usually the case on the railways, female members are few; in this case counting for less than 4 per cent of the total.

FINANCE

German unions are among the most prosperous in Western Europe and their vast wealth and diverse commercial operations are one of the distinctive features of the country's labour movement. Between 1971 and 1973 the metalworkers' union alone had an average annual income from all sources of £38 million. In this union dues are paid on a graded scale according to the level of wages. They can be any-where between £1·12 and £7·66 per month, but the average is £1·60. The average textile union member's dues are about the same, while in the railway union the average contribution is £1·43 per month. Contributions are divided between different levels of the union in such a way as to leave the bulk of the spending power with the national unions. The standard remittance by all unions to the DGB is 12 per cent of dues income. Between 15 per cent and 20 per cent of contributions are allocated to cover local expenses.

DENMARK

BACKGROUND

Like the German and British labour movements, the Danish trade unions have a unitary structure with one major central confederation, LO (Landsorganisationen i Danmark). LO was founded in 1898 following a joint conference of Scandinavian unions in Stockholm at which it was decided to form a national federation of unions in each country. The decision to create a central union body was very much a product of a period of intense industrial unrest, and unlike the British TUC, which was originally conceived of as a lobbying organisation, LO was designed as a general staff of the trade union movement with an important co-ordinating role in industrial conflicts. From the earliest days affiliated unions had to notify it of intended bargaining demands, and LO maintained its own strike fund which gave it a certain amount of influence over affiliates. However, the present centralised system of industrial relations did not develop fully until after the war, and today individual Danish unions still retain more autonomy than their Swedish and Norwegian counterparts.

The Danish unions maintain a close relationship with the Social Democratic Party and although there is no collective affiliation of trade union members, organic links are maintained through the practice of having two representatives from the party on the LO executive, an arrangement which is reciprocated on the party executive. It is also normal for high-ranking union leaders to join social democratic governments.

MEMBERSHIP

The combined membership of all LO's affiliates is 953,000.

STRUCTURE

The structure of Danish trade unionism closely resembles the British system in that there is a considerable number of craft unions still in existence. This is a legacy of the earlier, well-established guild system in the country. LO has some 44 affiliated unions, a drop of 20 during the last half-dozen years. Craft unionism still persists and a union like the metalworkers is essentially a composite body of boilermakers, blacksmiths, pipefitters, and so on. On the railways Denmark is one of the few European countries to have a separate union for locomotive engineers. The craft element is preserved by union control over apprenticeships. However, the textile and clothing unions have always organised on industrial lines. Today there is a very definite tendency to restructure the labour movement so as to have a few unions based on broad industrial groups. In 1970 the LO conference decided to reduce the number of affiliates to seven industrial unions. Already two unions account for 40 per cent of LO membership. And in 1972 the engineers retitled themselves 'metalworkers', thereby staking their claim to the leadership of a future unified industrial union.

General policy guidelines for LO are laid down at a conference held every four years. It is attended by the executives of all the affiliated unions plus one representative of each local trades council. This body also elects the principal officers of the confederation and an executive board. In between conference a general council made up of representatives of the different affiliates, one per 2,000 members, meets at least annually to decide policy. But in practice it is the executive board with some twenty members including the principal full-time officers of LO which directs policy, only needing to consult the general council on important matters.

METALWORKING

Metalworking is a long-established industry in Denmark with shipbuilding and agricultural machine manufacturing two of its more traditional areas. Most industrial operations are small scale and in 1967 the country had less than 100 enterprises with over 500 workers. The principal union is the metalworkers' union (Metalarbejderforbund Dansk), with 108,000 members. However, with the proliferation of craft organisations the overall spokesman for the metalworkers is a body known as Centralorganisationen which is equivalent to the British Confederation of Shipbuilding and Engineering Unions. It has fifteen affiliates and is run by a small secretariat staffed mainly by officials from the metalworkers' union. The second largest affiliate of Centralorganisationen is the general workers' union representing unskilled employees in the industry. This is in fact the largest Danish union with over 250,000 members, 50,000 of whom are in the metalworking sector.

The metalworkers' union has no white collar members; these belong to a separate organisation, and less than 1 per cent of the total membership is women. There is in fact a separate LO affiliate catering exclusively for women. One-third of the metalworkers' members are located in the Copenhagen district. The largest group of members, some 15,000, is in ship-building, with 9,000 in car repairing and 6,000 in government establishments. The different sectoral groups have their own informal representative meetings two or three times a year but these only have an advisory role.

TEXTILES

The textile union (Textilarbejderforbund Dansk) has 14,300 members : clothing and leather workers are organised in separate unions. The union claims to represent 90 per cent of the organisable workforce. Two-thirds of the members are located in the thinly populated Jutland peninsula, with 5,000 of the members in the Ringkøbing district. The membership includes workers in all sections of textile working. Hosiery accounts for 28 per cent of them, the woollen and worsted trade 16 per cent, cotton 12 per cent, and carpet weaving also 12 per cent. Women make up 9,000 of the total membership. The union does not organise any white collar workers.

RAILWAYS

There are two railway unions in Denmark. The general railway union (Jernbaneforbund Dansk has 8,700 members, while the locomotive drivers (Lokomotivmands Forening Dansk) has 1,600 members. Union membership is practically 100 per cent among both groups.

FINANCE

Danish unions charge some of the highest dues in Western Europe, with members paying 2–3 per cent of their wages. However, this includes a contribution to the state-run unemployment scheme for which the unions act as government agents. In metalworking the total weekly dues are £1·51 on average. This amount includes a variable contribution charged by the branches for their own purposes. The national union itself receives just over half the total contribution. Dues to the national union are scheduled to rise to 97p per week in 1976. In the textile union dues amount to 2 per cent of weekly wages. In general LO receives about 10 per cent of the dues paid.

SWEDEN

BACKGROUND

Early union organisation in Sweden was largely the product of agitation carried out by Danish trade unionists living in the country.

The Swedish central union organisation, LO (Landsorganisationen i Sverige), was founded in 1898, the same year as the Danish LO. Besides this, there is a confederation of salaried employees, TCO (Tjanstemannens Centralorganisation), as well as a separate organisation for professional workers, SACO (Sveriges Akadamers Centralorganisation).

From the start there was a very close relationship between the unions and the Social Democratic Party. Indeed LO was brought into existence largely through the efforts of the party. At the outset there was compulsory collective affiliation to the party together with an arrangement whereby two of the five members of LO's executive were to be nominated by the party. Both of these provisions were abolished in 1900. However, a 1909 declaration of the LO congress, stating that the Social Democratic Party is regarded as the natural political leader of the Swedish working class, still stands. A system of collective affiliation by union branches is now practised, with a provision for individuals to contract out. More than one-third of LO's members are affiliated to the party in this way.

MEMBERSHIP

LO has a membership of 1·8 million, while TCO claims to have 650,000 members.

STRUCTURE

In terms of Scandinavian trade unionism with its tendency towards centralisation, Swedish unions stand midway between their Danish and Norwegian counterparts – more centralised than in Denmark but less so than in Norway. LO was originally formed as a loose confederation of national unions. Its function was to co-ordinate defensive action in the event of lockouts by providing dispute benefit. In 1912 it was decided in principle to adopt a form of industrial unionism, to reduce the number of unions from 41 to 22 and to give LO more positive powers. The rationalisation process was slow and even after the adoption of a policy of 'wage solidarity' with the lowest paid workers in 1922 there was an unwillingness to hand over to LO the powers necessary to co-ordinate the policy. It was not until the late 1930s and early 1940s that LO acquired its present far-reaching powers over its affiliates. The structure of the movement has been changing gradually as the goal of full industrial unionism has come closer to achievement. There are now some 25 national unions as compared with the target of 22 affiliates.

Only the national unions in Sweden are entitled to send delegates to LO's five-yearly conference: unlike in Denmark and Norway, trades councils are not represented. The 300 conference delegates are elected in ballots held at the local level of the affiliated unions. Conference is the highest policy-making body and sets guidelines for future wage policy. But the long period between conference means that the more detailed policy decisions are left to a general council of 140 members elected directly by the national unions and meeting several times each year. However, real power in the movement undoubtedly rests with the twelve-man executive board meeting weekly. This consists of the full-time president and secretary of LO, and the presidents of the ten largest affiliated unions. As LO's own handbook concedes, this body has 'a decisive influence in the conduct of the organisation's business'.

METALWORKING

Metalworking is Sweden's biggest industry. Traditionally this has been based on the manufacture of high quality steels and specialised products such as ball-bearings. Engineering accounts for 35 per cent of the country's production. Over 40 per cent of the manufacturing labour force is employed in metals and among the most important sectors are shipbuilding, car manufacturing and electrical engineering.

The metalworkers' union (Svenska Metallindustriarbetareforbundet) is the largest Swedish union with a membership of 443,000, 51,000 of them women. This represents 96 per cent of the organisable workforce. During the 1960s the union expanded twice as fast as LO as a whole. Of the total membership some 210,000 are employed in metal manufacturing; 50,000 members are employed in iron and steel production; 30,000 in shipbuilding; 22,000 in automotive repairs; and 6,000 work in foundries. The union has no formal system of sectional representation for these different groups. All members are manual workers, white collar employees belonging to a separate organisation. On a regional basis most members are located in an area from approximately 150 miles north of Stockholm down to the southern tip of the country, with an important concentration on the west coast. In the southern part of the country there are approximately 5,000 engineering enterprises, mostly small scale. The chief centres are Gothenburg, Stockholm and Malmo. In 1961 the ILO reported that 75 per cent of industrial enterprises in Sweden had fewer than 26 workers and only 172 plants employed more than 500 people.[9] There are some 125 shipyards in the country, mostly small or medium sized, with Gothenberg, Malmo and Halsingborg the main centres.

The metalworkers' union stands out among Swedish unions as one of the few organisations which still maintain a formal commitment to the socialisation of industry.

TEXTILES

In line with the general post-war contraction of the textile industry, Swedish textile trade unionism has declined in strength in the past two or three decades. In 1968 the textile union merged with the clothing union and the shoe and leather union to form the present amalgamated body (Bekladnadsarbetarnas Forbund), with a current membership of 56,000 or some 90–95 per cent of organisable workers in the three sectors. The membership includes 21,000 textile workers, 29,000 clothing workers, and the remainder in the shoe and leather industry. The textile membership has declined from a level of 52,000 in 1950. Within this sector knitwear now provides the largest number of members with 5,200. There are a further 5,000 members in synthetic fibres, 4,500 in cotton textiles, 3,000 members in woollen textiles, and the remainder work in smaller sectors such as hemp and silk manufacturing. In textiles women comprise 50 per cent of the membership, while in the union as a whole female members con-stitute two-thirds of the total. As in metalworking, all members are blue collar workers. On a regional basis two-thirds of the members are in western Sweden and a further 20 per cent are in the south. Only relatively small numbers are to be found in the north and east in old textile centres such as Norrköping to the south of Stockholm.

RAILWAYS

Since 1970 the railway trade unionists in Sweden have been part of the general public service union (Statsanstalldas Forbund). As in the textile industry, the railway labour force has been declining rapidly and with it union membership has fallen. The total number of railway members in the union is now just under 38,000 compared with 65,000 in 1952. However, the railway members are still the largest group in the union whose four other sectors organise post office, telecommunications, defence and power workers.

FINANCE

In metalworking, dues to the national union amount to £3·01 per month. The textile union head office receives an average of £2·07 per month, and railway workers pay their national union 1 per cent of their wages in the form of contributions. All unions remit 38p monthly to LO. On top of national dues local branches can charge their own subscriptions. In metalworking these tend to range between 94p and £1·41 per month, making total monthly dues in some cases as high as £4·40. In textiles the average contribution to the branch is 57p, whereas local dues for railwaymen are approximately £1 per month.

NORWAY

BACKGROUND

The emergence of the Norwegian labour movement coincided with the growth of an agrarian movement hostile to Swedish rule in Norway. When eventually Swedish domination was ended in 1905 Norway was left with no native aristocracy, without an urban tradition, but with a strong egalitarian tendency rooted in agrarian values. From its inception in 1899 the central confederation, LO (Landsorganisasjonen i Norge), developed very close links with the Social Democratic Party, and as in Sweden the original arrangement was for the confederation and the party to have reciprocal representation on each other's national executive. This was terminated after the First World War and today there is a joint advisory council. However, voluntary collective affiliation to the party by union branches still exists and up to 45 per cent of the party's members are recruited in this way.

MEMBERSHIP

LO affiliates have a total membership of 642,000.

STRUCTURE

The Norwegian trade union movement is the most highly centralised in Scandinavia. Many of the unions have their headquarters in the same building as the central confederation, LO, and there is a strong reliance on services provided by the latter. From the outset LO was given extensive powers over affiliated unions. However, as in a number of other European countries, it was not the interests of union bureaucracy but a desire to create a general staff for a militant labour movement that prompted the centralisation. From the Danish sector of the First International a strong Marxist influence was imported into the labour movement in the 1870s. And in the early years of this century Norwegian emigrants to the United States who had experience of the Industrial Workers of the World brought back notions of the One Big Union that would organise all industrial workers.

The structure of the movement still bears the marks of the early syndicalist influence in the trade unions. LO's thirty-five affiliates are organised basically along industrial lines, but there is also a system of geographically-based trades councils. At the turn of the century, and again after the First World War, attempts were made to increase the influence of these within the movement. However, the national unions resisted this development, and although the twenty or so trades councils are still represented in LO policy-making bodies their tasks are limited to propaganda, education and other supporting activities.

The supreme policy-making body is the four-yearly conference with 300 delegates, 260 of them elected by the national unions and 40 by the trades councils. In between conference the direction of policy is in the hands of a 120-man general council, again comprising a similar proportion of directly elected national union and trades council delegates. The council meets at least once a year. But as in other countries where a multi-tier system of union government operates, it is the executive board meeting weekly which really controls the federation, this body being made up of the top four full-time officials of LO and the presidents of eleven of the confederation's largest affiliates.

METALWORKING

Metalworking is one of Norway's most important export industries. The metalworkers' union (Norsk-Jern- og Metallarbeiderforbund) has 105,000 members with some 25 per cent of them, the largest group, in Norway's key shipbuilding industry. Some 30,000 members work in mechanical and electrical engineering, and the remainder are to be found in small sectors such as steel (5–6,000 members), auto repairing (4,000 members), and aircraft (1,000 members). Most Norwegian industry is very small scale. In 1968 less than 300 plants employed more than 200 workers. Only 5,000 of the members are women, and the union does not organise white collar workers. Geographically 45 per cent of the members are in the Oslo region and the majority of the remainder are to be found in the south-western region of the country.

TEXTILES

The textile union (Bekledningsarbeiderforbundet) organises workers in the clothing, leather and shoe industries, and following the pattern of the Swedish textile union it was formed by a merger of three pre-existing unions in 1969. The total union membership is 19,400, of whom 5,000 are pensioners. This represents some 80 per cent of the organisable workforce. 12,000 of the total membership are in clothing, 6,000 are in textiles, and the remainder work in the shoe and leather sector. Figures for the different sub-sectors of textiles do not exist. Three-quarters of the membership are women, and there are no white collar workers in the union. Oslo has the largest single group of textile and clothing workers, but generally the biggest concentration of members is in the south-western provinces of Bergen and Hordaland.

RAILWAYS

Like Denmark, Norway has a general railway union (Norsk Jern-baneforbund) and a locomotive engineers' union (Norsk Lokomotiv-mandsforbund). The former has 15,000 members, 95 per cent of the organisable workforce, while the latter has 1,800 members. In the general railway union 900 members are women.

FINANCE

In metalworking and textiles the amounts paid in union dues range between 1·2 per cent and 1·4 per cent of wages. The metalworkers' top level of dues is 83p per week. In textiles basic weekly dues are 58p, and for railwaymen the contribution is about 36p per week. LO receives 11p per week per member from the national unions. Local branches also charge their own dues. In textiles this might be anywhere from 3p to 19p per week, and if there is a full-time branch secretary to maintain they may be as high as 32p.

CONCLUSION

STRUCTURE

In all the countries examined, except Denmark, the unions are basically organised on industrial lines, with one union recruiting all the workers in a particular industry. Even in Denmark, which has a tradition of craft unionism, there is a tendency to merge existing craft unions into larger industrial units. The system is more developed in some countries than others. The Germans, Belgians and Dutch have the greatest concentration of members in the smallest number of unions, while in France, Italy and Norway there are still comparatively large numbers of separate unions.

POLITICAL AND RELIGIOUS DIVISIONS

In a number of countries the advantages of the industrial form of organisation are largely cancelled out by the fact that the labour movement is divided along religious and political lines. In Belgium there is a basic two-way division between Catholics and socialists. Holland, Italy and France have three major union confederations, each one with unions competing for membership in every industry and sector. The overall effect of this, at least in France and Italy, is that the total number of unions in existence is probably about half the number of British TUC affiliates. On the other hand, Denmark, Sweden, Norway and Germany do have unitary systems of organisation.

UNION MEMBERSHIP

The degree of unionisation varies from country to country, though different systems of counting members and different definitions of what is an organisable worker make precise comparisons difficult. At the upper end of the scale are the Scandinavian countries and Belgium with perhaps as much as two-thirds of the workforce organised. Here the fact that unions also act as social welfare agencies clearly makes union membership a more attractive proposition. At the bottom end of the scale come France and Italy, with between one-fifth and one-quarter of all workers organised. In both countries the divisions in the labour movement and the long history of manipulation of the unions by political parties have combined to deter potential members from joining. Today France has only the same proportion of the labour force organised as Sweden had in the first decade of the century.

RELATIONS BETWEEN NATIONAL UNIONS AND CENTRAL CONFEDERATIONS

Within the general framework of industrial unionism the focal point of power in the labour movement varies from country to country. The most centralised movements are the Scandinavian, especially the Swedish and Norwegian, and also the Dutch. In these countries the central confederations traditionally play a major role in actively co-ordinating the activities of their member unions, and even take part in collective bargaining. Close behind in terms of centralisation come the German unions. At the other extreme are the French and Italian unions with a federal structure and full local autonomy, at least in theory. In practice there is rather more centralisation than the federal structure would lead one to believe. In both countries the labour movement is organised horizontally, by regions, as well as vertically, by industries, and this tends to enhance the power of the confederations. Beyond this the political faction system which operates widely in the French and Italian movements enables the dominant political tendencies to impose uniform policies on the federated units.

FINANCE

In France and Italy the financial weakness of the individual unions and the dependence of some of them on the confederations for support has strengthened the tendency towards centralisation. Indeed finance is another area where French and Italian union practice is markedly different from that of other continental labour movements. In these two countries dues tend to be low, are very irregularly paid, and with the exception of one French confederation, the CFDT, unions are incapable of paying strike benefit. Elsewhere in Europe the level of union dues is at least as high as the highest amount charged by most manual unions in Britain, and very often considerably more. Most unions aim to set dues at 1 per cent of wages. The highest contributions are charged by some of the Scandinavian unions with total contributions amounting to 2–3 per cent of wages. And the degree of centralisation in most continental labour movements is reflected in the fact that a relatively high proportion of dues, usually ranging between 10 and 15 per cent, is remitted by the unions to the central confederations.

3

Union Organisation in the Plant

This chapter considers the nature of trade union workshop representation within different organisations. The aim is to discover how powerful the shop level organisation is; how it relates to higher levels in the union structure; and whether it is actually controlled by the workers themselves. The point of asking these particular questions rests on the importance of plant level trade unionism for the ordinary member. This is where workers come into direct contact with the union, and it is this level of organisation that can have the most profound influence on their detailed conditions of employment. Thus it is here that the foundations of democratic structures and procedures must be laid.

The first factor to be considered is whether or not there is a direct union presence in the plant. If so, the question arises as to whether this is the sole form of employee representation at work. The existence in many countries of works councils, for the most part non-union bodies, means that plant-based union organisation is only one of two channels of representation, and in certain countries labour law accords the non-union channel a more important role.

Where in-plant union representation exists it is necessary to examine its effectiveness and responsiveness to membership wishes. We need to measure the extent of plant-level representation. Is there a sufficient number of representatives to look after the interests of the members adequately? From the point of view of democracy it is important to know how they are chosen, whether they are selected at the base, or if they owe their position to higher union officials. This leads on to the wider question of the representatives' formal status in so far as the employers and the unions are concerned.

In consequence of being officially recognised, plant representatives may be accorded certain facilities and rights which can influence their effectiveness. The actual power in the hands of workshop spokesmen must be considered, especially with regard to their ability to represent their members directly before the employers in collective bargaining. And finally we need to examine the existence of direct links between workshop groups in different locations such as are likely to increase their overall strategic importance *vis-à-vis* the employer and the official union.

Ideally for workshop democracy one would like to see a network of lay union representatives at the plant level sufficiently extensive as to be able to give detailed attention to members' grievances. They should constitute the sole channel of representation of workers to the employer, and not be bypassed or undercut by competing non-union or employer-dominated bodies. Workshop representatives ought to be elected by the union members and directly answerable to them through a regular system of re-election. They must have full rights to negotiate with employers over issues arising at the point of production, being granted adequate facilities and time off work to fulfil their functions properly. And the official union ought to give full support and encouragement to attempts to link up with workshop groups in other locations in an effort to create wider combine organisations.

NON-UNION REPRESENTATION: THE WORKS COUNCILS

First of all we need to isolate those institutional forms of representation that are not strictly trade union in origin, particularly works councils. Here we propose to look briefly at their basic features and common characteristics, and to highlight the contrast between them and trade union forms of plant-level organisation.

The ideological basis of works councils can be traced back to the mid-nineteenth century European liberal notion of the 'constitutional factory' in which workers were to be granted some say in how it should be run.[1] In their modern form they are essentially a product of early post-war reconstruction, created at a time when more radical ideas on the democratic restructuring of industry were gaining currency among European workers. The works councils were designed to tap this urge for greater worker involvement in the management of firms, without actually changing the reality of the industrial power structure. They were to be the organs of 'social partnership' through which workers and management would combine to deal in a bi-partisan way with a limited range of issues. A consensus rather than a conflictual view of industrial relations was fundamental to their operation, and this was written into some of the laws and agreements which established the systems. The French law on works councils (comité d'entreprise) called for 'the union of all elements of production, to return to France its prosperity and greatness', while maintaining the authority of the head of the undertaking.[2] The relevant Italian collective agreement required works councils (commissione interna) 'to maintain relations between workers and management in a spirit of collaboration and mutual understanding to ensure the smooth running of the firm's production'.[3] And under Dutch law a works council (ondereningsraad) was expected to 'do all in its power to ensure the best possible running of the enterprise'.[4]

There are certain superficial differences between works councils in various countries. German councils (Betriebsrat) can have as many as thirty-five or so members in the largest factories,[5] whereas in France there are never more than eleven. The term of office also varies. In France it is two years, in Belgium four years. The composition of works councils differs from country to country. In Germany they meet independently as a workers' body. In France and Holland the employer acts as chairman of what is otherwise a workers' body. And in Belgium the council (conseil d'entreprise) is bilateral, with equal representation of worker and employer representatives.[6] Here the composition reflects different notions of how the councils should operate, the Dutch and French models suggesting a highly paternalistic system, whereas the Belgian arrangement does at least recognise the equality of the two sides.

In each case the councils are non-union bodies in that workers, whether unionised or not, may vote in elections or stand for office. The election procedure varies slightly from place to place, giving unions in one country a greater influence than in another. In Germany unions have no formal role in the works council elections, but they support their own preferred candidates and claim that as many as 90 per cent of them are successful. In France only the unions are allowed to nominate lists of candidates for the first ballot, but when a run-off vote is needed non-union lists may also be presented. The result is that nearly half the works council seats are held by non-unionists.

But throughout, the tendency is for the councils to undermine trade unionism at the plant level by creating a form of organisation that lies between workers and their unions. By taking on some of a union's natural representational functions, works councils have aimed at eliminating the need for a union presence in the plant, or at least, where the latter still persists, casting it very much in a secondary role.

The works councils generally have consultative and advisory functions in matters relating to the management of the firm, with occasional executive responsibilities in limited areas. In France, for example, they control the works canteens. But the reality of their influence differs from case to case. In Italy the advisory and consultative functions mean very little. In Belgium on the other hand, where the legislation governing works councils was strengthened in 1973, a considerable amount of information about the financial and commercial position of the firm must be given to the council at frequent intervals and in a format that does not disguise the reality of the situation. But information disclosed, even if it touches on important issues, is of considerably reduced value if, as in Germany and Holland, it has to be treated as confidential by the works councillors. It is at this point that the corporate nature of works councils comes into conflict with the essential oppositionary nature of worker–employer relations.

In general the councils do not negotiate on matters of plant wages and working conditions, though in Germany they do have a limited function in this area. The amended German Works Constitution Act of 1972 gives the works councils 'co-determination' rights in matters of plant rules, starting and stopping times, safety, the method of paying wages, and the plant wage structure. They can now negotiate over piecework rates, premiums and matters related to the measurement of productivity, and they have to be consulted before major decisions involving hiring and firing are made. However, their ability to negotiate over these various issues is severely restricted by the legal ban on works councillors calling strikes. Once again the corporate element in the works council system clashes with the reality of industrial life. German works councillors who are involved in strikes normally resign from the council as a precaution.

Finally, the overall impact of works councils depends on the extent to which they in fact exist. In Germany they are supposed to operate in any firm with five or more employees, and in practice they do exist in the vast majority of firms with fifty or more workers. French works councils are supposed to be set up in firms with over fifty employees, but only between one-quarter and one-third of the firms covered by the law actually have a council. In Belgium, where much industry is small scale, the requirement that they should exist in every firm with 150 employees means that many enterprises have no council. And in Holland, where the system has generally been regarded without much enthusiasm, a recent upward revision of the legal minimum workforce necessary for their establishment in a factory (the figure is now 100 workers) has not induced much more than 50 per cent of the firms covered to set up a works council.

Who then negotiates wage and working conditions at the plant level? The answer, as we shall see, is that this is either not done at all or is perhaps handled by one of the newer forms of institutional representation created in recent years to make up for the deficiencies of the works council system.

WORKPLACE UNION REPRESENTATION: BACK-GROUND AND EXTENT OF COVERAGE

BRITAIN

In Britain workplace organisation is characterised by the shop steward system, arguably the most distinctive feature of British trade unionism. Shop stewards made their appearance in British craft unionism in the closing decades of the last century. They were a local innovation without official status. Gradually their functions were extended to fill gaps in areas such as plant wage bargaining untouched by the official union machinery, and yet for a long time they remained outside the confines of union constitutions. After the end of the First World War they came to be officially recognised by most trade unions, but even so rule books tended to leave their functions very vague.

Extent

Studies of shop stewards have proliferated of late and in particular the investigations of the Donovan Commission and the Commission on Industrial Relations (CIR) have, for the first time, given us a global view of the nature and extent of shop steward organisation. For many years there was no accurate count of the number of shop stewards operating in Britain. Estimates ranged from the Donovan Commission's guess of 175,000 to the TUC's own figure of 200,000. However, it is now evident from the CIR's researches that the total number is much more likely to be 300,000.[7] This is a striking statistic. It indicates a considerable network of lay officialdom in the trade union movement, with a density of representation of something like one shop steward per thirty-five members for the 11 million or so trade unionists in Britain.

FRANCE

Plant union organisation in France is so recent as to date only from 1968, and the union presence on the shop floor is still quite limited.

Apart from works councils, the traditional form of in-plant worker representation has been via 'personnel delegates' (délégué du personnel) first introduced by collective agreement in 1936. These delegates were given the job of making individual or collective representations to the employer over grievances arising from labour legislation or wage rates. They also have a general brief to report to government labour inspectors any breaches of the law. But like works councils, they are elected by and from the entire workforce, unionised and non-unionised, and for this reason they have always been inadequate as representatives of the organised workforce.

During the 1960s the unions began to press for a direct physical presence in the plant, and in December 1968 a law granted each union, for the first time ever, the right to set up plant sections (section syndicale) in firms with more than fifty workers. These union sections have a spokesman or union delegate (délégué syndical). In the larger firms with over 1,000 employees the unions are allowed two of these. Thus there now tend to be three types of representative at the shop floor level – works councillors, personnel delegates, and union delegates – each speaking for the workers in some capacity. But it is around the unions' plant sections, and in particular their delegates, that union activity revolves, and it is with them that employers negotiate in cases where workshop bargaining exists.

While unions have begun to make inroads into plant organisation since 1968 there has also been a counter move in the growth of the number of employer-dominated company unions. For example, in the car industry both Citroen and Simca (Chrysler) have given encouragement to house unions. Despite the unions' legal right to a plant section the issue is still very much contested, and by 1972 only 35 per cent of the firms eligible to have a plant section had one. Most large firms fell into this category. In over half the firms in metalworking union sections had been created, while only 34 per cent of textile firms had been affected. In textiles the only real breakthrough in plant-level organisation has been in the synthetic fibres section, especially in the textile division of the giant chemical multi-national, Rhone-Poulenc. In the traditional textile areas such as Roubaix–Tourcoing near the Belgian border, unions still meet a lot of employer opposition to the creation of plant sections. In only one factory in Roubaix has this opposition been overcome and the problem is accentuated by the small-scale, diffuse nature of much of the textile industry.

Extent
The number of in-plant union delegates is difficult to discover from the unions directly. Membership and dues records are often very

unreliable and likewise a precise knowledge of their strength of representation in a plant escapes the unions. The CGT's metalworking, textile and railway unions are unable to say how many plant delegates they have. However, the CFDT unions tend to be more aware of their organisational strengths and weaknesses. The CFDT metalworking union has around 3,500 plant delegates, a ratio of one delegate per thirty-five members. The CFDT textile union has 1,000–1,200 delegates in a ratio to the membership of 1 : 50. And the CFDT railway union's 380 shop delegates represent the membership in a ratio of 1 : 65. Since the French railways are nationalised the unions are not confronted by any great problem of obtaining recognition for their delegates, and an institutionalised pattern of relationships exists between union and employer representatives at every level.

To be fair it should be pointed out that the unions themselves do not regard the number of plant delegates or the number of recognised sections as an indication of their organisational strength. They prefer to gauge this in terms of the number of 'militants' who identify with the unions, and this, of course, can give a more favourable picture. But whether it is a better yardstick is rather doubtful. Basically a militant is an active rank and file member. In most cases he holds no official position, though sometimes the term is used to include local union office holders. French unions tend to hold to the generalisation that militants constitute 10 per cent of the overall membership. As a general policy they do attempt to have one dues collector for every ten members, but in many cases the 10 per cent figure is more a statement of policy and an expression of hope than an attested fact. The CGT metalworkers, for example, reckon to have 15,000 militants, 'representing' members in a 1 : 26 ratio. Yet the fact is that there can be no real head count of what is, by definition, an amorphous group of activists with varying degrees of commitment to the union. The CGT metalworkers' total number of miltants is, in fact, derived from the number receiving a copy of the union's publication for militants. But this is issued free and therefore indicates no special commitment on the part of the recipient. They are subject to no organisational discipline beyond that applicable to ordinary members; only the self-discipline they themselves impose. The fact is that French trade unions have traditionally operated more as political propagandist bodies than as organisations geared to making tangible economic gains, and this emphasis allows them to do without a more formally structured system of workshop organisation. Of course, lay activists such as the militants, operating in an unofficial capacity, are indispensable for any voluntary organisation. But where bread and butter issues are concerned, a union's organisational strength at the plant level is probably better judged in terms of something more concrete than the existence of a highly notional number of sympathisers and voluntary workers.

ITALY

For most of the post-war period there was no direct union presence in Italian factories and plants, only representation of workers by the non-union works council. As the structure of centralised national collective bargaining started to breakdown in the 1960s the unions began to think in terms of devolving power to the local level. But action was slow in coming, and when a wave of strikes broke out in 1969 most of the early running was made by workers at the base, much of it necessarily unofficial.

In a situation where no acceptable agency existed for handling the local demands that were being made, a new form of shop floor organisation had to be set up. The workers elected their own delegates, established their own factory committees and in most cases insisted that these be unitary bodies, bridging the three-way structural division between the official unions. Bargaining demands were put forward on a plant by plant basis and a system of ultra-democratic control began to evolve on the workers' side with delegates accepting a mandate from mass meetings and reporting back progress at every stage.

In the aftermath of the 1969 strikes a new Act of May 1970, the Statute of the Rights of Workers, gave formal blessing to the system that had emerged. Factory committees (consigli di fabbrica) were to be allowed in enterprises with forty workers or more. In plants with up to 200 workers one shop steward (delegato) from each of the three rival unions is recognised. With up to 3,000 workers a firm is allowed a total of thirty shop stewards, with one additional steward per union for every 500 extra workers. Rule book revisions since 1969 have also formalised the role of shop stewards within the union. In metalworking the factory committee is declared to be the basis of trade union organisation and the only representative body of workers, having replaced the discredited works councils. In fact the old works councils are now being phased out, though in some cases they exist side by side with the new factory committees. The unions' long-term policy is to have the factory committees combine the functions of shop stewards and works council.

However, the shop steward system that has emerged is not entirely under trade union control. Non-union workers can vote in elections and perhaps as many as half the shop stewards are not in a union. This is an inevitable consequence of the disillusionment with unions that developed in the long post-war period when they were seen as the instruments of the political parties to which they were tied. The unions are now trying to live this down. The strong non-union element in factory committees is something that worries them and they have made efforts to influence the composition of the committees. Their aim has been to have 40 per cent of a factory committee's members elected solely by trade union members, but this policy has not been altogether successful.

Extent
In the federated metalworking unions approximately 22,000 shop stewards are elected in some 1,400 factory committees and represent the combined membership of the unions in a ratio of 1 : 45. In the textile industry, which is less well organised, the total number of shop stewards in the three principal unions is 13,300.

BELGIUM

Apart from the system of works councils discussed above, in-plant worker representation in Belgium is also via two other bodies, the safety committee (comité de securité et d'hygiène) and the union delegation (délégation syndicale). The personnel of these three bodies tend to overlap and the different channels of representation are complementary rather than in competition. Representatives on each of the bodies are elected by the workforce at large, whether unionised or not, but only union members are included in the delegation. The deeply-rooted tradition of unionism among Belgian workers and the organisational strength of the labour movement ensures that these plant bodies are under firm union control.

Of the three forms of representation the union delegation is the most important and the one that comes closest to the British shop steward system. Under a national collective agreement of 1947 delegations may be elected in firms with more than twenty workers. However, the small scale of much Belgian industry means that up to one-fifth of all workers are not eligible to be represented in this way. The size of delegations has recently been increased to a maximum of thirty.

Extent
In metalworking the FGTB and CSC unions each have around 1,000–1,500 members whose sole representative function is as union delegates. This gives a delegate–membership ratio of 1 : 100–150. However, this is an understatement of the real density of representation since some works councillors and safety committee members are also elected as delegates. Like the French unions, Belgian unions

also tend to gauge their organisational strength in terms of the number of militants, but here the term refers chiefly to members involved in one of the three forms of plant representation. The CSC metalworkers claim to have 11,000 militants in a ratio to members of 1 : 13.

On the railways the unions reckon that they have one union delegate for approximately thirty members.

Neither of the two major textile unions has a separate breakdown of the number of delegates. The FGTB textile union has 3,500 representatives on works councils, safety committees and union delegations, while the figure for the CSC textile union is around 6,500. In both unions the ratio of all forms of plant representative to members is approximately 1 : 18.

HOLLAND

Dutch trade unions have a long history of conservative, bureaucratic government. Neither before nor since the war has there been a tradition of strong union organisation at the workshop level. Works councils have been the only recognised channel of representation since 1950, but the unions have become increasingly dissatisfied with their operation and in recent years have attempted to increase their influence on them. For example, NVV members who hold positions on works councils are taught that their primary allegiance is to the union rather than the company. In smaller plants, especially where no works council exists, the unions have introduced 'trust men' (vertrounsmen), union activists who, while having no executive responsibility, are given the job of liasing between the union and the workforce. And since 1972 district union officials in metalworking have been allowed access to the shopfloor to see members.

In the last few years the unions have gone further than this and have attempted to establish a direct presence in the plant, a presence that is sometimes seen as a form of opposition to the works councils. The aim has been to inject some vitality into trade unionism at the grass roots level. The system adopted involves the formation of union plant committees composed of trust men who now operate more cohesively under the leadership of specially trained and appointed lay co-ordinators. The co-ordinator, or 'contactman', is the chairman of the committee and acts as a link between the official union and its members in the plant. The committees are formally integrated into the union structure in that they, as well as local branches, are entitled to representation on the district committee.

The plant committees are carefully nursed and supervised by full-time specialist officials whose sole job is to liaise with wokshop groups. The NVV industrial workers' union has one such specialist in most of its fourteen districts and the NKV industrial union has two officials at head office fulfilling a similar role. In the initial stages the factory committee system is seen by the unions not so much as a way of developing plant bargaining but as a means of training members in union methods, stimulating union consciousness, and generally presenting some opposition to management by insisting that social as well as technical and economic considerations be taken into account in the management of the plant.

Extent

The unions are vague as to how many trust men they have. Sometimes they have difficulty in getting people to take on the job; and even after the position is filled it may take some effort to keep the incumbents functioning. The NVV transport union has 1,000 trust men among its railway members. This is a ratio of 1 per 11 union members. The ex-Catholic transport union affiliated to NKV also regards 10–12 per cent of its members as trust men. However, the union admits that not all these are active. The NVV industrial workers' union estimates that about 7 per cent of its membership are trust men, while the NKV industrial workers' union reckons that 10,000 of its 136,000 members hold such positions; 5,000 of them in the metalworking sector in a ratio to members of 1 : 12.

In 1973 the NVV industrial workers' union had no more than 250 union plant committees organised on the 'contactman' system, and in the NKV industrial workers' union the number of such committees was no more than 75.

GERMANY

The works council system is probably the most highly developed in Germany, and here the unions have recognised the danger of the councils becoming a mere appendage of management. Consequently they have tried to tighten up the connection between themselves and the works councils. Direct participation by a union official in the council has long been possible if one quarter of the members request it. In this case the official attends only in an advisory capacity. Since 1973 full-time union officials have also had the right of access to their members in the plants, though this is still contested by many employers. In general, however, the unions' attempt to increase their influence on the shop floor during the past decade has been through the introduction of trust men (Vertrauensleute) along the lines we have seen in Holland.

Their function is to bridge the gulf between union members and works councillors and to foster trade unionism in the workshop. They have only limited executive responsibilities and little status. Between a quarter and a half of them also act as works councillors and so there is some confusion of role. But those who are trust men pure and simple are obliged to assist the works councillors, an indication of their subordinate status.

Extent

In metalworking there are 121,000 trust men, a ratio of 1 to every 20 union members. In textiles there are 8,300 trust men, meaning a ratio of 1 per 35 members. In the railway union the 30,000 trust men represent the members in an approximate ratio of 1 : 15.

DENMARK

Danish unions share in common with British trade unions the fact that, to a large extent, they are organised on a craft basis and have a highly developed shop steward (tillidsmand) system. The Danish shop steward function is long established, and indeed stewards were recognised a number of years before they were in Britain. Workshop representatives began to appear in Danish manufacturing industries about 1870, and by 1900 the main engineering union, the Smiths and Engineers, had succeeded in obtaining a special provision in the collective agreement covering the recognition of shop stewards. Moreover, two years later, in 1902, the engineers won a further provision in the collective agreement which guaranteed shop stewards protection. This was nineteen years before the British Engineering Employers Federation conceded recognition to shop stewards. Of twenty-two large national unions in Denmark twelve had obtained recognition for shop stewards before 1920.

Extent

Shop stewards have to be recognised by firms employing more than five workers. Altogether there are more than 15,000 accredited shop stewards in Denmark, making an overall ratio of stewards to union members of approximately 1 : 55. The metalworkers are better organised at the shop level than the average union. Their 3,800 shop stewards ensured that in 1973 there was one workshop representative for every twenty-seven members. The textile union has a total of 283 shop stewards, or one steward per fifty rank and file members.

The greater number of members per shop steward in textiles suggests that there are many factories in this industry that have no shop stewards at all. In factories where the steward system operates the overall shop steward–member ratio is more like 1 : 30. During the last fifteen years the amount of shop steward representation in metal-working has improved, the ratio of stewards to members in 1961 being 1 : 41. On the other hand the trend in textiles has been in the opposite direction and there are now relatively fewer shop stewards than there were in the early 1960s.

SWEDEN

As in all Scandinavian countries, the plant-level unit of union organisation is the club which is a formally constituted sub-section of the local branch. In Sweden the club chairman, and only the chairman, is regarded by the employer as a shop steward (tillitsman). But the club committee can have up to nine members, and in prac-tice these committeemen tend to share the representational functions at plant level.

Extent
Counting only the chairman of the club as a shop steward, the metalworkers' union had one plant representative per 195 members in 1973. However, if it is assumed that all clubs have a nine-man committee, the effective ratio of representatives to members was 1 : 21.

The textile union has one shop steward per forty-four members. But more than two-thirds of these are single representatives in shops that are too small to warrant the creation of a club. In fact there are only 480 fully constituted factory clubs in the entire textile sector.

In the railway industry, where workplace organisation is less pro-nounced, the union estimates that there are 700–800 stewards repre-senting members in a ratio of 1 : 50.

NORWAY

Shop stewards (tillitsmann) are well established in Norwegian in-dustry, their rights and status being set out in great detail in a Basic Agreement between LO and the national employers' federation. Under the agreement shop stewards are permitted in any undertaking where there are at least twenty-five workers. This minimum qualify-ing figure is regarded by the unions as still too high since many plants, even in metalworking, employ less than this number. In a shop em-ploying twenty-five workers the number of shop stewards permitted is two and the figure rises to a maximum of ten in plants employing 750 workers.

Extent

In 1973 the metalworking union had 1,600 factory clubs and claimed to have 12,000 shop stewards representing the members in a ratio of 1 : 7. However, many of these people did not have the full status of shop stewards under the terms of the Basic Agreement. In larger factories the union tends to subdivide the club into groups and the elected officers of these have some representative functions without being recognised by management. Semi-official shop stewards such as these may constitute as much as two-thirds of a plant's corps of union representatives.

In textiles the union has 956 shop stewards, a ratio of approximately one steward per fifteen members.

A ratio of one shop steward per fifteen members is also found in the general railway union.

THE SELECTION AND CONTROL OF PLANT REPRESENTATIVES

Whether or not in-plant representatives are under the close control of higher level union officials will have a considerable bearing on their value to the membership. Frequently the rank and file and the leadership perceive problems differently, and on matters where the rank and file are intimately involved democracy demands that policy should be made locally. This can only be done properly if the union representatives speak for the members rather than the official leadership. It means that workshop representatives should be directly elected by the membership and subject to recall when they no longer have the confidence of their constituents.

The British shop steward system is basically democratic in that shop stewards are normally elected and theoretically subject to re-election at regular intervals. Often in practice positions are held for long periods without the incumbent being challenged in an election. But in general the circumstances under which stewards operate allow the membership a substantial amount of control. The average size of the steward's constituency is sufficiently small for him to be constantly observed by the members, and the close physical proximity of shop stewards to members at work is likely to heighten the transparency of the situation. Moreover, as in many parts of the trade union movement, there is a strong tendency for shop stewards to act as delegates or spokesmen for their shops, rather than to represent their constituents according to their own predilections in the manner of parliamentarians. The delegatory principle means that there is likely to be a continuing rendering of account by the shop steward.

And in practice an unsatisfactory person can be recalled and replaced.

However, the direct accountability of shop stewards to the base can lead to organisational problems. In Britain a potentially difficult situation arises from the fact that they are elected by workers locally to represent their interests and yet at the same time they have the status of official union representatives. Consequently where the wishes of the local membership and the official union conflict the shop steward is placed in a dilemma. Elected by his workmates, though accredited by the national union, he can easily find himself at the centre of a dispute in which the competing claims of local democracy and organisational discipline are involved. This was the issue that confronted the National Industrial Relations Court in the 1972 cases of the T&GWU's blacking of container bases. The question was what amount of control the official union had over shop stewards. Though the Industrial Relations Court has now been abolished, that sensitive question still remains largely unresolved.

FRANCE

The system of choosing union plant delegates differs from organisation to organisation, though appointment is more common than formal election. The CGT metalworkers' delegates are not elected but are designated by the leaders of the local union branch. They have no fixed term of office and hold their position at the convenience of the union. A similar practice prevails in the CFDT and CGT textile unions. But in the latter case there is at least a recognition among the union's national leadership that the system is not exactly open and democratic, and they hope in the future to move in the direction of holding open elections with secret balloting. However, the appointment of delegates is perhaps less of a bureaucratic procedure than it may seem, considering the fact that the decision is taken at the local union level or possibly by the leaders of the factory union section, both of which enjoy considerable autonomy from the central apparatus.

The unions differ in the amount of autonomy they grant to plant sections, but as a general rule the CFDT unions devolve more power to this level than is done in the CGT. Indeed, in most CFDT unions the plant sections are wholly autonomous in matters of industrial policy and finance, although the amount of funds at their disposal is very limited.

Union rule books do not deal with the question of controlling the activities of plant delegates or disciplining them in any way. Disciplinary action is a matter for the appointing body, and thus there

is little likelihood of higher level union officers being able to interfere in the relationship between a delegate and his section.

ITALY

In Italy the ground rules for the operation of shop stewards' committees have not yet been fully settled. Shop steward elections are
every two years in textiles, and though there is no fixed term in
metalworking the tendency is for elections to be held annually. However, a steward's mandate can be revoked by the workers in the
shops at any time. To date non-union workers have been able to vote
in elections, while unions have been trying to guarantee the existence
of a union majority on factory committees. But often elections are
not held at all and the rival unions simply divide between them the
number of seats on the factory committee according to their relative
strength, and local members are then appointed to fill the positions.

BELGIUM

Union delegations are supposed to be elected every four years, but
it is just as common for them to be appointed by the regional committee of the union. The FGTB metalworkers' union leans towards
election. The FGTB railway union insists on delegates being elected.
But this is by no means the practice in all unions.

In metalworking the decision to have or not to have elections is
made at the regional level between the two unions. Here the organisations may simply agree to divide the places up between them in the
same proportion that seats were won by the rival unions in the works
council elections. Thereafter, appointment of delegates for each
union is likely to be made by the twenty to thirty most active militants
deciding which ones among themselves should take the seats. It is
possible for a regional full-time officer to have a hand in this process,
but in metalworking it is unlikely that he could impose his will.

In textiles neither the FGTB nor CSC union bothers with elections.
Under an inter-union agreement that has been in effect since 1947 the
two unions divide the seats on the union delegation between them
equally. This is done even though the CSC union has grown more
since 1947. The reason behind the agreement is to prevent the
employers from knowing the relative strength of the unions. In both
unions the delegates are selected by the regional full-time officer in
consultation with local militants.

Once elected, works councillors and safety committee members
are not subject to recall. But members of union delegations can be
removed during their term of office. The decision is normally taken

at the regional level at the instigation of dissatisfied members. In general the unions keep delegates under firm control, and a CIR investigation of shop floor practices in Belgium discovered that one union required all members of delegations to sign an undated resignation slip.[8]

HOLLAND

In the NVV industrial workers' union and transport union trust men are appointed by the full-time district organisers. The same practice applies in the NKV industrial workers' union. Indeed, of the unions studied, only the NKV transport union attempts to elect its trust men, and even here the union is confronted by widespread apathy so that about 50 per cent of its numbers have to be appointed to make up the complement.

In the case of the factory committee contactmen, all are carefully selected by the district officials.

GERMANY

Trust men may be elected, but more commonly they are appointed by the local full-time officials. For example, this is the case in textiles though the union would prefer to see more of them elected, thereby investing the position with rather more prestige among the workers. The term of office is three years, appointments being made just prior to the works council elections. Where elections take place they must be confirmed by the union and the union can withdraw approval of a trust man at any time.

DENMARK

The shop stewards are elected every year or two years. The metalworking union opts for biennial elections; the textile union shop stewards are elected annually. Not all industries have shop stewards exclusively drawn from trade union members. In metalworking, however, only union members may stand for election. All workers in the shop, whether unionised or not, may vote in the election if they have worked there for at least two years. And a steward's election is not valid unless at least half the workers in the shop vote for him. These are not merely internal union rules but are part of the national agreement. After the election the union must ratify the result and then notify the employer whose approval is also necessary. This is usually a formality, but there is a recognised arbitration procedure in the event that the employer does object. Once a steward is recognised it is a breach of contract for the employer to refuse to deal with him.

In larger plants shop stewards will normally be elected in each shop, but the national agreement gives the employer the right to oppose the election of a separate steward for every union represented there. In such a case one workplace representative might be permitted to speak on behalf of a number of union groups. In any event if there are more than four shop stewards in a plant one will normally be elected as the chief spokesman and as such may well be granted extra facilities and possibly full time off work with pay.

SWEDEN

The club chairmanship is always an elective position, as are the places on the club committee. Elections for these posts may be annual or biennial. The textile workers elect club officials each year. But in the metal union, and especially in the larger clubs, the preference is for elections every two years. The general principle is that half the committee is elected every year.

The granting of credentials to shop stewards is a matter that solely concerns the club. There are no procedures for higher level union approval of elected representatives. The national union has no right to intervene and dismiss, replace or discipline a steward. And even the local union branch does not have the right to interfere in such internal club affairs.

Workshop groups enjoy a considerable amount of financial independence from higher levels of the organisation. Club income derives from a special contribution that may be levied at the factory level. Besides this form of income, clubs in the shipbuilding industry are often paid lump sum amounts by the shipping firm on the completion of a vessel and the amounts involved can be very large. The national union has nothing to do with these types of payment and is frequently unaware of them.

NORWAY

Shop stewards are elected in accordance with union procedure and also in line with the terms of the Basic Agreement. In metalworking and railways elections are held every two years, and in textiles they are held annually. The Basic Agreement stipulates that only workers over twenty-one can vote in these elections and then only when they have been employed by the firm for two years. However, young workers are entitled to elect one shop steward as their own representative. The employer must be notified of the results and only then does a steward have full recognition. There are provisions for an employer to seek the removal of a shop steward who violates the Agreement, the final decision resting with the Labour Court. On the other hand the national union is not in a position to remove an elected steward, and the metal union clearly distinguishes between local branch officials whom it regards as union officers and club officers who are responsible to the membership.

FUNCTIONS OF PLANT REPRESENTATIVES – FACILITIES – COMBINE ORGANISATION

From a practical standpoint the most important consideration in connection with workshop representatives is what they can do in a concrete sense that will benefit the membership. They may act as union recruiting agents, disseminators of information and dues collectors, but these functions are basically geared to the organisational needs of the national union. More important from the members' point of view is whether their representatives can treat directly with employers and negotiate with them on issues that deeply affect the rank and file. In connection with this it is important to consider the privileges and facilities granted to plant representatives that can result in an increase in their effectiveness.

In Britain workplace representatives are frequently in a position to negotiate with employers on crucial questions of wages and working conditions. And while in theory this is often merely supplementary to negotiations at a higher level, in practice plant negotiations are often seen by the members as the most important stage of collective bargaining. Indeed, to a large extent the job situation as it affects the workers and the level of take-home pay are likely to be decided here.

Another aspect of workshop organisation that can have a bearing on local negotiations is the element of inter-shop steward co-ordination by means of combine committees. In Britain, just as joint shop stewards' committees within plants have helped to cement over the fragmentation caused by multi-unionism, so also have attempts been made over many years to run combine committees of shop stewards from different plants of the same company or even of shop stewards from different firms within an industry, as was the case in the car industry in the 1950s. Some of these have suffered and subsequently declined because they were essentially Communist Party creations rather than broadly-based co-ordinating bodies. More recently some unions have begun to encourage inter-plant shop steward connections within the framework of official union machinery. But achievements here have been limited and much more needs to be done to connect plant representatives in different sections of national enterprises, as well as to develop more ambitious links within multi-national corporations.

FRANCE

Prior to 1968 unions did not have any recognition within factories. Dues collecting and the distribution of union literature were rarely permitted. Such functions are now the legitimate responsibility of the plant sections, though even these limited activities are still opposed by many employers. Consequently there is a constant trial of strength over the question of workshop recognition, and even where the union presence is established the balance of forces is such that employers often refuse to negotiate with the unions at this level.

Because of the autonomy enjoyed by local bodies in French unions the question of whether combine organisation is official or not does not arise. Combine meetings do take place within the confines of a particular union confederation. For example, the CGT metalworkers have a co-ordinating body for the twenty or so Renault plants. The CFDT metalworkers' union has similar regular meetings, and in both cases policy and strategy for negotiations are decided. The meetings are convened by the local bodies themselves and the costs are borne at this level. Yet the gatherings are not unofficial in any sense and they have the co-operation and participation of full-time officers. In textiles, the CGT's union takes the lead in co-ordinating meetings of delegates from the different plants of the individual large firms every three, six or twelve months. The CFDT textile union also has combine meetings for big firms like Provost and Agagio, but their policy is not to seek negotiations at the level of the company and consequently the meetings are seen as educational and propaganda events rather than for the purpose of determining bargaining policy.

As far as employer-provided facilities designed to assist the plant delegates are concerned, the French unions are rather badly served. Office space and access to a telephone are luxuries that escape many delegates, though they are allowed between ten and fifteen hours per month off work without loss of pay to attend to union matters.

ITALY

Shop stewards in Italy do negotiate with employers at the plant level and these negotiations may or may not be within the framework of official collective bargaining. The deciding factor is the particular balance of forces between unions and employers, and in many situations there is a continuing state of open industrial warfare.

Combine committees of shop stewards tend to be allowed by the union rules. Their role is informational and advisory, helping individual factory committees to initiate action. Combine committee members are elected by the various factory committees. Meetings are attended by officials of the provincial unions wherever the combines are located. And the committees are entitled to appoint their own full-time officials to be responsible for executing decisions reached by the committee.

Since 1970 shop stewards have enjoyed a number of statutory rights in the plants such as the right to hand out union literature. The law of 1970 also grants recognised shop stewards eight hours off work per month to attend to union business, and in plants with over 200 workers the shop floor representatives must be granted office space. If the unions request it general membership meetings can be held in the factories during working hours without loss of pay, up to ten hours per year being set aside for this. The employers have generally sought to regulate more closely the functions of the shop stewards, but the unions have resisted this on the grounds that it is purely an internal union matter.

BELGIUM

The task of union delegations is to process individual and collective grievances, to police the application of collective agreements in the plant and to conduct plant negotiations over wages and conditions. Within the plant delegations tend to be self-sufficient, and full-time union officials do not have automatic access to plants. The delegation is, of course, a mixed body with members from different unions and this means that there is always a need to co-ordinate union approaches. But unlike French unions between whom rivalry is often very pronounced, the Belgian unions tend to work closely together.

Since the early 1960s there has been less scope for independent plant negotiations as the focus of collective bargaining has shifted to the national level. This has caused a certain amount of tension between the workshop groups and higher levels of the union hierarchy, and in the late 1960s militant, unofficial shop floor groups began to emerge as a reaction against the centralising tendency. As a result the unions were forced to make special efforts to retain control of their delegates in some areas. In 1971 a national agreement extended the role of the delegates within the framework of the official national bargaining system, especially in connection with the policing of agreements.

Combine organisation of union delegates exists but it is part of the official union structure. The FGTB metalworkers' union has co-ordinating committees for delegates within all major multi-plant companies. These meet regularly and especially when company-level negotiations take place. Where company-level bargaining exists plant delegates participate alongside full-time officials.

The CSC metalworkers' inter-plant co-ordination is less well developed. Full-time officials sometimes convene meetings of the two or three principal delegates from each plant in a combine, and sometimes general meetings of militants from all the various plants are arranged for the purpose of exchanging views. But such events tend to be *ad hoc*.

Joint delegate meetings in the textile industry are even less common. The CSC textile union arranges half-yearly meetings of militants from the thirty or so cotton plants belonging to LUCO, but this appears to be an isolated case.

Since 1971 delegates have had more facilities in the factories for passing on information and holding meetings. They get time off from work with pay on a sliding scale depending on the size of the plant. In large plants of 11,500 or more workers the entire delegation share between them 2,060 hours off work per month, the equivalent of full-time release for a dozen or so delegates. And in practice it is quite common for the time allowance to be greater than this under the terms of local agreements.

HOLLAND

Local union organisation has atrophied over the years as the extremely centralised system of collective bargaining leaves little scope for local initiative. The trust men have no formal powers and little influence. In most cases they are simply a link in the union's informational chain, and more often than not this merely involves passing on to the membership the views of the leadership. The new plant committees have not been devised as a vehicle for collective bargaining in the workshop, though the 1972 national metalworking agreement did open the door for negotiations at this level. Since then trust men have been included in the union negotiating team in bargaining with Hoogovens, Philips, and some other firms in metalworking. The scope for lay involvement is greater in this sector than elsewhere because there are a number of big firms that conclude separate agreements outside the national agreement. In textiles, on the other hand, the general absence of company-level bargaining severely limits lay participation in negotiations. And in railways, where the plant union system does not operate, there is no scope whatever for local bargaining.

Following the 1972 metalworking agreement unions have moved

on to demand time off with pay for trust men and facilities for conducting union business during working hours. During the widespread strikes in manufacturing in spring 1973, which were largely about the granting of union recognition in the plant, demands were made that trust men be allowed 2½ hours per year per member off work with pay. Concessions have been won, but these are mostly in the metal industries. For the first time some trust men now have the right to hand out union literature and put up union notices at work. Meanwhile demands for the right to hold general membership meetings in the plant and to have time off from work for training continue to be made.

GERMANY

Despite the fact that trust men were introduced to mitigate the tendency for plant bargaining to take place independently of the union, they themselves play no part in negotiations unless they also happen to be works councillors. In individual cases a trust man may be asked to join a team of works councillors to advise them on a point in which he has some expertise, but this is as far as it goes.

Otherwise, their normal activities include the recruiting of new members and the collection of dues, though with the widespread use of the check-off there is little need for that. Generally, they have a role in spreading union information and acting as a link between local members and works councillors. They may also play a limited part in grievance handling, hearing complaints and passing them on to the works councillors whose job it is to take them up.

However, trust men have no special facilities or privileges in the plant. There is no protection against arbitrary dismissal such as works councillors enjoy. And they are not given paid leave to attend to union business.

DENMARK

A considerable amount of piecework is practised in Denmark and this means that there is plenty of scope for in-plant bargaining over rates and time allowances. But the distinctive feature about piecework is that it has traditionally been set on an individual rather than a group basis. This means that negotiations take place between the individual worker and the foreman. The shop steward intervenes if there is failure to agree at this level.

In the past, piecework often operated on a sub-contracting system with shop stewards acting as a sort of sub-contractor to his members. This placed him in a role halfway between management and union.

With the introduction of more sophisticated wage payment systems in the 1960s this practice has now died out. But the shop steward still fulfils the role of a 'broker' standing somewhere between management and workers. The metalworking collective agreement, for example, specifically states that it is the shop steward's duty to maintain and promote co-operation at the work place. This is a reflection of a general trait of Danish trade unionism in which union leaders at all levels of the hierarchy are seen as mediators rather than sectional representatives of the membership. And shop stewards can be sued for negligence by the employer if they fail to carry out their responsibility of maintaining the peace.

In most cases workshop representatives are allowed considerable time off work with pay. And stewards are protected from arbitrary dismissal. Since 1926 metalworking shop stewards have had the right to two months (now four months) notice before dismissal, and the notice must be worked. The onus is on the employer to show 'compelling reasons' for the steward's dismissal. During the period of notice arbitration proceedings begin, and if the award is in favour of the shop steward the employer will be ordered to retain him.

SWEDEN

Despite the centralisation of collective bargaining in Sweden there is still some scope for plant level negotiating. Central agreements set a framework for lower level negotiations, but within this many details have to be resolved. And the traditional reliance on piecework means that a considerable amount of negotiating must take place in the plant. In the late 1950s two-thirds of all work in the metal industries was paid on an incentive basis, but this is now declining. In textiles 50 per cent of workers are still on piecework. In metalworking a national agreement specifies how piece rates are to be computed. But times for jobs are negotiated in the plant on the basis of work study and a procedure exists for resolving piecework disputes at this level. The fact that earnings tend to be considerably higher than basic rates reflects the importance of shop floor bargaining. Aside from this it is at plant level that such matters as shop steward rights and status are decided.

The experiment in centralised economy-wide bargaining since the war has in fact produced strains which can only be eased by devolving bargaining power to the local and plant level. This poses something of a problem in terms of central union control over clubs. In any system of decentralised bargaining the club must have a large amount of autonomy. Yet in theory clubs are required to carry out instructions from the local branch or the national union on the

handling of internal workshop problems. Indeed the club is constitutionally a creation of the local branch, and the channelling of the
stewards' lines of communication through the local branch is supposed to prevent workshop groups from evolving a separate power
base. For all this the club rather than the local branch tends to be
the effective bargaining agency.

To maintain the influence of the national union at this level the
metalworkers' union is now pioneering a system of 'contact men'
somewhat akin to the trust men of Holland and Germany. Such
people may be club committee members or they may simply be rank
and filers. Contact men are selected by the local branch and the
union then gives them a special training in courses organised at the
local level by national officers. Their role is that of a two-way information agency between union and member. They take no part
in collective bargaining and are only likely to engage in grievance
handling in small factories where there are no clubs. In the present
stage of the system's development some contact men are required
to service several thousand members. But the long-term aim is to
have one for every 20–25 members.

Combine committees of shop stewards are only in a formative
stage. In individual firms in metalworking such as SKF, combine
organisation among shop stewards has existed unofficially for a
number of years. The metalworkers' union is now thinking in terms
of giving official encouragement to such developments. Local training courses for shop stewards are being organised officially with a
view to giving workshop representatives from different locations an
opportunity to meet, while an official eye is kept on developments.
And some consideration is being given to changing the union's rules
to allow combine groups to be set up constitutionally. However since
the question involves other unions too, the metalworkers are waiting
for a lead from the central union body, LO, before proceeding.

Shop stewards are allowed paid time off work and plant agreements occasionally provide for a steward to be freed entirely from
work, but full-time workshop representatives are not very common.
In the largest metalworking factories like Volvo or in the shipyards
there might be as many as three full-time shop stewards. But in
textiles there are no plant representatives permanently released from
work.

NORWAY

The role of shop stewards within the centralised Norwegian system
of industrial relations is to act as the first stage in grievance handling,
to supervise the application of collective agreements and to negotiate

over piece rates and wages in the plant. All this is within the framework of nationally negotiated agreements. Shop stewards do not have the right to call strike action over local issues during the term of these agreements. Indeed the Basic Agreement requires shop stewards to do their best to maintain peaceful and effective co-operation at work. Nevertheless occasional walkouts do occur. In railways opportunities for plant bargaining are limited to issues such as work scheduling and never touch on wage questions.

Joint shop steward bodies are permitted within the official union structure. The Basic Agreement provides for joint meetings of shop stewards from different unions within the same plant. In such a situation the entire body of union members is entitled to elect one of the stewards to the position of chief shop steward which then allows him greater freedom within the plant. The Agreement also provides for the establishment of combine committees. In multi-plant companies, or sections of companies covered by the same collective agreement, a co-ordinating committee composed of the various chairmen of shop steward groups must be recognised. And management are compelled to meet the body at least once a year.

Where the amount of a steward's work justifies it, the Basic Agreement requires the two sides to negotiate at plant level over the provision of office space. Normally the three leading officers of the club constitute the union side in plant negotiations and these three are all granted unrestricted access to the various departments of the plant. Ordinary shop stewards are allowed to go about their union tasks unimpeded, and while they are not allowed any specific amount of time away from their work the Basic Agreement stipulates that time off should not be refused without very good reason. In the metalworking industry nearly every big factory of, say, 1,000 workers has at least two full-time shop stewards whose wage is paid by the employer. Shop stewards generally are granted some protection against arbitrary dismissal under the Basic Agreement in that they must be given four weeks notice. And if the union challenges this the person must be kept on by the firm until the Labour Court makes a ruling.

CONCLUSION

Union workshop organisation is at different levels of development in the countries examined, but everywhere its importance is coming to be recognised by the unions. Recent years have witnessed considerable growth in the strength of union representation at this level and improvements in the facilities accorded to union delegates. In a number of countries this must be seen, at least in part, as a means of compensating for the inadequacies of the works council system.

The amount of workshop-level union representation does not appear to differ greatly from country to country. The best organised unions in France and Italy have a similar ratio of representatives to members as have British trade unions in general. Figures for the Scandinavian unions suggest that their best organised unions may have a denser ratio of shop stewards to members than is the general case in this country, though in Sweden and Norway not all of those included in the calculation have the full status of shop stewards. And in most countries it is the metalworkers rather than the textile or railway unions that are best organised at the plant level.

However, it is not simply the number of representatives that is important, but what they can do for their members. Here only the British, and to some extent the Italian, shop stewards appear to combine a reasonably dense network of plant organisation and substantial freedom to negotiate on behalf of the membership. The Donovan Commission estimated that four out of five British shop stewards negotiate over one or more issues with their employer, and that plant bargaining exists in practically all unionised firms in engineering with more than 250 workers. In other countries such as Germany and Holland there are no union negotiating rights at this level. In France the unions have often not had the strength to force employers to bargain with them. And in Scandinavia, where the workshop group has the right to negotiate, its capacity for bargaining effectively is reduced by the widespread restriction on local strike action.

Finally, there is the key question of how democratic the shop floor organisation is. Only the Scandinavian unions have all their shop stewards elected by the membership at large. In Belgium, Germany, Italy and France both election and appointment is practised. In each of these countries except Germany elections usually imply competition between unions for places on a joint union body, with each organisation's candidates being put forward by list. Who gets on the list is not so much a matter for election as for the union machine to decide, though the process of natural selection may not differ all that much from the way some British shop stewards emerge. At the same time, however, it is clear that the system of workshop representation in most countries, again with the exception of Britain and Italy, has developed under the close supervision of the official union. In a number of cases the unions seem well able to control the activities of the plant representatives. And this suggests that there may be grounds for doubting their ability to represent their members adequately at all times.

4

Union Conference

This section deals with the legislative process in trade unions as embodied in the system of regular conferences. The aim is to describe how conference works and to see to what extent the system is susceptible to control by rank and file members. Conference is usually represented as the supreme policy-making body in a union. In many cases it is at conference that the top officials of the organisation are elected. And often conference acts in a judicial capacity as the final appeal court for members' complaints against the leadership. Because of the importance of these various functions, the question of how conference goes about its business is fundamental for any study of democracy in an organisation.

In their analysis of trade union democracy the Webbs regarded the development of union conference as an important and welcome step towards representative democracy in the labour movement. Indeed, the emergence of a system of periodic conferences of elected union representatives was a necessary means of coming to terms with the problem of running a large-scale, national organisation. But it would be wrong to conclude that trade unions now operate a full-blown system of representative government.

Until well into the second half of the nineteenth century, and for as long as unions were sufficiently small and manageable, the general preference was for a form of direct democracy that involved policy-making by mass meetings or through referenda, with the responsibility for initiating policies firmly lodged in the hands of the members. Much of the thinking that lay behind this system of government still has an appeal in contemporary trade unionism. The conversion to representative democracy has never been complete; and as was suggested earlier, rank and file union members in Britain have tended to venture no further away from direct democracy with its emphasis on active participation by members, than they have been compelled to by the sheer size of organisation.

Union conference is a form of representative government. But the 'representative' element can vary from union to union. Conference delegates may have all the freedom of parliamentary-style representatives, or they may be strictly mandated by their branch to speak and vote in a particular way. In between these polar positions is a range of options, each one reflecting a greater or lesser degree of direct democracy. For as J. A. Banks rightly suggests, a conference representative who reports back to his branch on his activities is moving in the direction of becoming a delegate.[1]

This distinction between, on the one hand, direct, and on the other hand, representative, democracy in unions is something that must be borne in mind in dealing with the operation of conference. Our examination of the legislative and judicial system involves consideration of those aspects of conference organisation that add to or detract from the ability of the rank and file to maintain control of the decision-making process. First of all we must look at the size of the assembly. Is it small and business-like, or large with a tendency to be unwieldy? If it is a small gathering, is efficiency bought at the price of having a system of indirect selection of delegates which militates against direct democracy? The frequency with which conference is held and the length of time the proceedings last are additional factors that affect the members' capacity for influencing detailed policy-making. Brief, infrequent conferences are unable to transact as much business as lengthy conferences held at short intervals. At conference itself the balance of forces between the organisation's officialdom and the rank and file representatives is of prime importance. We need to look at the percentage of full-time officials attending conference and the number of these entitled to vote. Beyond this it is important to consider how open and subject to rank and file influence is the procedure for deciding the order of business and treating resolutions, in short the whole process of managing the conference. With regard to the voting on conference resolutions, we need to have some idea of how extensive is the practice of branches mandating their delegates. And finally, we must look at the judicial role that conference may have. Do members have the right to appeal to a third party against leadership decisions, and does the conference have a part to play in this?

If conference is to be a truly democratic institution it is probably preferable to have a small deliberative assembly even though this involves fewer people participating, provided that the delegates are elected directly by the membership and there is a full system of reporting back to local branches. More important still for union democracy is the need to have frequent conferences. Held at intervals of more than twelve months, conferences can do little more than lay down general policy guidelines, leaving the executive bodies to interpret these and elaborate the details. To ensure rank and file control of conference, attendance should be restricted to lay members, with an absolute minimum number of full-time officials present with a voice but no vote. Equally, conference procedures need to be decided by the delegates themselves without interference from the union leadership. And as much as possible, conference voting ought to be on the basis of mandates from the local constituency, based on a thorough, prior consideration of the agenda at the local level.

CONFERENCE SIZE

The optimum size of conference delegations is an issue over which there are likely to be nearly as many differing views as there are unions. The simple argument in favour of the smaller body is that it lends itself to more workmanlike proceedings. Policy can be discussed and decided in detail. The relatively low cost of maintaining a small number of delegates permits conference to go on for a longer period. And the physical layout of a small conference can lessen the gulf between the platform and the floor.

On the other hand a small conference in a large union may involve a form of indirect selection of delegates and this conflicts with the ideal of direct democracy. Larger conferences can avoid this with direct election of delegates and more or less mass participation of lay members. The gathering together of large numbers of members also serves as an essential emotional rallying point in many general unions whose heterogeneous membership may need an occasional reminder of their community of interests. On the other hand the atmosphere of large conferences is better suited to the needs of the accomplished platform speaker than the unpolished contributions of ordinary delegates.

British unions provide examples at both extremes. The conferences of the large general unions such as the Transport and General Workers Union (T&GWU) and the Union of Shop, Distributive and Allied Workers (USDAW) have in the region of 1,000 delegates. At the other end of the scale the engineering section of the Amalgamated Union of Engineering Workers (AUEW) has a 52-man policy-making body. A proposal in 1974 to increase the size of the AUEW's national committee from 52 to 300 was fiercely opposed and defeated when it was put before the union's policy-making body for decision.[2] Most unions fall between these two extremes and B. C. Roberts' investigation of seventeen major unions concluded that the average size of union delegations was something under 500.[3]

Our study of unions on the continent shows a somewhat similar situation, the average size delegation for twenty-nine unions examined being rather more than 400. Three-quarters of these unions had delegations of 200–500 people, and as Table 4.1 shows these included each of the Dutch, German and Scandinavian unions studied.

Table 4.1 *Approximate Number of Delegates Attending Union Conference*

France	CGT metalworkers	1,000+
	CGT textile workers	300+
	CGT rail workers	900+
	CFDT metalworkers	700
	CFDT textile workers	300
	CFDT rail workers	600
Italy	CISL metalworkers	500
	CISL textile workers	250
	CGIL rail workers	1,000
Belgium	FGTB metalworkers	350–400
	FGTB textile workers	300
	FGTB public service workers	750
	CSC metalworkers	600
	CSC textile workers	1,000
	CSC rail workers	400
Holland	NVV industrial workers	300+
	NVV rail workers	200
	NKV rail workers	200+
Germany	DGB metalworkers	470
	DGB textile workers	200
	DGB rail workers	300
Denmark	metalworkers	430
	textile workers	225
Sweden	metalworkers	300
	textile workers	250
	public service workers	300
Norway	metalworkers	300–350
	textile workers	124
	rail workers	210

None of the unions operates a conference as small as the AUEW's 52-man, or the National Union of Railwaymen's (NUR) 77-man, conference. For the most part the assemblies are medium-sized gatherings, the major exceptions to this rule being found among Belgian CSC unions and certain French and Italian communist organisations.

The actual size of delegations at various CGT union conferences reflects certain interesting aspects of their policy-making system. The

CGT metalworkers' rule book permits each of its 1,800 local branches to send a delegate to conference. In practice by no means all of the branches avail themselves of this right, largely for financial reasons. Similarly, only about three-quarters of the CGT railway union's branches eligible to be represented at conference do in fact send a delegate. To some extent this is part of a deliberate policy to restrict the size of the conference to manageable proportions, and the practice of imposing an unofficial limit on the size of delegations also exists in the CFDT unions. In the case of the CGT textile workers, however, the union's problem is not to limit the size of the delegations but to encourage local branches to send more delegates to conference. As in other CGT unions, all branches are entitled to be represented. But although the union has 400 branches, only 121 of them were represented by delegates at the 1973 conference. The union leaders explained that the national parliamentary elections held that year had served to divert the attention and energy of their members. But they also recognise that an important factor in the poor attendance is the membership's low estimation of the practical value of conference in the policy-making process, a point we will return to in more detail.

FREQUENCY AND DURATION OF CONFERENCE

The most common arrangement in Britain is for union conference to be held every year or every two years. V. L. Allen's survey of trade unionism in 1952 showed that more than half of eighty-four large TUC affiliates studied had annual policy-making conferences and 75 per cent had conferences at least every two years.[4] Of the various unions in metalworking, textiles and railways, the AUEW and General and Municipal Workers Union (GMWU) have annual conferences, as do the railway unions, the Associated Society of Locomotive Engineers and Firemen (ASLEF), the Transport and Salaried Staffs Association (TASSA) and the NUR, together with the National Union of Hosiery and Knitwear Workers (NUHKW) and the National Union of Dyers and Bleachers (NUDB) in textiles. The T&GWU and the National Union of Tailors and Garment Workers (NUTGW) meet to set policy every two years.

However, as Table 4.2 shows, the continental practice is for conferences to be far less frequent. Of the various unions examined, the minimum period between conferences is three years and it is not uncommon for conference to meet every four or even five years.

Once again the practice in the French CGT unions is particularly worth noting. Until the early 1970s CGT unions held their conferences

Table 4.2 *Frequency and Duration of Union Conferences*

		Interval (in years)	Duration (in days)
France	CGT metalworkers	3	5
	CGT textile workers	3	4
	CGT rail workers	3	4–5
	CFDT metalworkers	3	4
	CFDT textile workers	3	3–4
	CFDT rail workers	3	3
Italy	CISL metalworkers	4	4–5
	CISL textile workers	4	3
Belgium	FGTB metalworkers	3	3
	FGTB textile workers	3	2–3
	FGTB public service workers	4	4
	CSC metalworkers	4	–
	CSC textile workers	4	1
	CSC public service workers	4	1–3
Holland	NVV industrial workers	3	3
	NVV rail workers	3	1
	NKV industrial workers	3	2–3
	NKV rail workers	3	1
Germany	DGB metalworkers	3	5
	DGB textile workers	3	5
	DGB rail workers	4	5–6
Denmark	metalworkers	3	5
	textile workers	4	5
	rail workers	4	3
Sweden	metalworkers	4	5
	textile workers[a]	5	5
	public service workers[a]	4	–
Norway	metalworkers	4	5
	textile workers	4	5
	rail workers	4	5

[a] The rules of the Swedish textile and public service unions do not specify how often conference must be held. The figure for textiles is based on past practice. The recently formed public service union has no established practice yet, but it is thought that conference will probably be every four years.

every two years, but now the interval has been extended to three years. The CGT metalworkers cite increasing costs as one important reason for this change. But it is apparent too that the task of organising a conference every two years placed a strain on the union's administrative machinery that it found difficult to bear. Another reason for the change cited by the CGT textile workers is that the new system enables the union to organise more specialist regional and sectoral conferences of militants. There is, indeed, a tendency for CGT unions to convene an increasing number of *ad hoc* conferences on particular issues. But however laudable this may be as a way of decentralising decision-making, the effect is also to devalue the national conference.

In this and other instances where conference is convened relatively infrequently the question arises as to how rank and file members can possibly maintain reasonable democratic control over union activities. In practice it means that most unions have to introduce an additional level of government in the form of a general council or its equivalent, fitting somewhere between conference and the national executive committee, and this body tends to acquire some of the powers of conference. The work of the general councils is considered later, but here it is sufficient to note that their existence tends to reduce the overall importance of conference.

Compounding the inadequacy of infrequent conferences in some unions is the fact that when they do take place they last for only a very short period. In Britain most union conferences last from three to five days, though in some cases much more time is taken up. In particular the AUEW and NUR policy-making bodies may sit for as much as two weeks and even then the agenda may not be completed. Table 4.2 shows the prevailing practice in the European unions studied. In many cases the duration of conference is much the same as in Britain. However, the railway sections of the two Dutch transport unions only hold a one-day conference every three years to discuss policies for the rail sector, and in the Belgian CSC textile union the national conference amounts to no more than a one-day gathering every four years. In such cases we must conclude that conference is purely a symbolic rite and that policy decisions are effectively taken elsewhere.

PRESENCE OF OFFICIALS AT CONFERENCE

Full-time union officials can, and often do, have interests different from those of the people they represent. One of the problems of democracy in large-scale, professionally administered organisations is to ensure that the wishes of the rank and file membership prevail over any narrow, professional interests that the leaders may have. However, at conference the influence of lay members can be limited in many ways, and there is often considerable scope for union officials to dominate proceedings and to guide the course of events in directions that suit their own purposes. There are various dimensions to the problem and a multitude of ways in which officialdom can impose its influence. Much of this boils down to the way conference proceedings are conducted. But prior to that the balance of forces between union officialdom and the rank and file can be decided by the number of full-time officials who are allowed to attend conference and participate.

British unions demonstrate a range of approaches to this problem. By and large most conferences do have a number of full-time officials in attendance, though it is common practice for them not to have a vote, merely the right to speak. In the textile industry the NUHKW exemplifies one extreme, its rule book specifying that all full-time officials attend conference and are regarded as fully accredited delegates. On the other hand the NUTGW constitution permits only two full-time officials among its general officers to be present. In engineering the AUEW takes the greatest precautions against domination by officialdom with the rule that only the president and general secretary and three of the full-time executive members are allowed to attend the national committee meeting, without the right to vote. Among the general unions the GMWU represents the opposite pole, its annual conference being open to general officers, the national industrial officers, the ten regional secretaries, one-third of the field officers, and one-third of the branch administrative officers. In the railway industry the NUR adopts a system similar to that of the AUEW in that only the president, the general secretary and assistant general secretaries are allowed to attend the annual conference, and then without the right to vote.

Opportunities for the entire corps of full-time officials to vote at conference, such as exist at the NUHKW conference, are rare. Nor is it necessarily the case that officials who have a voice but no vote will dominate debates. However, there is no need for officials to play such an open part for their influence to be felt at conference. The psychological effect on delegates of seeing officials there in strength can be to inhibit lay participation. But beyond this, full-time officials may play a significant part behind the scenes in mobilising support for the leadership position, and this is especially so in cases where the officials present owe their appointment to the union leaders.

FRANCE

The CGT metalworkers' union estimates that up to 20 per cent of the people present at conference are full-time officers of one description or another. However, it is likely that the majority of these are people employed by local unions or even plant delegates on full-time release from work rather than officials employed by the national union and therefore members of the central apparatus. Still the full complement of around forty full-time officials who make up the national administration do attend conference. And bearing in mind that large assemblies are often more easily manipulated and swayed by the platform than smaller gatherings, this gives the union leadership a substantial body of supporters at conference.

The CFDT metalworkers has a similar ratio of lay delegates to full-time officials. Again many of the full-time officials probably hold their position at local level as employees of an autonomous local group. But the sixty to seventy full-time officials from national and regional level are likely to attend.

In the CGT railway union the thirty or so full-time officials attend conference. However, neither the CFDT nor CGT textile unions has large numbers of full-time officials at conference since both unions only have a handful of staff representatives.

ITALY

In both the CISL metalworking and textile unions the average number of full-time officials present at conference is 25 per cent of the total delegation. However, the vast majority of these are people employed at regional or provincial level by bodies who enjoy a considerable amount of autonomy from the central administration.

BELGIUM

In the FGTB unions the full-time officials can have full voting rights at conference if they are elected as delegates by a regional body. If they are not so elected they can attend with a voice but no vote. In the FGTB metalworkers' union some indication of the possible influence of the official element is given by the union rule stating that regional bodies that are entitled to more than three delegates must chose 50 per cent of them from among lay members working on the shop floor. The union claims that in practice the percentage of lay delegates is considerably higher than this. And in any case the union's full-time officials at regional level are essentially employed by the governing body at that level and cannot be presumed to be supporters of the national administration.

The CSC unions display different approaches, the railway union debarring all officials from being delegates, while the textile and clothing union has thirty officials at conference out of a total delegation of 1,000.

HOLLAND

The NVV industrial workers' conferences are attended by all full-time officers down to and including regional organisers. Along with seventy-eight members of the general council who attend in a consultative capacity, they constitute a bloc of non-voting delegates accounting for one out of three of the total number present. And since all full-time officials owe their appointment to the national leadership this provides the administration with a considerable number of potential workers and lobbyists at conference.

GERMANY

In the three German unions studied a situation exists similar to that in the NVV industrial workers' union. In the metal union only 78 per cent of the delegates are laymen. In the railway union the figure is 80 per cent, and in the textile union lay members barely constitute more than two-thirds of the overall delegation.

DENMARK

In most Scandinavian unions conference is dominated numerically by rank and file delegates. In the Danish metalworkers 90 per cent of the delegates are reckoned to be from the shop floor, and the balance tends to comprise local full-time officials employed by the local body.

SWEDEN

In the Swedish unions examined full-time officials can be voting delegates at conference. In the metalworkers union the vast majority of delegates are shop stewards and local branch officers. In the public service union, however, full-time officials constitute 25 per cent of those in attendance at conference and 15 per cent of the voting delegates.

NORWAY

The metalworkers union allows its twenty-five or so full-time officials to attend conference with a voice but no vote, and the textile union claims that all voting delegates are lay members.

In summary, the situation is that many unions permit their full-time officials to attend conference in a voting or non-voting capacity. In either case their presence can be important, whether they actually vote in support of the leadership position or simply use their influence as lobbyists among lay delegates. However, a general distinction has to be made between full-time officials who are genuinely to be seen as part of the central administration and those employed by another level of the hierarchy. The latter situation applies to many of the full-time officials attending union conferences in France, Italy and Belgium as well as some in Denmark. In these cases the fact that up to 20–30 per cent of the total delegation are not lay members would seem to be less likely to favour the central administration than is the case in, for example, Holland and Germany where all full-time officials are directly responsible to the national leadership.

CONFERENCE PROCEDURES

In discussing conference procedures it is helpful to distinguish between two general approaches that tend to be found in European unions. In the first place there is the system in which conference considers only one or a few general resolutions prepared by the leadership. In the second place there are conference systems in which some semblance of initiative rests with the membership. In the latter case the chances of resolutions from the grass roots meeting with success will depend largely on how free the conference arrangements committee or standing orders committee is from control from above : in the former case there is rarely any great difficulty in getting conference to endorse the leadership's proposals placed before it. The two styles of conference are broadly associated with, in the first case, unions that exist within a divided labour movement and, in the second, with organisations that belong to a unified movement. In France, Italy, Belgium and Holland where there is dual unionism, to be a member of a particular union is to show a commitment not simply to trade unionism in general but also to a particular strand of trade unionism. Here the amount of potential internal conflict and disagreement within a union is likely to be less than in unions such as in Germany and Scandinavia where the organisation may embrace a wider range of viewpoints. Because of this, union conferences in the former group of countries are less likely to witness factional divisions based on competing ideologies. If members find themselves out of sympathy with the general perspectives and orientation of the union they can presumably leave and join a rival union. But where the labour movement does not tolerate dual organisation the only alternatives for a dissatisfied member are to oppose the dominant philosophy from within the union or to leave the movement altogether.

British unions fall very definitely into the second category described. Union conference is frequently the place where real alternative philosophies and programmes are counterposed, and consequently the procedure followed at conference is very important. On the whole there is a basic similarity between the way conference is conducted in various British unions. Essentially the meeting is intended to hear an account of the officers' stewardship and to make policy for the ensuing period. This involves receiving and discussing the report of the leadership and also debating the various resolutions and motions that may be proposed by the leadership or the local branches and districts.

Conference procedure is a highly specialised matter and a familiarity with this on the part of delegates is necessary, for although the event is meant to give the membership an opportunity to make policy there are many ways in which the will of the members can be frustrated. The precise wording of reports and resolutions matters a great deal. Resolutions from the branches may seek to tie the hands of the leadership very tightly on a particular issue. On the other hand the leaders may attempt to place the widest interpretation on a resolution so as to have the greatest possible freedom of manoeuvre. The way in which resolutions are composited, the order in which business is called, and the management of the debates can also seriously influence the democratic process. This is fully appreciated by experienced delegates, so that before the substantive issues are decided there tend to be struggles over procedural issues aimed at giving one or another faction the upper hand.

The first point that needs to be considered is the way resolutions are treated. In Britain it is customary for branches or divisions to send in motions before conference. A preliminary agenda is circulated and proposed amendments to the resolutions invited. In order to keep conference within manageable proportions the number of resolutions has somehow to be limited, and it is in the arrangement of the agenda or the compositing of resolutions that the initial struggles between different viewpoints often take place. The battleground is the conference arrangements committee, the standing orders committee or the resolutions committee. The purpose of these bodies is to condense the business of conference so that the agenda can be completed, to allow the delegates a chance to vote on the major different points of view put forward, and possibly to give them some guidance on this in the form of a recommendation for or against acceptance.

These committees are thus strategically important bodies, and it is over their composition and the manner of selecting them that the first struggle is likely to take place. In terms of democratic procedure it is essential that they be elected by rank and file members and that they should be completely free from any direct or indirect pressure from the leadership. This may not be possible if there are full-time officials either on the committees or acting as advisory members.

In practice the committees tend to include full-time officials, executive committee members and laymen in various combinations. The National Union of Boot and Shoe Operatives (NUBSO) uses a mixture of officials and executive members. TASSA tends to have a committee made up of executive and lay members. The AUEW, NUR and T&GWU, on the other hand, have bodies composed entirely of lay members. Within these various forms there are different methods of selection. For example, a T&GWU biennial conference elects the standing orders committee for the subsequent conference. TASSA's membership elects its conference committee well in advance of the event, usually in the proportion of two rank and file members to three executive committee members. And the NUTGW executive committee appoints a standing orders committee in advance of conference from among the delegates elected by the branches. This committee then elects its own chairman.

FRANCE

The procedure in France differs considerably from British practice. National officers' or executive committee reports are presented and debated, but the basis of future policy tends to be a programme drawn up by the leadership rather than a collection of resolutions originating with the local branches. And frequently the conference will have a particular theme or themes for discussion decided on in advance by the leadership. For example, the national officers may decide that the conference should discuss its approach to incomes policy, industrial democracy, or the restructuring of aspects of the union's internal organisation. Such predetermined themes then become, in effect, a substitute for resolutions from the base. And consequently the practice may well result in conference debates revolving around leadership priorities rather than around the issues that concern the rank and file. Given this system, it is hardly surprising that the resolutions committee or its equivalent does not figure prominently in conference arrangements.

In the CGT metalworkers' union the main conference debate is on the report of the general council. It is essentially a report prepared by the national officers who constitute the secretariat and then approved by the general council. The report and a proposed policy programme prepared by the secretariat are circulated among the branches in advance. In conference a dozen or more amendments to the programme might be introduced, but the main lines of the final product tend to correspond closely to the original draft.

Sometimes the policy programme will deal specifically with collective bargaining demands, but in the CGT textile union these are treated as a separate issue. At its 1973 conference the CGT textile union adopted a single resolution some seven pages long. It amounted to a short essay on the state of the textile industry within the framework of world capitalism, but it included very few positive proposals other than some non-contentious suggestions such as to intensify the effort to get CGT propaganda accepted. The separate bargaining programme endorsed was simply an updating of the union's long-standing aims. The full list of bargaining demands extended over fourteen printed pages and touched on almost every conceivable subject including a demand for a cease-fire in Cambodia and a settlement to the Middle East question. But none of the decisions taken at conference is so precise as to tie the hands of the national officials. From the broad list of demands approved they are, presumably, free to decide their own order of priorities. As the conference call stated, the aim is to 'define the general orientation for future struggles'. It is, therefore, only within this general area of approving 'the orientation' that the conference has a role, and the assembly can hardly be seen as the occasion for detailed policy-making by the rank and file.

By comparison with CGT practice, the conference procedure in the CFDT is perhaps a little more open, though basically it is the same system. As in the CGT, the agenda is prepared by the national office in the name of the general council, the themes for discussion being pre-selected and circulated to branches in advance in the form of reports. The CFDT metalworkers' conference spends a day debating each of the reports placed before it by the leadership. Afterwards the national officers introduce resolutions on the reports. In 1971, seven resolutions were debated including a general one on policy, one dealing with the bargaining programme, another with the role of the plant branches, and the remainder on union finances, publications and the war in Vietnam. Again each of the resolutions amounted to a short essay taking up on average about six printed pages. During the debate amendments were proposed from the floor on many issues and votes were taken on contentious sections. In some cases up to 40 per cent of the delegates voted against the official view, but no resolution or section of a resolution was rejected. In any event, when resolutions are as long and discursive as these it may be impossible to change the general tone and intent without a complete rewriting, and this is outside the scope of most conferences. The fact is that in drafting the resolutions before congress the leaders make an effort to appeal to all sides, and the final product is more like a compromise communique than a specific directive.

The CFDT textile union goes a little further in attempting to involve the conference delegates in policy-making. After hearing the report of the national officers, a report which deliberately sets out to raise questions rather than to supply pat answers, the delegation divides itself into working parties on different themes that have been highlighted by the report. It is in these groups that the work of drafting the different parts of a single all-embracing resolution begins. The net result is a generally-worded resolution-cum-communique which has the broad approval of the bulk of the delegates and may touch on anything from detailed decisions relating to union finance to a wider philosophical discussion of the best forms of struggle.

BELGIUM

The CFDT textile union approach, with its greater scope for rank and file initiative, is also found among some Belgian unions. In the FGTB metalworkers' union conference is the final stage of a process that begins a full year earlier with the choice by the executive of three or four conference themes. In 1973 the themes were inflation, multinational companies and European trade unionism. The union draws up working papers on each of the themes and these are circulated, along with the national officers' report of activities, to the regions in time for the triennial regional conferences. There each region adopts a collective position on the various documents. At the subsequent national conference there is a general debate on the report and the working papers lasting one and a half days, after which conference divides into various groups to begin drafting the resolutions. A similar style of conference was started in the CSC metalworkers' union in 1972. And while this system of collective drafting of resolutions represents an advance over the procedure where a prepared resolution is placed before the delegates, it is easy to see how, with very wide-ranging, general statements, the union leaders are left with considerable flexibility of action.

By contrast with the relatively open conferences of the two metalworking unions the CSC textile union provides a classic example of a conference controlled by the leadership. This one-day event held every four years leaves no time to discuss anything in detail, while at the same time the leaders are in close control of all matters coming before conference. The leadership sends out drafts of up to half-a-dozen general resolutions to the branches before the conference. Branches that wish to propose amendments do so, and the leadership can decide whether to accept the proposal or not. A second agenda is then distributed incorporating the amendments accepted and stating briefly why other proposals have been rejected. But the full text of the amendments, whether accepted or not, is not published. The amendments that are accepted tend to qualify the original proposal rather than negative it. And at all times the resolutions stick to a high level of generalisation. One of the five resolutions dealt with at the 1972 conference was on the subject of wages and employment policy, and an amendment proposing the incorporation of specific demands relating to job security and bonus payments was rejected by the leadership on the grounds that this was too detailed for a medium-term programme. At the conference itself the officers' report of activities is debated in the morning and voted on in its entirety. And in a single afternoon session all the lengthy resolutions prepared by the leadership have to be debated and voted on.

HOLLAND

In the NVV industrial workers' union, policy is contained in a single official resolution submitted to conference by the leadership. The first day of conference is given over to debating the report of activities and the financial report. Elections of officers are held at conference, and only on the final day are resolutions discussed. The main focus of attention is the single, all-embracing resolution that has been prepared over the preceding year and a half by various working parties made up of laymen and full-time officials. These working parties have responsibility for different sections of the resolution, their work being co-ordinated at all times by head office. At the same time local branches and factory committees are invited to submit resolutions of their own. If they do they are published in the union newspaper, but resolutions from this source are rare. The general council and the executive committee usually make a joint recommendation for or against acceptance of resolutions and their advice tends to be decisive. But the occasional situation does arise when these two bodies are split and submit conflicting recommendations to conference. And in these rare instances the delegates can be confronted with a real choice. The union's leaders believe that the strength of this system lies in the prior preparation for conference at the local and regional level over the year or so before conference when the feeling of the rank and file is being gauged. But in the NKV industrial union, where a similar system is used, some officials have doubts about the whole conference procedure. In this union it is admitted privately that everything is decided in advance and that conference is more a social than a legislative event. The leadership's policy proposals are never rejected, and at the same time very little ever becomes of resolutions sent in by the membership.

GERMANY

German union conference procedure more closely resembles British practice than any of the arrangements so far dealt with. In the metalworkers' conference two out of the five days are given over to debates of officers' reports, and the balance of the time is spent debating resolutions submitted by local branches or the executive. In 1974 800 resolutions came from the branches. A nine-man resolutions committee composed mainly of rank and file delegates from each region and elected at regional conferences has the job of recommending acceptance or rejection of each proposal. The committee begins its deliberations before the start of congress and a member of the national executive sits in with it. Resolutions committees made up of representatives of each of the regions are standard practice in German unions. In the textile union the rank and file have less control over the handling of resolutions at this stage than is the case in the metalworkers' union since the resolutions committee tends to be made up of three members of the national secretariat and between eight and eleven full-time regional officers.

DENMARK

The debating of resolutions takes up most of the time at Danish union conferences, and the tendency is for the resolutions committee to be quite a large body. Both the textile workers' and the metalworkers' unions have fifteen people on their committees. In both unions it is predominantly a lay body with perhaps one or two full-time officers. The committee does not meet before conference and is only elected at the first session. The union president will have drafted out an official position on the various resolutions sent in by branches in advance and this is made known to the committee when it meets. The committee then submits a compromise draft to the conference at large which is debated and voted on.

SWEDEN

One of the distinctive features about Swedish trade unionism is that members have a constitutional right to submit their own motions and resolutions direct to conference without having to go through any prior vetting at branch or regional level. This is a reflection of the unions' regard for the individual rights of members. Consequently much of conference's time is taken up with debates on large numbers of motions from branches and individual members. Some indication of the number of resolutions that may be dealt with is given by the fact that at the 1973 public service union conference there were 1,800 resolutions from this source. Most of these were grouped together for purposes of voting, but the proposer of a resolution retains the right to have his original motion voted on separately if he wishes.

The standard practice is for the national office to receive resolutions in advance and to draft out an official position on each one. This then has to be approved by the general council. In the metalworkers' union all resolutions, together with the official reaction to them, are circulated in advance of conference, and at the conference the voting is on the general council's recommendation to accept or reject a resolution, or alternatively on a statement from the general council that it proposes to do such and such a thing on the issue.

NORWAY

The Norwegian metalworkers use a six-man committee to composite resolutions. The members are proposed by the executive committee and confirmed at congress, thus in effect they are the leaders' choice. Of the six the chairman is the full-time vice-president of the union, another is a full-time district official and the balance are lay members. Voting is mainly on composite resolutions, but as in Sweden a delegate can insist on an original proposal being voted on. In the textile union the resolutions committee has seven members elected at conference in a similar way, only one of whose members is a full-time official. The railway union's standing orders committee is a five-man body nominated by the executive committee and including two national officials.

THE CHAIRMANSHIP OF CONFERENCE

European unions display a variety of arrangements for chairing conference. In France the standard practice is for a number of people to be elected to a conference committee at the first session. Sometimes this will include a full-time official from the secretariat, but most of the members are laymen. Each one then takes it in turn to chair a session of conference. Belgian unions, although their conference style is much the same, do not follow this practice and it is normal for them to have a full-time regional officer chosen by the executive or general council in charge of conference proceedings. This is the system used by both the FGTB metalworkers' and textile unions. In other cases, for example the CSC textile and railway unions and the FGTB public service union, the full-time president of the union presides over the conference sessions. A similar situation applies in the various Dutch unions where a national officer, usually the president, chairs conference.

In Germany conference may be chaired by a lay member or a full-time official. In the metalworking and railway unions national officials from the secretariat preside. But the textile union elects an eight-man body at the start of conference to chair its sessions in rotation. The group includes the union's president plus one other national official, two full-time officials from the local level and four lay delegates. This system is used by the Danish metalworkers' union whose six-man conference committee, or praesidium, will normally include lay members. Again the chairmanship of the various sessions is rotated. Neither the Danish textile nor the railway union follows suit in this practice, each relying on a national officer to preside. Elsewhere in Scandinavia the custom of having a praesidium with half or all its members laymen is well established. The Swedish unions have a three-man committee, all laymen, in the textile and railway unions, but including one official in the metalworkers' union. In Norway the metalworkers and textile workers have four laymen and the rail union has eight laymen elected as co-chairmen at the start of the conference.

In cases where conference is unlikely to reflect deep internal divisions or to give rise to contentious debates, such as in some French unions, the use of laymen as conference chairmen may make little difference to the outcome of the conference. In this situation there is perhaps no need on the part of the organisation to have proceedings controlled by someone of standing who is likely to be able to dominate the discussion. However, it is noticeable that the Belgian and the Dutch unions, whose conference style closely resembles the French, still choose to have a senior full-time official in charge of proceedings. Equally it is interesting that a number of unions in Germany and the Scandinavian countries, notably Norway, leave the control of conference debates in the hands of elected laymen, even though the business under discussion may not have originated with the leadership and may not bear its stamp of approval.

MANDATED DELEGATES OR FREE REPRESENTATIVES

The question of mandating delegates is one that frequently arouses strong passions in the labour movement, and not surprisingly since it goes to the heart of the democratic process. Essentially the matter boils down to whether or not union bodies should be delegate or representative in nature; whether a spokesman should be bound to speak and vote as his constituents feel he should or whether he should attend conference with an open mind, deciding how to vote after hearing the merits of each case. Proponents of the former view are acutely conscious of the possibility that lay delegates will be unduly influenced by the oratory of seasoned platform speakers. And there is also the fear that, in the course of the banquets and social occasions that often surround conference, impressionable delegates may be swayed from the position they would otherwise have taken on important issues. Certainly people who are unaccustomed to the expense account living that conference delegations often enjoy, may be exposed to a variety of external pressures not normally experienced in the work situation. Supporters of representative conferences invoke the ideal of parliamentarism and point out that not all issues before conference are clear cut enough for a mandate to be exercised. Behind this there is often the fear that a mandated delegate may be acting more on behalf of a political grouping than for the broad mass of members.

FRANCE

In France the tendency is for delegates to be mandated, at least on important issues. This applies equally to the CGT and CFDT unions. Delegates cast votes for the number of members they represent, but in the CGT metalworkers' union the delegate is supposed to cast his votes for, against and abstentions in proportion to the divisions that exist in his local. The same union has a rule that permits a branch which is not represented at conference to transfer its voting power to another branch which is represented. Alternatively the mandate may be deposited with the general council which will see that it is taken into account in the voting. Of course such casual arrangements as these are not as important as they might be elsewhere since close voting is not a feature of CGT conferences.

ITALY

In Italy the practice varies. Some conference delegates, such as in the CISL metalworkers, are mandated on clear-cut issues. On the other hand the CGIL railway union maintains that there is no such arrangement at its conference.

BELGIUM

Mandating is practised in Belgian unions and sometimes it is specifically required under the formal procedures. In both the FGTB metalworkers' and textile unions the national conference is preceded by regional conferences, and it is here that attempts are made to develop a collective viewpoint on the national conference agenda. In the metalworking union the chief full-time official from each region will normally state the majority viewpoint of his members at the conference. But this does not rule out the possibility of a dissenting member of the delegation stating his opposition publicly. In the csc textile workers' union the chairman of congress asks each speaker to say whether he is speaking on behalf of his constituent members or simply in his own capacity.

HOLLAND

Dutch union leaders are generally hostile to the idea of mandating delegates. The NKV industrial workers' union officials claim that it does not take place in their union, and the NKV transport union forbids it by rule. Similarly the NVV industrial union opposes the mandating of delegates. The union's officials stress that this would kill debate, whereas under the present system discussion is reckoned to be a very important part of the decision-making process.

GERMANY

German union officials tend to be opposed to mandating and the metalworkers' and railway unions maintain that it does not take place. But the textile union quietly admits that the practice cannot be stopped, although if a delegate is suspected of being mandated official pressure will be brought to bear by the union at the local level to see that he is not chosen as a delegate again.

DENMARK

Union leaders in Denmark unofficially try to prevent their conference delegates from being mandated. At each metalworkers' conference the platform tends to lecture the delegation against coming with closed minds. But in practice the system still prevails. Efforts by the textile workers' leadership to eliminate the practice have also failed.

SWEDEN

Swedish unions tend to believe that mandating is not very pronounced and their rule books make no reference to the matter.

In the Norwegian textile union the leaders believe that there is a lot of secrecy surrounding the practice which prevents them from knowing exactly how common it is. And the metalworkers' experience is that the rule banning mandating is frequently ignored.

FINAL APPEALS

Conference, or a body elected by conference, might sometimes seem to be the most suitable agency for hearing appeals, and it is important to see whether or not in fact individual unions entrust their delegate meeting with the task of safeguarding the rights of individual members by providing for a system of appeals against governing body decisions.

British unions operate a number of types of appeal system. Most common is the arrangement whereby conference acts as a final appeal court. This is the standard practice in each of the three railway unions, NUR, ASLEF and TASSA. Some unions have a special appeals board which acts as a sub-committee of conference. NUBSO and the T&GWU have such a body. The former is made up of three people chosen at congress from among delegates who are not on the executive committee, and the T&GWU body has six members. The AUEW has a very elaborate system which separates the judiciary from the legislative and executive arms. An eleven-man final appeal court is elected by the membership at large every three years and sits annually to hear complaints. On the other hand there are unions whose rule books deal rather casually with this whole question and leave final disciplinary decisions to the executive committee. This is the case in the NUTGW and in the NUDB. And in the GMWU, the general council is invested with sweeping powers to discipline members for breach of rules or for other actions not covered by the rules.

One feature that is immediately evident in studying the constitutions of some European unions is the absence of a meticulous, legalistic approach to internal union affairs such as is encountered in many British unions. In European unions the rule book is often a very slight document with whole areas of union government left untouched or treated in the most cursory way. In such cases there is little question of members having clearly defined rights and obligations that can be backed up by reference to the rules. Equally, there are few strict limitations placed on the freedom of action of officers. And, not surprisingly, these same unions rarely have a well-defined appeals procedure. Thus, to the extent that democracy prevails in these unions it certainly does not do so on the basis of respect for extensive *written* rights and obligations of members and officials.

FRANCE

French unions tend to fall into this category. For example in the CFDT unions appeals are to the general council, and there is no fixed procedure in the event that the appeal is *against* a decision of the general council. The CGT unions have a disputes commission which operates as an arbitration panel in any internal disagreement. The two sides to the grievance each select two men from the panel and they in turn choose a chairman. The purpose of the body is to hear the complaints and issue a judgment. In the CGT metalworkers the commission is made up of ten men selected from within the general council. A grievance panel makes its recommendations to the general council which then chooses whether to act upon them. In the final analysis an appeal can be made to conference. But the commission does not figure prominently in the activities of most unions and in the CGT metalworkers it has not been called into action for twenty-five years.

ITALY

Unions tend to have a five-man appeal tribunal to hear the complaints of the membership. In the CISL unions the body has three full-time officers and two lay members elected at conference.

BELGIUM

In the FGTB the textile union allows appeals to the general council, while the metalworkers' and public service unions have a hierarchy of appeals for members of different standing. Thus in the former case ordinary members can only appeal to the regional executive, plant delegates can appeal to the regional conference, and only the full-time officials have a right to appeal to the national conference. In the CSC unions a formal appeals system is virtually non-existent. The metalworkers' union rule book mentions the possibility of appeals to the executive committee, and the leaders indicate that an appeal might be heard by conference. But in the textile and railway unions members with complaints to make are simply expected to write personally to the president of the union, or possibly to the president of the CSC, and ask him to mediate the dispute.

HOLLAND

The unions affiliated to the NKV tend to follow the same practice as the CSC textile and railway unions in Belgium. In the NVV unions the general council appears to act as the final appeal body, though the rule book of the NVV transport union does indicate that appeals to conference can be made in the case of expulsions.

GERMANY

It is standard procedure in Germany for union conferences to elect a five-man lay appeal board. In the case of the metalworkers final appeal can be made beyond this to the general council, and in the railway union cases of expulsion can be appealed in the last resort to conference. But while the rule books establish these boards as the custodians of constitutional rights, the appeals procedure tends to be resorted to relatively infrequently.

DENMARK

In Denmark the textile union permits appeals to be made first to the general council and ultimately to conference. But in the metal-workers' union the system used is similar to that of the Belgian CSC unions. Aggrieved members write directly to the union president who deals with the complaints as they come in, and attempts to resolve the dispute himself. There is no formal machinery involved, though this arrangement may take up a lot of the president's time.

SWEDEN

The metalworkers' union employs a system of arbitration in cases of expulsion. The two sides each choose two people to represent them, the arbitration board is chaired by an independent fifth person, and recommendations are made to the executive committee for final decision. Where ordinary appeals are concerned in both the metalworkers' and textile unions, the first stage is to the executive committee and then to the general council. Theoretically there is a further appeal to the conference, but in the metalworkers such a step has never been heard of.

NORWAY

In Norway all the unions studied designate conference as a theoretical final appeal body. But in the metalworkers' union at least, most appeals do not go beyond the executive committee. It is rare for the next stage, the general council, to be reached. And there are no recorded cases of appeals going as far as conference.

CONCLUSION

We began this chapter by contrasting representative democracy and direct democracy, and suggested that even within representative forms of government it is possible for varying degrees of direct democracy to exist. In the process of describing the various facets of conference organisation the intention has been to see how much scope for direct involvement and control by rank and file delegates is permitted by the different systems.

The frequency, duration and size of conference have a considerable bearing on the nature of the assembly as a policy-making body. Our study indicates that the frequency and duration of conference are often such as to suggest that close rank and file control of the legislative process can only exist with difficulty. This is especially so in the cases where conference is less frequent than every three years, and when the entire event lasts for less than three or four days. In general the size of conference delegations is not so large as to make the gathering unmanageable as a working body. Some European union conferences do have in the region of 1,000 people present, but this is no more than attend the larger union conferences in Britain.

In terms of the influence of union officialdom at conference the factors considered were: the number of full-time officials present at conference, the control of standing orders or resolutions committees, and the method of chairing conference. It appears that many unions permit their entire body of full-time staff to be present at conference. In a number of cases these constitute more than one-fifth of those present, and in some instances these staff people are eligible to vote. However, in other cases the situation is tempered by the fact that many officials are actually employed by lower levels of the hierarchy and they sometimes enjoy a degree of autonomy from the national administration. In such circumstances the officials in question should not be regarded as automatic allies of the union's central leadership. Nevertheless, the impression is that at many continental union conferences the presence of full-time union representatives may be a very significant factor.

In connection with the control of strategic conference committees, our examination highlighted the different styles of conference as between unions that operate within the context of a divided labour movement, and those in countries where dual unionism is not a problem. In the former situation, a particular union is less likely to encompass a wide spectrum of views than in the latter case where, with a single movement, a more diverse union membership might be expected. In the first group of unions, in countries such as France, Belgium and Holland, where a greater unanimity of views may exist among the members, the close control of conference procedures by the leaders is perhaps less important as a means of ensuring the adoption of their policy proposals. In the latter case, where in theory more initiative in proposing policies lies with the rank and file, the question of who controls these strategic conference committees can be important in deciding the balance of power in the assembly, and in a number of countries, especially in Scandinavia, these committees are predominantly rank and file bodies. It is also chiefly in the Scandinavian unions, together with the French, that the chairmanship of conference is often left in the hands of elected lay delegates. In other countries conference sessions are controlled by appointed officials.

The democratic control of delegates by a system of mandating appears to exist to some extent in a number of union movements. The practice is most common in France and Belgium where it tends to be part of the official system. Elsewhere, mandating tends to operate unofficially, and in most cases is opposed and often vigorously resisted by the union leadership. Sometimes it is even proscribed by rule. However, union leaders themselves are often vague about the extent of its use; and the occasional official claims that mandating does not exist must be treated with caution.

Finally, our look at the judicial system within unions shows that in many cases there are only informal and often ill-defined appeals procedures. Few unions allow final appeals by members to the conference. In any event the individual's right to appeal to a conference which might not be held for another three or four years is of doubtful value. In the cases where this right exists in theory there is little evidence that it is exercised very often in practice. And in general it seems fair to conclude that in many organisations there is a total absence of a meticulous, legalistic approach to the question of members' rights.

5

General Councils and National Executives

Internal union democracy depends not only on conference decisions reflecting the will of the membership, it also requires the existence of democratically constituted bodies to supervise the execution of policy in between conferences and to make policy when conference is not in session. However precise and comprehensive conference decisions may be, and however frequently the event is held, full-time leaders always have a certain amount of leeway in interpreting and applying policy, and it is to prevent abuses at this stage that ongoing supervision of the national officers is needed. Among the necessary ingredients for a democratic supervisory body such as this, is that it should meet at frequent intervals. It must be fully accountable to the membership, and as an aid to this there should be full publicity of its proceedings, with rank and file members having a chance to judge the performance of their elected representatives and also an opportunity to express their opinion publicly through the medium of the union press. Ideally the supervisory body should be largely, if not entirely, made up of rank and file members. Of course the argument is sometimes made that the professional expertise of full-time national leaders enables them to dominate rank and file bodies more easily than they could a group of full-time officers. There is some truth in this, though the argument presupposes a lower level of ability among rank and file members than is often the case. In any event it is not beyond the bounds of human ingenuity to devise some institutional arrangement for compensating for any weaknesses in the supervisory body.

In Britain the body normally required to fulfil this supervisory function is the executive committee. Historically national executive bodies first made their appearance when unions began to centralise their activities in order to increase the level of organisational efficiency. Until well into the second half of the nineteenth century unions tended to decide policy on the basis of referenda of the whole membership, and such central administration as existed was conducted by branch executives on a rotating basis, or possibly by the branch in the most important town. For example ASLEF's affairs were conducted by its Leeds branch from its foundation in 1881, and until nearly the end of the century the engineers' union was managed by a local council in London. As unions grew bigger and administration became more complex there was need to have some central control over union funds and industrial policy. This naturally meant reducing local autonomy and direct democracy as practised hitherto. As the instrument of centralisation the union's national executive thus stands at the point of balance between membership concern for internal democracy on the one hand and administrative efficiency on the other.

This chapter considers the role of the different governing bodies within trade unions, examining facets of their structure and operations as well as their relationship to other levels of the union hierarchy. The relevant factors here are the size of the body; the frequency with which it meets; the method of selecting the members; whether it is composed of rank and file members, full-time officials, or some combination of the two; and the particular powers it enjoys. The supervisory body's relationship with other levels of the hierarchy will largely be determined by the way in which its members are selected and the number of full-time officers among its members. If the body includes a large proportion of national officers its ability to take decisions independently of the national office may be less than would be the case if all its members were drawn entirely from the rank and file. And if the members of the governing body are elected directly by the branches or districts, its relationship to conference will probably be different from what would be the case if the members were chosen at conference. The point is that the governing body ought not simply to be considered in isolation; the overall relationship between conference, the executive committee and the national officers has to be taken into account.

In many European unions the situation is further complicated by the fact that there is often yet another level of union government in the form of a general council, a body larger than the executive interposed between the latter and conference.[1] This adds to the paraphernalia of government and tends to make it more difficult for observers to unravel the lines of authority between the different levels of the hierarchy. The relationship between conference, the general council, the executive and the national officers varies from union to union, and it is important to try and identify where power lies in the different situations.

GENERAL COUNCILS

In recent years only one large union in Britain, the GMWU, has had a general council as well as a union conference and a national executive. Until 1975, when the union decided to amalgamate the general council and the executive, the council was composed of full-time regional secretaries and lay members, the executive being elected from among the council members. Quarterly meetings were held to receive reports from the executive. The council also acted as the union's final appeal board. And when a situation arose which was not covered by the rule book the council had the power of decision. It was thus a very important body, but it still had to operate within the framework of annual union conferences.

By contrast, most European unions find it necessary to have a general council precisely because of the infrequency of conference. With conference held at three- or four-yearly intervals, in some cases as infrequently as every five years, and then perhaps for only three days, the general council must assume some of its legislative functions. At the same time it is required to act as a watchdog over the national executive and the national officers in the secretariat. The danger here, as we shall see, is that with the introduction of another tier of union government the tendency is for the national leaders to become more remote from the rank and file.

METHOD OF ELECTION

The relationship between general councils and conference takes three basic forms. The first situation is where the members of the council are elected at conference. Alternatively the members may be elected directly by the regions or districts. A third possibility involves a mixture of these two systems. Union structure tends to be a product of the forces that operated on the organisation at the time of its foundation. The explanation for these different systems lies in the different way unions have reacted to the problem posed by infrequent conferences. In many cases unions are not prepared to hand over ongoing control of the organisation to a central body elected indirectly at three- or four-yearly conferences. They prefer instead to vest this power in a body composed of direct regional delegates susceptible to closer control by the regions and possibly subject to recall in between conferences. But whether or not the general council members are elected at conference, with an express mandate to watch over the implementation of its decisions, may well have a bearing on the extent to which they regard themselves first and foremost as the custodians of conference policy, with a primary obligation to render account at the next conference. Delegates elected directly by the districts or regions to represent them on the general council may regard themselves as having a mandate to take decisions that supersede conference policy. In this case the general council effectively replaces conference as the legislative body and conference becomes little more than an occasional symbolic rite. The three following examples will help us to categorise the systems used to select general councils in the different unions.

In the Norwegian metalworkers' union the four-yearly conference elects a general council to take all necessary policy decisions until the next conference. It is also responsible for overseeing the national executive and indirectly supervising the work of the national officers. In this case, as Figure 5.1 shows, the national officers and executive committee members all belong to the general council and between them they account for almost half the council members.

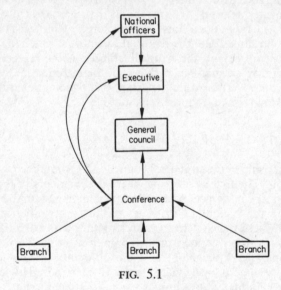

FIG. 5.1

Unions in which this relationship between conference and the general council applies include:

France	CGT metalworkers
Belgium	CSC textile workers

Denmark	metalworkers
	textile workers
Sweden	metalworkers
	textile workers
Norway	textile workers

An example of the second type of system is provided by the railway sector of the Belgian FGTB public service union. In between the four-yearly conferences of railway members the control of the sector is left to a general council whose members are directly elected by the regions (Figure 5.2). In this particular case the regional delegates may change from meeting to meeting so that in effect the council becomes a mini-conference.

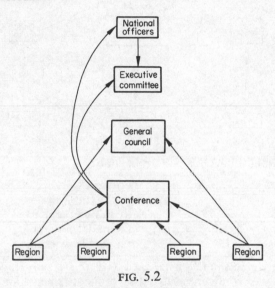

FIG. 5.2

The unions in which this relationship between conference and the general council is to be found include:

Belgium	FGTB metalworkers
	CSC metalworkers
Holland	NVV industrial workers
	NKV industrial workers
Germany	metalworkers
	textile workers
	rail workers

The two systems of electing general council members are sometimes combined as they are in the French CFDT metalworkers. In this case just over half the members are elected at conference while the remainder are elected directly by the regional bodies and the different trade sections (Figure 5.3).

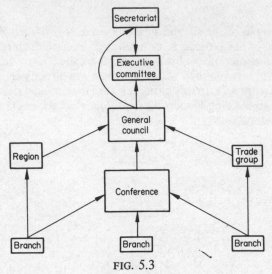

FIG. 5.3

Unions that follow this pattern include:

France	CFDT rail workers
	CFDT textile workers
	CGT rail workers
Italy	CISL metalworkers
	CISL textile workers

There are points in favour of each of these systems. If, despite the infrequency of conference, its policy pronouncements are regarded as being solemnly binding, then a general council elected at conference, with a specific mandate to watch over the implementation of the policy and to report back to conference, provides some continuity in the chain of authority. And indeed, some might even argue that, for all the defects of the conference system discussed in Chapter 4, the event is the one occasion when a reasonably large number of rank and file members are brought together to consider matters of policy, and therefore all possible effort should be made to see that the authority of conference is preserved. On the other hand it might be argued that a system in which the general council is composed of directly elected regional delegates keeps on-going policy more closely in the hands of the rank and file and compensates more for the infrequency of conference. Under certain circumstances a general council such as this might effectively replace conference. The deciding factor will be whether or not the council has the right to initiate policy. If so, it can act as a conference in miniature. But if, as is sometimes the case, its role is more that of an advisory body, ratifying and confirming decisions taken elsewhere, then it will not be a real substitute for conference. And whether or not the rank and file are able to maintain closer control of policy under such an arrangement depends on how the regional or district delegates are chosen and what proportion of them are full-time officials. The third alternative, a composite general council with some members elected at conference and others representing districts directly, attempts to preserve the best of both these systems.

The variables are complex, but as a second best alternative to frequent, full-scale, democratically run conferences we would prefer to have a system with a general council made up of rank and file delegates directly elected by their region or trade group and attending the council with full powers to initiate policy, even if this tends to make conference redundant. However the general council is not simply to be judged on the basis of its legislative function. In most cases it is also responsible for supervising the work of the executive committee and, indirectly, of the national officers on the secretariat. Here, as we shall see, the situation is complicated by the fact that the general council, the national executive and the secretariat have overlapping memberships. Frequently the entire executive sits on the general council, and a close-knit executive committee might be able to control the council, especially if a significant number of members are full-time officials.

A few unions do not have a general council at all. Among these are the French CGT textile workers and the Norwegian railway workers. The case of the CGT textile union is interesting in that the general council was only abolished quite recently, largely for financial reasons. The council had been a 95-man body that met every six months, and the union found that the cost of maintaining such a body was beyond its means. In addition it was coming to be seen as a barrier preventing closer contact between the membership and the national leaders. With the abolition of the general council the union has reconstituted its national executive committee on a bigger scale and this is backed up by a number of flexible *ad hoc* committees on special subjects.

SIZE OF GENERAL COUNCILS

The size of membership of general councils in the unions studied ranges from relatively small bodies of 20–30 people to gatherings of up to 150 people. At the latter size the general council begins to assume the proportions of a full-scale conference. In fact, as Table 5.1 shows, most general councils are sufficiently compact for them to be able to operate as workmanlike mini-legislatures.

Table 5.1   *Size of General Councils*

		Approxi- mate Size of Union General Councils	Full-time Officials on General Councils
France	CGT metalworkers	66	41
	CGT rail workers	150	30 (minimum)
	CFDT metalworkers	50	22
	CFDT textile workers	39	30
	CFDT rail workers	92	24
Italy	CISL metalworkers	136	80
Belgium	FGTB metalworkers	132	50
	FGTB rail workers	120	–
	CSC metalworkers	40	0
	CSC textile workers	44	8
Holland	NVV industrial workers	78	0
	NKV industrial workers	75	0
Germany	textile workers	32	7
	rail workers	99	30 (non-voting)
Denmark	metalworkers	32	7
	textile workers	24	3
Sweden	metalworkers	36	12
	textile workers	31	5
Norway	metalworkers	34	3
	textile workers	27	4

However, in terms of rank and file control of proceedings this factor may be counter-productive where full-time officials are included on the council in significant numbers. In such a case the influence of officialdom may be even greater than it is at full-scale conferences. We must now consider the position of general councils in the various unions in more detail.

FRANCE

The CGT metalworkers' union's sixty-six general council members include the entire body of elected full-time national officials, some eighteen in all, together with a number of members who hold full-time positions at the regional level. Altogether, it is estimated that no more than 25 out of the 66 may be rank and file members from the shop floor. The selection process at conference involves the outgoing general council and representatives of each of the union's districts drawing up a slate of candidates aimed at balancing the various regional and trade interests, as well as having adequate representation of both sexes and members of different age groups. Conference approval of this slate is normally automatic. The general council convenes once a month. It is responsible for policy decisions in between conference, and it is the general council's report, together with its proposals, that constitute the main business of conference.

In the CGT rail union the general council has a similar structure. The full staff of thirty or so head office officials sit on the council and the balance of the membership reflects an attempt to have all regions and grades represented. Unlike the CGT metalworkers' general council, this body only meets twice a year.

The CFDT metalworkers' general council is composed of members elected at conference and of delegates sent directly from the regions and trade groups. Twenty-six of the total number of fifty are elected at conference and there is an even balance of regional and trade group representatives among the remainder. All the union's full-time national officers plus the entire national executive committee belong to the general council and no more than twenty-eight of the members are from the rank and file. The council meets every four months.

Like the CFDT metalworkers, the CFDT textile union's general council has a composite membership of nine direct regional delegates and thirty members elected at conference. About three-quarters of the members are from the rank and file, the balance being made up of the national officers and other full-time officials on the national executive. The different trade groups are represented in proportion to their size of membership. As well as being responsible for policy in between conference the general council acts as the final appeal body in any internal dispute. It meets to conduct its business four times a year.

In the CFDT railway union the majority of the ninety-two general council members are the direct representatives of regional and sectional groups and no more than forty are elected at conference. Twenty-four of the present total are full-time officers, including the entire body of head office officials. The council meets every six months.

ITALY

The CISL metalworkers' union's general council has seventy-one members elected at conference and sixty-five direct delegates of the different provinces. Those elected at conference hold office for four years, the others serve a two-year term. Only 40 per cent of the members are laymen. However, an interesting feature designed to keep the council more under rank and file control is that the direct provincial representatives, who are in the main lay members, are subject to recall at any point during their term of office. The council receives a report from the national officers each year, it interprets policy and acts as the custodian of the union rules. Meetings are held at least twice a year.

A similar form of general council operates in the CISL textile union, with full-time officials in a clear majority. Indeed, this sort of balance between lay members and full-time officials is also common to a number of CGIL and UIL unions.

BELGIUM

The FGTB metalworkers' union has a general council entirely made up of regional delegates. By rule 60 per cent of the members must be lay members. The remainder are full-time national officers or regional organisers. Council meetings are held every second month.

As we have seen, a similar type of general council operates in the railway sector of the FGTB public service union. Its 120 regional delegates may include full-time officials apart from the sector's national officers, but for the most part the council members are lay.

The CSC metalworkers' union utilises a much smaller general council than either of the two FGTB unions. Its forty members are all lay delegates sent directly from the regions with representation proportional to membership. The regions select their delegates annually. The national executive and full-time officials generally can attend the council meetings but they have no vote. However, the council itself is not empowered to take any decision unless there is a two-thirds majority in favour. According to union rules meetings must be held once a year, but in practice they tend to take place quarterly.

The CSC textile union's general council consists of thirty-six lay members chosen at conference to represent the different regions on a proportional basis. In addition to these, full-time officials, including the national officers, can sit on the council provided that they do not constitute more than one-quarter of the total membership. At present there are eight such full-time officials on the council. This body, which meets quarterly, is responsible for electing from among its own members the executive committee and the national officers who constitute the secretariat.

HOLLAND

In both the NVV and NKV industrial workers' unions the general council is composed of members delegated directly by either their district or trade group. In the NVV union the seventy-eight members are all lay members and are all selected in their districts. There is no formal arrangement aimed at reflecting the mixed industrial composition of the union, though since the merger a majority of seats have been reserved for members of the old metalworkers' union, the senior partner in the amalgamation. Meetings are held quite frequently, usually every six or eight weeks.

Two-thirds of the NKV industrial union's 75-man general council are delegates of the different trade groups, and the remainder are selected in the districts. All are lay members. Full-time officers have the right to attend council meetings with a voice but no vote. Meetings are held at least every four months.

GERMANY

As in Holland, all three German unions examined have general councils made up entirely of direct regional delegates elected at regional conferences. In theory all the voting members are lay, but in practice in metalworking very few of them may be actually on the shop floor, many being works councillors on full-time release from their jobs. The entire national executive plus the senior full-time regional officials attend the meetings with a voice but no vote. In metalworking the total number present at council meetings can be as high as 105. In the railway union nearly one-third of those in attendance are full-time officials. The council has responsibility for making the final decision on internal appeals, based on the recommendations of the appeals committee. But in policy matters it has only an advisory role, supporting the executive committee, the highest decision-making organ in between conference. Its meetings are held three times a year.

DENMARK

The Danish metalworkers elect their entire general council at conference. Its thirty-two members include the seven national officers and ten lay members of the executive, but otherwise members are laymen holding no higher office than branch chairmen. The council meets four times a year.

The textile union's general council of twenty-four includes the entire national executive committee, but only three of the total number, the union's national officers, are full-time officials. The lay members elected at conference who are not on the national executive constitute a majority on the council.

SWEDEN

The Swedish unions, like others in Scandinavia, tend to elect their general council at conference. In metalworking the 36-man body must have two-thirds of its members working on the shop floor, but included among these are lay members of the national executive. A solid bloc of full-time officials comprising the five general officers, five national organisers and two full-time branch officials make up the balance. Meetings are held at least every six months, though in practice they may be every two months or possibly more often.

In textiles the weight of officialdom within the general council is less. The five national officers are the only full-time officials on the 31-man body, and although the general council's lay members include lay national executive committeemen, those not on the executive are in an overall majority on the council. The union only has a small number of branches and each of these is represented on the council. Meetings are held twice a year.

NORWAY

The general council of the metalworkers' union has a majority of lay members. The three general officers of the union are the only full-time officials on the body, and although the national executive is included *in toto* a majority of the general council members are laymen elected at conference. The council only meets annually, or when a round of collective bargaining is pending.

In the textile union the general council has a similar composition. The four general officers of the union are the only full-time members of the 27-man council. The rest are lay members, the majority being people elected at conference who do not hold seats on the executive committee.

As Table 5.1 shows, several unions have general councils with substantial numbers of full-time officials among their members or present at their meetings. In some cases these people are actually in a majority, and in about one-half of the unions considered the full-time officials on the general council constitute at least one-quarter of its members. Even where lay members are in an overall majority it is often the case that their numbers are largely made up of lay representatives from the national executive whose involvement in the on-going process of government may result in their being closer to the leadership than to their fellow rank and file members. In some cases, such as in the Dutch industrial workers' unions, only the lay members specifically elected to the general council have the right to vote, but even so the mere presence of union officials can still influence the tone of the meetings and affect the outcome of business. Indeed this seems more likely to happen in the general council than at conference proper since the size of most general councils is quite small and the numbers of full-time officials present is proportionately greater than at conference. In these circumstances there is no guarantee that the general council will enable the rank and file to control policy any more than they can through the medium of infrequent conference.

However, the general council's role is not simply to take policy decisions but also to supervise the executive committee and, through that body, the national officers. Its effectiveness in this area will depend to some extent on the frequency of its meetings. The monthly meetings of the CGT metalworkers' general council would seem to be often enough to enable it to exercise on-going control of the union. In some other unions, however, the general council meets only at six-monthly intervals, and even once a year. In these cases the likelihood is that the national executive and full-time officers will have considerable freedom of activity. But the power of the executive committee depends not only on the effectiveness of the general council's supervision, but on the executive's structure, composition and method of election, a subject we must consider next.

NATIONAL EXECUTIVE — METHOD OF ELECTION

The predominant method of electing national executive committees in British unions is by referendum ballot of the membership. Indirect election at conference is relatively rare and tends to be confined to smaller unions. The Union of Post Office Workers is one of the largest unions to elect its executive in this way. In TASSA a minority of the executive are elected at conference, but most are directly elected by the membership. The GMWU use a third method, the executive committee being elected from among members of the general council.

Among the European unions studied there are examples of each of these different methods, though election at conference or by members of the general council is far more common than direct election by the membership at large.

Unions in which the executive is elected by conference include:

France	CGT textile workers
Belgium	FGTB railway workers
Holland	NVV industrial workers
	NVV railway workers
	NKV railway workers
Germany	metalworkers
	textile workers
	railway workers
Denmark	metalworkers
	textile workers
Sweden	metalworkers
	textile workers
Norway	metalworkers
	textile workers
	railway workers

Unions in which the effective selection of the executive members is made by the general council from within its own ranks include:

France	CGT metalworkers
	CGT railway workers
	CFDT metalworkers
	CFDT textile workers
	CFDT railway workers
Italy	CISL metalworkers
	CISL textile workers

The unions whose executive committee members are selected directly in the regions are:

Belgium	FGTB metalworkers
	FGTB textile workers
	CSC metalworkers
Holland	NKV industrial workers

The method of selecting the executive can be an important determinant of its power and status in the union. Just as the relationship between the general council and conference may be influenced by whether or not the one is elected by the other, so also the general council's effectiveness in supervising the executive committee may depend on whether the latter is a creature of the council. If the national executive is chosen by the general council from among its own members, the executive becomes, in effect, the executive arm of the general council. But, of course, if the council itself is chosen at conference this system means that the election of the executive is two stages removed from the rank and file, and the hierarchy of governing bodies is based on a pyramidal system, with successive tiers ever more remote from the membership. However, if conference is responsible for electing the executive, the latter being ultimately accountable to conference, the same direct chain of authority between executive and general council may not obtain, especially if the general council itself is chosen directly in the regions rather than at conference. The third alternative, where executive members are chosen directly by districts or regions, may give the committee a power base of its own independent of conference, the general council and the national officers. If it is also a rank and file committee it may be the best way of ensuring that policy is implemented in conformity with the membership's wishes, and as such would probably be preferable to the other two systems. However, in those unions examined in which the executive members are sent directly by the regions, there is a tendency for the committee to be made up of the senior full-time regional officials sitting *ex officio* rather than as members elected in open contest. In the CSC metalworkers the executive is made up of the most important regional officials. The NKV industrial workers' executive comprises the secretariat, the seven most senior district officers, and the eight heads of the trade groups. In the FGTB textile union the committee is made up of the chief organisers of the most important regions. Under this system the executive is certainly a most powerful body, though whether it is likely to represent the membership better than a rank and file group would is another question, especially in view of the fact that these full-time officers tend to hold office permanently.

FREQUENCY OF MEETINGS

Often rule books in British unions do not specify how frequently the executive committee meetings are to be held. However, it is normal practice for them to be monthly or at least quarterly, and sometimes, as in the AUEW, meetings are held weekly. The frequency of executive meetings can provide an indication of how close is that body's control of day-to-day union activities.

Many of the European unions studied do not stipulate the frequency of executive meetings by rule, but for those that do have a fixed arrangement the number of meetings per year is:

Table 5.2   *Annual Number of Executive Meetings*

France	CFDT metalworkers	3 (minimum)
	CFDT textile workers	12
	CFDT railway workers	12
	CGT metalworkers	52
Italy	CISL metalworkers	6
	CISL textile workers	4
Belgium	FGTB metalworkers	26 (minimum)
	FGTB textile workers	26
	CSC metalworkers	4
Holland	NKV industrial workers	52
Germany	metalworkers	24
	textile workers	6
Denmark	metalworkers	4 (minimum)
Sweden	metalworkers	12 (minimum)
	textile workers	8
Norway	metalworkers	12
	textile workers	12
	railway workers	6

In practice the differences suggested above may not be quite so great since some unions tend to have more than the minimum number of meetings. However, there are still significant differences and these do give some idea of where power in the unions lies. Most noticeable of all are the very frequent meetings in the FGTB metal and textile unions and also in the NKV industrial workers' union. The fact that in each of these unions the executive is also directly chosen in the regions and usually comprises full-time officials would seem to indicate that this is the most powerful body in these particular organisations. In other cases, where executive meetings are perhaps only quarterly or three times a year, the likelihood is that on-going decisions are made by an inner group of executive members dominated by the national officers. This is something to look at in connection with the size and composition of executive committees.

NATIONAL EXECUTIVES — SIZE AND COMPOSITION

The size of British union executive committees varies considerably. At the lower range of the scale the AUEW has only seven members on its full-time executive while at the opposite extreme the T&GWU body is among the largest with thirty-nine members. Within this range the NUR executive has 24 members, TASSA's has 28, the NUTGW has 15 and ASLEF is governed by a 10-man body. Small executives are often more business-like, and for the sake of efficiency large executives sometimes have to establish an inner cabinet. However, this sort of arrangement can lead to a loss of lay control especially when, as in the NUHKW, three-quarters or more of the inner group are made up of full-time officials.

Table 5.3 shows that the range of executive committee sizes among the European unions considered is much the same as in Britain.

Table 5.3   *Size of Executive Committees*

		Total Membership of Executives	*Full-time Officers on Executive*	*National Officers Among Full-time Executive Members*
France	CGT metalworkers	18	18	3
	CGT textile workers	40	5	5
	CGT railway workers	30	30	8
	CFDT metalworkers	14	14	8
	CFDT textile workers	14	8	4
	CFDT railway workers	27	12	12
Italy	CISL metalworkers	15	5	5
	CISL textile workers	20	5	5
Belgium	FGTB metalworkers	20	20	4
	FGTB textile workers	18	18	4
	FGTB railway workers	22	18	10
	CSC metalworkers	14	14	4
	CSC textile workers	7	7	5
Holland	NVV railway workers	12	3	3
	NKV railway workers	11	4	4
	NVV industrial workers	12	12	12
	NKV industrial workers	22	22	7
Germany	metalworkers	30	11	11
	textile workers	20	7	7
	railway workers	27	7	7
Denmark	metalworkers	17	7	7
	textile workers	11	3	3
Sweden	metalworkers	11	5	5
	textile workers	13	5	5
Norway	metalworkers	15	3	3
	textile workers	13	4	4
	railway workers	26	6	6

The table also indicates the large number of full-time officials who hold seats on union executives. This is in sharp contrast to the practice in many British unions where executive committee membership is restricted to lay members. This is the situation, for example, in the T&GWU, the NUR, TASSA, NUDB and the NUTGW. The GMWU and the NUHKW have mixed executives of full-time and lay members, while the AUEW provides the major example of a full-time executive.

Among the European unions studied nearly one-third have executive committees made up entirely of full-time staff. This is not to say that the executive as such is full-time as is the case in the AUEW, merely that its members are all on the union payroll in some capacity, as national officers or regional organisers. Apart from these organisations a further ten of the twenty-seven unions examined have executive committees in which full-time officials account for one-third or more of their members. In most cases the full-time officers on the executive are made up, in whole or in part, of the national officers who constitute the secretariat. This means that they are likely to be a cohesive group, in constant communication with each other, and well organised within the executive. The secretariat is usually responsible for preparing the agenda for executive meetings, it is the instigator of much of the executive's business, and constitutes a *de facto* inner cabinet whether the constitution provides for one or not. And the fact that the members of the secretariat constitute a collective leadership, often being elected on the same official slate rather than as the preferred candidates of rival factions, tends to make them an extremely powerful bloc at the centre of the union's government.

Some unions do attempt to limit the power of the national officers within the executive. For example, the Belgian FGTB textile union only allows the members of the secretariat to speak in the executive and not to vote. In some other unions such as the Belgian CSC metalworkers and the French CFDT railway union the executive committee as such is responsible for choosing the principal national officers from among its own members and is therefore theoretically in a position to exercise closer control. But in neither case does this provide for more direct rank and file control since almost half the CFDT railway union executive is made up of full-time officials, while in the CSC metalworkers the executive has no lay members. If anything, the system of indirect election moves this important function one stage further away from the membership at large.

COMMUNICATIONS AND THE NATIONAL EXECUTIVE

The picture presented suggests that in most unions there is a great concentration of executive power in the hands of the national officers who are present in strength on both the general council and the executive committee. The very composition of these governing bodies would seem to limit rank and file influence in many cases. Whether this is so in practice depends in part on whether internal union communications are such as to keep the membership adequately informed about the nature of general council and executive proceedings, and to enable members to engage in public criticism of these bodies in the union press. A detailed analysis of the content of union newspapers is beyond our scope, but it is possible to give an indication of the type of publication unions produce and its accessibility to the members.

For the most part the European unions studied recognise the power of the union press as a force for shaping the thinking of the membership. Journals tend to appear frequently, at weekly, fortnightly or monthly intervals, and are usually provided free, with copies often being mailed directly to members' homes. The exceptions to this rule are to be found chiefly in Belgium and Italy where the individual unions either choose not to produce, or have difficulty in producing, a regular paper of their own.

Where union journals do exist they are invariably house organs, under the control of the executive and reflecting the position of the leadership. Reports of the decisions taken by the general council and executive committee are usually carried, but detailed accounts of the proceedings are unlikely to be published and it is very rare for the voting record of the various members to be announced. Often the papers do not even publish letters or contributions from the rank and file, and in cases where they do there is a strong tendency for the debate to be closely controlled from above. As a matter of policy, correspondence from members is not normally published in the journals of the CGT metal and railway unions, the CFDT metal and railway unions, the German textile and railway unions, and the NKV industrial workers' union. Unions that do make a practice of regularly publishing members' letters in their paper include: the NVV industrial workers' union, the Danish metalworkers' union, the German metalworkers' union and the Swedish metal and textile unions. Other organisations such as the NVV and NKV transport unions and the various Norwegian unions do sometimes publish rank and file contributions, but this is not something that is openly encouraged and the result is that few members avail themselves of the opportunity.

CONCLUSION

The on-going process of union government between conferences in most of the European labour movement involves two bodies, a general council and an executive committee. Between them they combine some legislative functions as well as being responsible for overseeing the execution of policy. European organisations find it necessary to have general councils because of the infrequency of union conference and the consequent need for a representative body able to take important decisions in between conference. The general council, usually the supreme authority between conference, is also responsible for supervising the work of the executive and, through the executive, of directing the activities of the national officers. The councils are clearly necessary but the overall effect of adding another tier such as this to the levels of government is often to make the relationship between the different governing bodies complex and, if there is a pyramidal relationship between the different bodies with each electing the next highest one, to make the top leadership more remote from the rank and file.

General council meetings are reasonably frequent, and they are usually large enough to be representative while still being sufficiently compact to deal with questions of policy in a workmanlike way. However, these bodies also tend to have a substantial number of full-time officials, sometimes even a majority of such people, present at their meetings, which means that the official viewpoint may well carry more weight there than at the union conference proper. The dangers for democracy in such a situation are manifest.

The weight of officialdom in many general councils also makes them unlikely agencies for effective rank and file supervision of the national executive. This is even more so if the executive committees themselves are dominated by full-time officials, and often this is the case. In a number of instances full-time officials constitute a majority on the executive, and sometimes the entire body is made up of people who hold full-time office in some capacity. This is the situation, for example, in some Belgian and Dutch unions where the executive members tend to be regional officers who hold their executive seats *ex officio* and consequently have a very secure power base. In these cases the executive also tends to meet very frequently, sometimes weekly, so that it is in effective control of on-going decision-making. In other unions the executive may meet less frequently, possibly at monthly intervals, but most of these executive bodies include among their members up to half a dozen national officers who, as a cohesive group in constant communication with one another, are in a position to act as an inner cabinet of the executive, often becoming in effect a central repository of much of the executive power. Even if the general council is able to exercise control over the wider executive its chances of being able to do so effectively in the case of the secretariat's day-to-day activities would seem to be much less.

The fact is that the weakness of conference, and the transference of power to a general council comprising many staff officials, a body which in turn is responsible for supervising an even more compact group of officers, tends to result in a concentration of power in the hands of those full-time officials who are represented at every level of government. The situation is compounded by the fact that in most unions official control of the press is such as to prevent this medium from being used as a platform for membership criticism of, and organisation against, the executive body. How the full-time officials are chosen and the extent to which they are accountable to the membership is a subject to which we now turn.

6

Full-Time
Union Officials

An examination of internal democracy and administrative efficiency in trade unions must take into consideration the question of full-time officials and their place in the organisation. This chapter sets out to examine the role of these officials, concentrating especially on their power and status and their accountability to the membership at large. What we are trying to assess here is the relative strength of the corps of full-time officials and the extent to which unions might be said to be dominated by them.

In the first place we need to have some idea of the number of officials and the ratio of these to members. A related issue is the number of administrative and professional–technical staff they have under their control. This factor has a bearing on the efficiency of union administration, but it can also reflect the degree of centralisation of organisational power in the hands of national officials. Next we must consider the key question of how officials are chosen. If they are appointed rather than elected it means that they are less directly accountable to the membership for their actions, and democracy is likely to suffer in consequence. Beyond this a source of potential competition for the highest elective office in the union will be eliminated, since it is from second- and middle-ranking officers that the most likely challengers for national office tend to emerge. If these people are the appointees of the incumbent national officers they are most unlikely to challenge their benefactors for the highest office. And in this sense democracy is doubly affected.[1] If officers are elected we need to know whether they are required to stand for re-election, and if so, how often. Finally, it is important to look at the pay of full-time officials since this is also a factor that influences their relationship with the rank and file. Merely by the fact of becoming full-time officials their life-style tends to change and the immediacy of their contact with the rank and file is often reduced. And if the officials are also paid unduly large salaries, the tendency is likely to be sharply accentuated.

There have always been different views within the labour movement about the role of full-time officials. The divisions stem largely from different emphases placed on the somewhat conflicting aims of internal union democracy and administrative efficiency. And even more fundamentally they may originate out of conflicting views about the ultimate purpose of trade unionism. Some unions with perhaps only a small staff of elected full-time officials will place great emphasis on the work of lay officers. At the other extreme there are unions that employ a large corps of appointed officials. The one may pride itself on its democratic structure; the other may stress its administrative efficiency. But beyond this the former type is often the product of a school of thought which sees trade unionism as a do-it-yourself training ground for socialism, while the latter derives from a more pragmatic concept of the union as the provider of a range of tangible services to the membership.[2]

At various times in the history of trade unionism deeper philosophical questions such as this have led to major divisions in the labour movement, the differences crystallising around the role of full-time officials. In the first decade of the century the Industrial Workers of the World split off from the mainstream American labour movement largely over the question of union 'bureaucracy', and in the course of establishing their own system of government they abolished the position of union president and replaced it with the collective leadership of an executive committee. Similarly before the First World War the South Wales Miners' Reform Movement issued a seminal document, *The Miners' Next Step*, in which they elaborated a programme for curbing the stultifying influence of the full-time miners' agents and for bringing the union under a more direct system of lay control. In effect *The Miners' Next Step* sought to do away with the whole idea of 'leadership'.

Even within the official union movement of today there are living reminders of different concepts of trade union organisation. The two biggest unions in Britain, the AUEW and the T&GWU, have quite dissimilar systems of internal government. Historically the AUEW structure was created and developed in such a way as to emphasise the principle of local autonomy. And forty years after its formation in 1851 the engineers' union still did not have any full-time central staff. By contrast, the T&GWU, an organisation with roots in the mass unionism of unskilled workers that first emerged in the 1880s, has always stressed the need for strong, central leadership. Under the leadership of Ernest Bevin and Arthur Deakin much attention was devoted to perfecting the union's administrative machinery. Even so, in 1952 when the union's total staff reached 1,400, 40 per cent higher than at the start of the war, Deakin wondered whether or not the union was providing too much 'service' and thereby sapping the vitality of the membership to the point where they were not able to help themselves.[3]

Britain has often been noted for its generally small number of full-time officials relative to the size of union membership. The Donovan Commission estimated that there were approximately 3,000 such officials in the country, giving a ratio of officials to members of 1 : 3,500. As between unions this ratio varies quite considerably. For example, in 1959 one survey showed that the NUBSO had a ratio of one official to 1,700 members, while at the other extreme the NUR employed only one official for every 16,200 members.[4] Within this range come most of the big unions. The Donovan Commission estimated that the T&GWU has an official for approximately every 2,700 members. The GMWU officials each service approximately 3,800 members, while in the AEUW there are approximately 6,800 members per official.[5]

Of the 3,000 officials in Britain, the TUC has estimated that about 17 per cent are national and regional officers; 2 per cent fulfil some specialist or administrative functions, usually at head office; and the rest fall into the general category of field officers and organisers.

NATIONAL OFFICIALS: NUMBERS AND METHOD OF SELECTION

BRITAIN

The most usual situation in British unions is for a general secretary to be in charge of the union's administrative machinery as chief executive officer. A minority of unions have a full-time president as well as a general secretary and in these cases there tends to be a more or less even division of power, as in the case of the miners and engineers. The general secretary will normally have one or more assistant general secretaries working with him and between them they will be responsible for the day-to-day running of the union under the executive committee. However, in practice the power of a general secretary is likely to be greater than his theoretical position as principal administrator might suggest. Very often he is the most influential member of the union's policy-making bodies, and sometimes he may play a decisive role in interpreting the union's rules and members' rights under the rules. In this sense he may be simultaneously engaged in the union's legislative, executive and judicial processes. And where the general secretary also holds his job for life his powers can be very considerable indeed.

Election

The most common practice is for the principal officers to be elected by referendum vote of the entire membership. This has the advantage of allowing the widest possible rank and file participation in the selection of the leader. On the other hand the task of supervising the national officers may be more difficult for the executive committee when the officer owes his position to a direct vote of the membership. A small number of unions including TASSA, and especially some textile unions like the NUDB and the Amalgamated Weavers Association, hold elections for general secretary at conference. Very few unions, notably the British Iron, Steel and Kindred Trades Association and the National Union of Public Employees, have their general secretary appointed by the executive committee. Even where general secretaries are chosen by referendum vote it is frequently on a once and for all basis, the job then being held until retirement. In some engineering unions such as the AUEW the basic term of office is three years. In the NUBSO the general secretary holds the job for four years at a time. But in a large number of unions including the NUR, TASSA, the NUTGW and the two general unions, the T&GWU and GMWU, jobs are for life. Assistant general secretaries may be elected just like their superiors as in the case of the AUEW and the NUDB. But in other unions such as TASSA and the T&GWU they are appointed by the executive.

When elections are held to fill vacancies the position is usually contested. A survey of twenty-five elections for general secretary in sixteen unions between 1919 and 1951 indicated that there were on average four candidates for each post.[6] How many of these were serious candidates with a real chance is, of course, another question, and where the incumbent official contests the post it is extremely rare for him to be defeated. However, by comparison with unions in many other countries the electoral process is a relatively vigorous one. In the United States only 20 per cent of top union offices are contested. Electioneering takes place in most British unions, but in only a few is this officially sanctioned. For example, the AUEW prints and circulates the election addresses of all candidates; the NUR allows nominating branches to advertise the qualifications of their candidate in the union's paper; and the NUTGW publishes a short biographical sketch of each candidate on the ballot paper, though of course potted biographies are no substitute for a full statement of views on policy.

FRANCE

As in many other areas of internal government the French unions provide a sharp contrast with British practice. In common with other European unions their group of principal officers tends to be rather large. The CGT textile workers' union has five national officers, while the CFDT metalworkers and the CGT railwaymen have eight principal officers. The CFDT textile workers are led by a four-man body. In each case the group of officers collectively constitute the secretariat. In most cases there is a general secretary or a president, an assistant general secretary and a number of national secretaries. However, there is usually little or no difference between them in status and they operate on a collegial basis.

Besides these the larger French unions also have a group of full-time officials, most elected but sometimes appointed, who share the task of running the national office. The CGT metalworkers' union has fifteen such officials who, together with the three principal officers, constitute the Federal Bureau. This body is in effect a full-time executive committee in that it is responsible for overseeing the work of the secretariat. Yet the relationship between the ordinary members of the bureau and the secretariat is complicated in that the former also assume a variety of administrative and representational responsibilities in different sectors and as such take their lead from the principal officers. Apart from the Federal Bureau members there are nine appointed officials at head office. The CGT railway union's Federal Bureau has thirty members including the eight members of the secretariat. In addition the national office has the services of eight other appointed full-time officials. The CGT textile workers' union has no such large headquarters staff of officials and relies solely on its five-man secretariat.

Neither the CFDT metalworkers nor textile union have full-time officers at headquarters other than the members of the secretariat. But the CFDT rail union has a total of ten full-time staff at its national office apart from the president and general secretary.

Election
The system of choosing officers is much the same in all French unions. Practically all offices are elective and yet there is hardly ever any fierce, open contest for positions. In most unions it is the general council which elects the members of the secretariat and the Federal Bureau from among its own members. In a formal sense the conference must confirm the choice made by the general council, but there is little likelihood of this confirmation being withheld. And because conferences are only every three years there is every chance that the general council may have to fill a vacant position in mid-

term, with no immediate prospect of its choice being ratified. There is never any electioneering on the basis of rival policy programmes. The fact that French workers join the union whose policies they identify with means that there is a general lack of sharp internal ideological conflict over policies, and the whole electoral system is really a process of evolving a consensus. As the general secretary of the CGT textile union points out, the task is really to slot everyone willing to work for the union into a job, having in mind their particular talents. The union encourages as many people as possible to put their names forward for office so as to have sufficient hands for the full-time and lay activities that need to be undertaken.

Terms of office theoretically last for three years but in most cases the officers are re-elected. However, the CFDT unions have introduced a more democratic practice designed to rotate office under which three terms are regarded as the maximum period for any person. Consequently nine or ten years is the limit for office holding. But even in a system like this, where the rotation of office is required, only about 50 per cent of retiring officers rejoin the rank and file in the CFDT metalworkers' union.

The rapid turnover of officers in the CFDT, coupled with the fact that the unions have been going through a period of radicalisation, has had the effect of lowering the age of officials. In the CFDT metalworkers' union the average age of the national officers is thirty-eight, the youngest one being only twenty-eight. Indeed, the leaders of many French unions are comparatively young, and in the CGT unions examined the average age of the leaders is forty-one.

ITALY

In Italy a very similar system of union administration obtains. Unions tend to have secretariats numbering four or five people, usually comprising a general secretary and three or four national secretaries. As in France, the collegial system of leadership means that the general secretary is only the first among equals. The power of union secretariats in relation to other levels of the hierarchy is considerable, and in the CISL metalworkers they are allowed to co-opt ten national officers. This represents quite an amount of patronage to be dispensed and suggests that the national officers need have no difficulty in erecting a protective barrier of sympathisers around themselves if they are of a mind to.

Election
In theory the secretariat is elected by the general council but there is never an open contest for office and electioneering is not practised.

Behind-the-scenes manoeuvring usually decides the outcome and the likelihood is that the most powerful regions represented on the general council will have their favourite son chosen. Terms of office are for four years. In recent years there has been a considerable turnover of national leaders, especially in the CISL unions, following the radicalisation of the membership in the late 1960s. There is no formal rule on the subject, but many CISL unions now operate a system of rotating office at the provincial level and it is likely that this will develop into a standard pattern in the future as is now the case in the French CFDT unions.

The turnover of leadership has had the effect of reducing the average age of national officers. The officers of the UIL metalworkers' union have an average age of forty. In CISL's metalworking union the normal age for national officials is about thirty-five, and the rail union officials in CGIL have an average age of thirty-eight.

BELGIUM

In Belgium the common system is for unions to be run by four principal officers. This is the situation in each of the unions examined with the exception of the FGTB textile workers which has only two national officers, a president and a national secretary.

Election
In the FGTB metalworkers' and textile unions the officers are elected at conference for a three-year term, while elections in the public service union are every four years. In practice most officers are returned unopposed, and in the FGTB textile workers' union the acceptance of the officers' report to conference is taken as a vote of confidence. On the other hand some CSC unions do not even pretend to have elections for office. In the CSC metalworkers the secretariat is appointed by the executive committee, and for all practical purposes the jobs are held until retirement. In the CSC railway union and textile union appointments of officials are made by the general council.

The age of national officers in the unions considered is generally higher than in France and Italy, averaging about fifty in each of the FGTB unions.

HOLLAND

In the NVV and NKV industrial workers' unions there are relatively large groups of national officers to handle the affairs of what were, until quite recently, several autonomous unions. Job security for the then officials of the various constituent bodies was an essential pre-condition for the mergers that created the new unions. But it is likely that the number of officials will be reduced by a process of attrition over time. The NVV industrial union has three principal officers, a president and two vice-presidents, together with nine full-time executive board members. The three general officers of the union are responsible for overall administration while the members of the full-time executive handle the particular affairs of each industrial sector. Two executive members have responsibility for textiles and two others look after metalworking. However there has been a tendency for power to be shared equally in recent years with a collegial system of leadership. This represents a big change from the mid 1960s when the president of the old NVV metalworkers' union stood alone as the most powerful officer.

In the NKV industrial union there is no hard and fast division of responsibilities along industrial lines among the seven-man secretariat. These include four principal officers – a president, vice-president, general secretary, financial secretary – and three national secretaries. In addition there are eleven appointed national officers.

The NVV transport union has a three-man secretariat for its rail sector elected at the triennial railway sector conference. One of these three is the overall president of the transport union and divides his time evenly between the affairs of the railway sector and those of the union as a whole. A similar situation obtains in the NKV transport union where the four leaders of the railway section include the president and treasurer of the entire union.

Election

National officers are elected at conference and they are the only full-time officials to be elected. The term of office is theoretically three years but in most Dutch unions office-holding tends to be permanent in practice. Certainly it would be quite out of character for a union election to be openly contested. Under normal circumstances it is left to the executive to decide who should fill a vacant position. In doing this they may well submit a list of candidates to the conference but with their own preference clearly marked. And the chances of the delegates rejecting the official choice are very slight. Thus the three general officers of the NVV rail workers' union are elected at conference on the nomination of the executive. In the NKV transport union official slates are prepared by the general council for elections for the presidency of the union and for the head of the railway sector. For other positions there is no slate and candidates are allowed three minutes or so at conference to give delegates a biographical outline of their union work. The union is conscious that the present elections are not really 'open', though they are hoping to make them more so.

The average age of national officers in the two industrial workers' unions is forty-six. In the NKV transport union, which is currently undergoing a process of radicalisation, the average age of its leadership is forty, while the NVV transport union officers tend to be in their mid-fifties.

GERMANY

In the metalworkers' union the secretariat comprises eleven people: a president, vice-president, treasurer and eight national secretaries. In both the textile and railway unions the secretariat is limited to seven members. In each case the division of responsibilities among national officers is along functional lines rather than on the basis of particular geographical or industrial sub-sectors. Thus the members of the metalworkers' secretariat each take charge of one of the following fields: collective bargaining, labour legislation, industrial engineering, shop stewards, work councils, co-determination, the European Coal and Steel Community, and education. Much the same sort of specialisations exist in the textile and rail unions. Often there is someone with particular responsibility for immigrant workers, and sometimes a member of the secretariat will specialise in international affairs.

Alongside the members of the secretariat there are large numbers of national officers appointed to particular functions. The metalworkers' union has no fewer than 111 officers and specialists in its headquarters. The textile union has fourteen national officers working directly under the secretariat, while the railway union has approximately fifty appointed officers at this level.

Election
Union secretariats are elected every three or four years at the national conference.

The average age of national officers in the railway and metalworkers' unions is around forty-eight, and in the textile union it is forty-two.

DENMARK

The number of national officers constituting the union secretariat ranges from three in the textile union and four in the general railway union to seven in the metalworkers. In the textile and rail unions this represents the entire body of headquarters officials, but in metalworking the national officers are supported by eleven other elected national officials whose main responsibilities are in the field of organising and negotiating. Two other officials of equal status to these are stationed in the provinces, but with similar responsibilities. The fact is that the union's membership is concentrated around Copenhagen and there is no need for a field staff as such.

Election

Danish union leaders must be re-elected at union conference. In recent years there have been contested elections in the metalworking and textile unions. Electioneering is not normally practised, but there is no rule against a candidate advertising himself by some means, and there have been occasions when this has happened in the metalworking union.

The average age of national officers is around fifty, though all three textile union officers are over sixty.

SWEDEN

Both the metalworkers' and textile unions have five principal national officers. In addition to these, the metalworkers have some thirty officials at head office; eighteen of them are negotiators and the remainder are involved in organising and senior administrative posts. The union has no field staff and some of these officials perform functions associated with field representatives elsewhere. The textile union has only five national officials, apart from its principal officers, working as organisers and negotiators. In the public service union there is a total of ten national officials working in the railway sector.

Election

Unlike in other Scandinavian countries, Swedish union leaders, once elected, are not normally required to stand for re-election. In metalworking the principal officers are originally elected by conference and then hold their position indefinitely. If a vacancy occurs in between conferences an appointment is made by the general council and the next conference confirms the choice. This was in fact the procedure adopted in the selection of the current president, Bert Lundin, in 1971. On that occasion the general council held a referendum in the local branches before deciding that he should succeed to the job. But the holding of a referendum is not a constitutional requirement, and in the same year a new general secretary was also chosen by the general council without the branches being consulted in this way. As in most Scandinavian unions, the average age of these officers is around fifty.

Apart from the principal officers, all the remaining national officials are appointed by the executive. Positions are advertised in the union and labour press, and the executive usually has total freedom to choose from the applicants, though the general council is formally supposed to ratify this choice. Most officials come from within the ranks of the union membership, but since a change of union rule in 1965 it is now permissible to recruit from outside. However, generally it is felt that it would be a poor reflection on the unions if they could not be staffed from among their own rank and file members.

NORWAY

The metalworking and textile unions have four principal officers and the railway union has six. In addition to these the metalworkers have fifteen appointed officials at head office with negotiating, organising and senior administrative responsibilities. Again these people often do the work performed by field representatives in other countries. The textile union has four officials in equivalent positions, but the railway union relies entirely on its six-man secretariat to represent the membership at the national level.

Election
Elections are held at conference where delegates elect committees with responsibility for proposing an official slate of candidates. In metalworking and textiles the committees are predominantly lay, but the members are all nominated by the executive committee. In the railway union the committee is exclusively made up of rank and file delegates. Inclusion on an official slate is a near guarantee of election. However, opposition candidates do sometimes stand, and at the last metalworkers' conference both the president and vice-president were opposed, albeit unsuccessfully. National officials other than the principal officers are appointed by the executive committee in metalworking. The officials invariably come from within the union's own membership, vacant positions being advertised in the union press. The system of appointing has only been in effect since 1949 when the union changed an earlier rule that all officers had to be elected.

FIELD OFFICERS

In most unions the bulk of full-time officials work at the regional or district level. Their functions involve negotiating, organising, liaising with the membership and supervising the administration of the district or individual branches within the district. How much emphasis will be placed on collective bargaining and grievance handling and how much will be devoted to more routine administrative tasks at this level will depend largely on the pattern of industrial relations in the industry. Where labour–management relations are highly centralised, as is generally the case in, for example, the railway industry, there may be very few and perhaps no field officers, while those that do exist will be mainly engaged in routine administration. In industries where centralisation is less pronounced or where collective bargaining takes place at the local level, far more of the officials' time will be taken up in direct dealing with the employers.

In Britain the system of selecting these officials varies. Some unions elect field officers, others appoint them, and in a few cases combination of the two methods is employed. The AUEW elects 26 divisional officers and assistant divisional officers and 112 district secretaries every three years. NUBSO appoints officials for four years at a time. The NUR has no field staff and relies instead on a group of national organisers who are elected once following a preliminary selection process and then hold their jobs permanently. But probably more common is the system whereby officials are simply appointed on a permanent basis. This is the practice in the T&GWU, the NUTGW, the TASSA and the NUHKW. In the latter case only full-time district officials are eligible for election to the union's highest offices. The GMWU adopts a hybrid system of selection. Prospective regional officials are taken on staff for a two-year probationary period after which, if they are considered acceptable, their names go forward for election in what is usually a one-horse race. Thereafter a full career structure is open to them with the prospect of elevation to the position of national industrial officer or regional secretary.

FRANCE

Field officers in French unions are almost invariably employed by the regional or local body, and the decision whether or not to have a full-time official at this level is not a matter for the national union. The salaries of such officials are met out of regional or local funds and the financial strength of these lower bodies will be a deciding factor in whether or not to employ somebody full-time. In the CGT metalworkers' union there are one or two instances where, confronted with a tough organising job, the national union has financed the employment of a full-time official. But such cases are exceptions.

The CGT metalworkers' union has no official count of the exact number of regional and local level full-time officials, but fourteen of its general council members are full-time officials employed at this level. The CGT railway union's corps of officials is almost totally centralised in Paris, with only three full-time people located outside the capital. Similarly, in the CGT textile union there are only two officials in the field, one at Lille and the other in Lyon. This situation is solely attributable to the financial weakness of the union and indicates how the labour movement has suffered from internal divisions. In the early post-war years the unified textile union had close to twenty regional full-time officials, while today all the officials of the various textile unions would not add up to this.

In the CFDT metalworkers' union there is a relatively large staff of fifty-nine regional officers. The CFDT textile union claims to have four such officials, while the CFDT rail union has a field staff of twelve.

Election

The officials are elected in, and employed by, the regional bodies of the various unions, though sometimes the national union will have some influence on the choice. Thus in the CGT textile union the national officers make it clear as to whether or not they regard a prospective candidate as being acceptable. Likewise, in the CFDT rail union the regional choice for officer has to be approved by the national executive.

Ratio of Officials to Members. Counting together national and regional full-time officials, the following approximate ratios of officers to members apply in French unions:

CGT metalworkers	1 : 19,000
CGT textile workers	1 : 7,000/8,000
CGT rail workers	1 : 3,000
CFDT metalworkers	1 : 1,800
CFDT textile workers	1 : 7,500
CFDT rail workers	1 : 1,000

ITALY

Unions in Italy adopt a similar approach to French unions in the employment of full-time field officers. The decision on whether to hire someone or not is left to the regional or provincial body, and the deciding factor will usually be the availability of funds.

In metalworking both the CISL and UIL groups have relatively large numbers of full-time field officers. In the former case there are 220 provincial officers and in the latter 160. In textiles the CISL union claims to have 147 provincial officers. An important reason for the relatively large staffs of officials is the recently developed system under which firms allow union members a six-month leave of absence from their jobs in order to undertake a probationary training as union officials. This also enables unions to avail themselves of the services of additional officers for limited periods, and in some of the smaller and poorer provinces part-time assistance of this sort is a common way round the problem of inadequate staffs. In a province like Reggio Emilia the CISL metalworkers have only one permanent full-time official but he is assisted by two people on temporary secondment. Members are not required to take a full six months away from work and this means that probationers can be used to supplement the union staff during passing emergencies.

Election
Office is theoretically elective, but as in France this is usually reduced to a process in which the most influential members at the level in question elevate a favourite son to the vacant position. In this process the need to maintain a balance between communists and socialists in CGIL and between socialists and Christians in CISL is an important factor. Terms of office are for three or four years and increasingly there is a tendency, especially in CISL unions, for the incumbent to be replaced after two or three terms.

Ratio of Officials to Members. Where figures are available they show the ratio of full-time national and provincial officers to members to be:

CISL metalworkers	1 : 1,200
CISL textile workers	1 : 1,300

BELGIUM

In metalworking the FGTB union has eighty officials at regional level compared with the CSC union's fifty-two. The FGTB textile union has thirty-five full-time representatives at this level, while its counterpart organisation in the CSC has thirty. In the public service unions field staff have responsibility for sectors other than railways and so no count of railway officials is possible.

Election
The method of selection of these officials ranges from straightforward appointment to methods that purport to be more democratic. Some unions leave the selection to the region, while in others the choice is made at national level. But there is rarely what could be described as an open election for the positions.

In the FGTB metalworkers officials are chosen at regional conference and are theoretically subject to re-election every three years. But in practice they are not normally challenged and in effect the jobs are held permanently. When a position has to be filled there is usually an attempt to avoid an open contest, and background manoeuvring will take place to try to find a candidate who is broadly acceptable. In this way the election is effectively predetermined. In the event that an official is ever removed from office it is practically unheard of for him to go back to the shop floor.

In the CSC metalworkers, when a job becomes vacant the senior full-time official in the region selects a few possible candidates from among the regional officials of the confederation itself, or possibly from among factory militants. These are considered by the regional governing body which will then state its preference. The general secretary or president of the union usually interviews the region's choice and the secretariat may then make the decision to hire him provisionally. After a probationary period of three months the general council normally confirms the appointment.

Both the FGTB and CSC textile unions adopt a similar system, their regional committees and national leaders contriving to find someone mutually acceptable. Because of the regional and language differences in the country what is often at issue in these backstage manoeuvrings is the need to balance the interests of Flemish and Walloon members. In the FGTB textile union candidates are proposed by the regional committee. The national officers sometimes arrange for a university to test the candidates' organisational and administrative ability, and the results are passed on for the region to make a final selection. But approval of this choice is still a matter for the general council. In the CSC textile union the initiative for choosing a regional officer will often lie with the committee of the region, but if there is no obvious candidate the national office may well assume the responsibility for appointing someone, possibly from somewhere else within the CSC hierarchy.

Ratio of Officials to Members. Altogether the ratio of national and regional officers to members is:

FGTB metalworkers	1 : 1,700
FGTB textile workers	1 : 1,400
CSC metalworkers	1 : 2,700
CSC textile workers	1 : 3,300

HOLLAND

The NVV industrial workers' union has a total regional staff of seventy-eight representatives. Each of its fourteen regions has a principal officer and from three to five organisers. In the NKV industrial workers union there are fifty regional officials. Neither of the two transport unions has separate field officers to look after the interests of their railway membership.

Election
There are no elections for positions at this level in Dutch trade unions. In both the industrial unions the national executive has the responsibility for making appointments and the successful applicant is then considered to be an employee of the national union.

Ratio of Officials to Members. The entire body of national and district officials in the NVV and NKV industrial unions represents the membership in the ratio of:

NVV industrial workers union	1 : 2,200
NKV industrial workers union	1 : 2,000

GERMANY

The metalworkers' union has a regional staff of forty-two, nine of them regional secretaries and the rest working under the secretaries as organisers. The railway union has forty regional officers and the textile union has sixteen. The functions of the field staff vary according to whether or not collective bargaining is centralised or decentralised. In metalworking and textiles this is a matter for the regions and the activities of the field staff are attuned to this. In railways the main collective bargaining activity is at national level and the role of regional officials is more an administrative one.

Apart from staff at this level German unions also have a highly developed system of full-time branch officers. These have to be acceptable to the national union, and since they are also paid by the latter rather than the local body they should therefore be counted as part of the corps of full-time union officials. In metalworking there are 263 full-time branch secretaries and 300 branch-based technical staff. The textile union has 115 full-time branch officials and 27 people undergoing full-time probationary training at this level. In the railway union there is a total of 110 full-time branch officers.

Election
None of the regional officers are elected in German unions: in every instance they are appointed by the national executive. In the case of branch officers, they are elected by the membership every three

years, but the branch choice has to be acceptable to the national union.

Ratio of Officials to Membership. Adding together the full-time officials employed at national, regional and local level gives a ratio of officers to members of:

metalworking	1 : 3,500
textiles	1 : 1,600
railways	1 : 2,000

DENMARK

None of the unions examined has a system of regional full-time officials. Unions like the textile workers make widespread use of full-time branch officers but, unlike the German officials at this level, they are simply employees of the local union and in no way part of the national administration.

Ratio of Officials to Members. Adding together the full-time full-time staff of the unions represent members in the ratio of:

metalworking	1 : 6,000
textiles	1 : 3,700

SWEDEN

Regional officers are not found in Swedish unions, though a system of full-time branch officials has been built up and the national union is in a position to exert some direct influence over these. The metalworkers' union has 100 full-time officials at this level, while in the textile union the number is 26.

Election

The selection of full-time branch officers is by appointment rather than election, and whether or not a branch has such an official is normally determined by its size. Branches over a certain size can appeal to the national union for financial assistance in employing a full-time officer. If the union agrees it will contribute up to 70 per cent of the wage costs. In a formal sense these officials are employed by the branch, but this system of financing obviously gives the national union some control over them. The appointment of a branch official begins with the national union advertising the post. The national executive shortlists the applicants and then discusses the various candidates with the branch committee which has the right to choose from the shortlist. Most applications come from the local branches' own members. Until ten years ago it was mandatory for them to be local members, but now this rule has been relaxed to allow mobility of union officials within the labour movement. By hurrying along a programme of branch mergers the unions are actively promoting an increase in the number of full-time local officers. Just under half the branches in metalworking now have full-time officials and in bigger branches such as Stockholm there are as many as seven such officials.

Ratio of Officials to Members. Taking together national and branch officials, the ratio of full-time officers to members is:

metalworking	1 : 3,000
textiles	1 : 1,600

NORWAY

With the exception of the metalworkers' union which has six regional officials, all appointed by the national executive, Norwegian unions follow the pattern of other Scandinavian unions in having no network of field staff. Full-time branch positions are also the exception rather than the rule, and where they do exist they are employed and paid by the local body.

Ratio of Officials to Members. Counting national and, where applicable, regional staff the ratio of officials to members is:

metalworking	1 : 4,800
textiles	1 : 2,500
railways	1 : 2,600

SALARIES

The pay of top union officials in Britain is generally regarded as being low. This is certainly so when compared with the salaries of leaders of industry. But the question of union salaries has an important bearing on internal democracy, and the relatively comfortable position of some officials compared with that of their members may well serve to divide the leaders from the rank and file. It is often said that without generous salaries unions would not be able to attract the best people. But there is rarely any response to the argument that those who will only work for a high salary are unlikely to be the best people for trade unions. Certainly it is difficult to find fault with the suggestion that officials should not be paid more than the highest paid members that they represent.

FRANCE

Where salaries are concerned, French union practices are very egalitarian. In all the CGT and CFDT unions leaders earn no more than the highest paid workers in their industry. On the railways, union officials are considered to be on paid leave of absence from their railway jobs and continue to receive from the railways the salary for their grade of work. The leaders of both the metalworkers' unions receive the rate for skilled men in the Paris region which in 1973 amounted to £2,400 p.a.[7] The CFDT metalworkers' general secretary receives a little more than this to compensate him for the drop in salary he experienced when going on staff. In textiles the same principle applies with both unions paying officials approximately £2,100 p.a. Some unions work on the assumption that an officer should not be worse off than he was when on the shop floor. But the general secretary of the CGT textile union claims to have earned double his present salary when he was an employee in industry. A further egalitarian feature of union salaries is that they are uniform for all officials. There is generally no hierarchy of rates that sets the general secretary apart, and even at the regional level the principle of parity applies, except in cases where the region simply cannot afford to pay this much. Financial weakness is the only limiting factor here.

ITALY

The CISL metalworkers pay the members of the secretariat £2,400–£3,000 p.a. National officials appointed by the secretariat earn £2,000 p.a. By comparison, average weekly earnings based on a forty-hour week for workers in the non-agricultural sector are £28.80.[8] In the UIL metalworkers the salaries for national officers are £1,800–£2,200 p.a. And as in France, Italian railway union officials are paid at the rate they would have received in their old job.

In general, field staff salaries are a little lower than for national officials. The CISL metalworkers' provincial officers are paid £1,500–£2,000 while their UIL counterparts earn £1,700–£2,000.

BELGIUM

Salaries of officials in all Belgian unions are kept confidential. This secretiveness over financial matters is something that clearly marks off the Belgian labour movement from the bulk of European unions. Not only is the information kept from outsiders, but even the members who provide the money for the salaries are left in the dark.

In the FGTB metalworkers' union the salaries of administrative and professional staff range from £2,200 to £4,500 p.a. The national secretaries are paid more than this and it seems likely that they earn at least £5,000 p.a. This compares with average weekly earnings of fractionally under £40 for a forty-hour week in manufacturing industry.[9] There are differences between the rates of pay for national and regional officials. And among regional officials there are also differences based on the number of members serviced, though in the FGTB textile workers' union there is said to be no great disparity between the highest and lowest rates. In the FGTB metalworkers' union there is a national minimum rate for regional officials, but decisions to pay above this can be made at that level if the region is financially capable of paying more. Salaries are determined in different ways in the FGTB unions. For the metalworkers' union the executive sets the salary. In the textile workers' union rates are decided by a commission elected from among the members of the general council. In the public service union, which pays its regional and national officials on a scale ranging from about £3,120 to £5,600, a three-man lay committee elected by conference examines the scale every four years.

So closely is this kind of information guarded that the rival union officials tend to have only a vague idea of what salaries are paid to their opposite numbers. The FGTB metalworkers suspect that their rates are higher than in the CSC union, while the FGTB public service union officials feel that their Christian counterparts may be earning a few thousand francs more than they. In fact information about salaries in the CSC is even harder to come by. The rail union officials receive the rate for their old job on the railways. Otherwise the system is that a scale of salaries for different posts for all affiliates is drawn up by the CSC itself after negotiations with the CSC clerical workers' union, to which all union officials belong. The body which actually makes the decision on salaries is the executive of the CSC which includes the presidents of all the individual unions. In principle the presidents of the different unions receive the same amount. However, for regional officers there are three grades of pay depending on seniority, size of the region, and personal merit rating. The spread is such as to give the president 30 per cent more than the lowest rated regional official.

It seems likely the CSC salary levels are generally lower than in the FGTB unions. The president of the CSC metalworkers admits that they have difficulty in recruiting officials from the shop floor. If a man goes on staff after the age of thirty-five his union salary may well be less than what he earned in industry, and in that case the union will probably grant him a number of years' seniority to enable his salary to be raised to a comparable level.

HOLLAND

Information about salaries in Dutch unions is freely available. The president of the NVV industrial workers' union earns £6,300 p.a. Executive board members and heads of regions are paid 81 per cent of this amount, and regional officers earn around £5,300 p.a.[10] A guideline for salaries is basically decided by the NVV for all its affiliates and most unions follow this.

Within the NKV industrial union rates of pay are much lower, ranging from £3,000 p.a. for the lowest level field officers to £5,200 p.a. for the president. The NKV transport union pays its officers slightly more than this on a scale ranging from £3,400 p.a. to £5,600 p.a. for the president. As in the Belgian CSC unions, the general rates for all NKV affiliates are proposed by the Confederation's general council after negotiations with the union representing salaried staffs.

GERMANY

Salaries in German unions are among the highest in Europe. The president of the metalworkers earns between £10,500 and £11,500 p.a. Ordinary members of the secretariat are paid £7,600–£9,600 p.a. By contrast, weekly earnings for workers in the non-agricultural sector are £56.[11] The scale is slightly lower in the textile union with national officers paid a maximum of £7,800 p.a. The salaries of regional officers are fixed on a national scale. In metalworking these average £6,700 p.a., while in textiles the rate ranges between £4,400 and £4,900.

DENMARK

The Danish metalworkers' union pays the highest salaries of any of the unions studied in Scandinavia. The president earns around £7,000–£7,200 p.a., the vice-president and treasurer earn a little less than this, and the remaining national secretaries are paid a little more than £6,200 p.a. In the textile union the collegial leadership is reflected in the fact that all three officers are paid £6,200 p.a. Compared with this, workers in the non-agricultural sector earn £68 on average for a forty-hour week.[12]

The level of salaries in Swedish unions is lower than elsewhere in Scandinavia. The principal officers are paid a little more than £5,300 p.a. in the metalworking and textile unions, with appointed national officers earning £4,600–£5,275 p.a. In the public service union the highest rate goes up to around £6,100, while appointed national officers can earn between £5,000 and £5,800 p.a. At the local branch level full-time officials in both metalworking and textiles earn around £4,500 p.a. These union salaries compare with average weekly earnings of £60·40 for a forty-hour week in manufacturing industry.[13]

NORWAY

Norwegian unions generally pay their officers the rates applicable to two civil service grades which are negotiated between the civil service union and the government. The railway and textile union presidents are paid £5,350 p.a. as are also the vice-president and secretary-treasurer of the metalworkers' union. The president of the metalworkers' union is on a higher rate than this and is paid around £5,700, roughly equivalent to the vice-president of LO. For national officials other than the principal officers the metalworking and textile unions pay £5,000 p.a. Compared with this, male workers in manufacturing earn £56 on average for a forty-hour week.[14]

ADMINISTRATIVE AND PROFESSIONAL STAFFS

As well as officials with representational and executive functions, unions sometimes employ large administrative staffs. Often there is no clear distinction between the two kinds of function, but it is important to try and discover how many people there are in strictly administrative jobs. The size of the staff can give a rough guide to the extent to which unions provide services to the membership. The number of people employed may reflect the financial strength of the union. But most important of all for this discussion, the size and the degree of centralisation of the union administration is an indication of the amount of organisational power in the hands of national leaders. If union leaders are to be regarded as bureaucrats, as indeed many of them are, then it is surely relevant to consider the scale of the bureaucracies they command.

In 1959 a survey of sixteen British unions showed that on average there was one staff employee for every 2,300 members.[15] Altogether 41 per cent of union clerical and administrative staffs worked at their respective head offices. In terms of concentration, the NUR was the most centralised with all administrative employees at national office. The T&GWU and GMWU were the least centralised with less than one-fifth of all staff at head office. And the AEU, with 59 per cent of staff at headquarters, was, perhaps strangely in view of its history, more centralised than most unions.

The following table shows the present ratio of administrative staff to members in those European unions for which figures are available:

Table 6.1 *Ratio of Administrative Staff to Union Members*

Belgium	CSC metalworkers	1 : 9,000
	CSC textile workers	1 : 6,000
	FGTB textile workers	1 : 3,300
Holland	NVV industrial workers	1 : 700
	NKV industrial workers	1 : 2,000
	NVV transport workers	1 : 650
	NKV transport workers	1 : 550
Germany	metalworkers	1 : 1,400
	textile workers	1 : 9,700
	rail workers	1 : 1,400
Denmark	metalworkers	1 : 400
	textile workers	1 : 1,250
	rail workers	1 : 2,500
Sweden	metalworkers	1 : 2,000
	textile workers	1 : 1,100
Norway	metalworkers	1 : 2,700
	textile workers	1 : 2,500
	rail workers	1 : 2,600

FRANCE

In France there are no figures for the total number of clerical and administrative staff who work for the unions at all levels. But figures for the headquarters suggest that in most cases unions are considerably understaffed. The largest unions such as the CGT metalworkers only have around thirty employees in clerical and administrative jobs, and in the poorer unions such as the two major textile unions, a head office staff of only three or four people is the rule. This means that the ratio of head office staff employees to members is at best 1 : 13,500 and in some cases as much as 1 : 20,000. Among these relatively small staffs there are rarely any professionals such as economists or work study engineers. The union leaders are traditionally expected to rely on their own ability in these areas.

BELGIUM

The CSC unions appear to have smaller staffs than their FGTB counterparts, but from the point of view of leadership control this is counterbalanced by the fact that the administration of CSC unions is rather more centralised. Some of the regional bodies in the FGTB metalworkers employ more staff than are to be found at the union headquarters, and in the FGTB textile union less than 25 per cent of the administrative staff work in the national office. By contrast 50 per cent of the staffs of both CSC metalworkers' and textile workers' unions are employed at head office.

Among their headquarters staff Belgian unions are also better served than the French in terms of professional and technical personnel. The FGTB metalworkers employ five professionally qualified people, including an economist and a work study engineer. The FGTB textile union has a technical support staff of five. And in the CSC metalworking and textile unions there are research and education staffs of seven and four people respectively.

HOLLAND

The Dutch unions generally have the lowest ratio of staff to members of any of the labour movements studied. And as in Belgium the Christian unions tend to have a more centralised administration than their socialist counterparts. In the NVV industrial workers' union less than 50 per cent of staff work at head office, whereas in the NKV industrial union two-thirds of the staff are attached to the national office.

The head office staffs of Dutch unions also include a number of professionals and technicians. The NVV industrial workers union has no less than fourteen professional staff members, while its NKV counterpart has two economists and two lawyers.

GERMANY

In both the metalworking and railway unions two-thirds of the administrative staff are in regional and local offices, while the majority of textile union employees work at headquarters. But in all three cases the degree of effective centralisation is considerable, with a direct line of command from the top down making branches the local agents of the national administration.

The headquarters' staffs also include significant numbers of professional workers. The metalworkers' union has twenty-four people in the capacity of economists, lawyers and sociologists. The textile union employs two economists, a lawyer and six textile engineers, and the railway union has approximately ten people working in a similar capacity.

DENMARK

The relatively large administrative staffs in some Danish unions, particularly metalworking, is attributable to the fact that they operate as government agencies in the field of unemployment insurance. One-half of the administrative workload in the metalworkers' national office is accounted for by this factor. Both the textile and metal unions employ people in the capacity of economists and work study specialists, but in neither case are there more than one or two.

SWEDEN

One-third of the textile workers' staff work at head office, while in metalworking the proportion is about one-half. Swedish unions tend to be better equipped than other Scandinavian unions in the area of professional staffing. The metalworkers' union employs eight economists as well as experts in the field of work safety and vocational training. The public service union has four economists.

NORWAY

Each of the unions studied has a totally centralised administrative structure with the entire staff under the immediate control of the national officers. But where professional research services are concerned centralisation has gone even further, to the point where the unions themselves do not maintain their own staffs and have to rely instead on the services provided by the central confederation.

The conclusion from this is that unions in Holland, Germany, Denmark, Sweden and Norway tend to have more administrative staff relative to members than in Britain, thus placing the union leaders in control of fairly large-scale administrative machines. The major exceptions are in France and Italy, where no overall figures are available, but where staffs are rather small, and in Belgium. How the professional and technical element in these staffs compares with their British counterparts we have no way of knowing, but it seems clear that certain German, Dutch and Swedish union leaders are much better supported in this respect than are leaders of British unions of comparable size.

The degree of centralisation of the administrations of European unions varies from case to case quite as much as it does in Britain and no hard and fast conclusions can be drawn from this. As the situation in the German unions studied shows, a certain decentralisation of administration does not imply any weakening of the national leadership's grip on the machine. But in the case of Holland and Belgium the relative centralisation of administration in the Christian unions does reflect the tendency for power to be more heavily concentrated in the national office than is the case in the socialist unions.

CONCLUSION

European unions display different approaches to the full-time staffing of their organisations. In the first place, unions have widely differing numbers of full-time officials, even after taking into account their size of membership. On the basis of the Donovan Commission's estimate of 3,000 full-time officials in Britain, the ratio of officials to members is approximately 1:3,500. Among the European unions studied this ratio is only exceeded in the CGT metal and textile unions, the CFDT textile union, and the metalworkers in both Denmark and Norway. The German metalworkers have a similar balance of officials to members as exists in Britain, but in most of the other countries considered the presence of full-time officers is much more noticeable.

Where the national leadership is concerned most unions have a larger body of officials than is generally the case in Britain, with secretariats numbering up to a dozen people. And it is the practice in a number of countries to operate a system of collective leadership of the entire secretariat, with the president or general secretary merely the first among equals. The generally large number of officials also carries over into the wider administration of the union, and many organisations have a much bigger head office staff proportionate to membership than one would expect to find in Britain. In this respect many of the unions examined might reasonably be described as being more bureaucratic than their British counterparts.

In the case of field officers, their numbers vary from country to country, the main distinction being between highly centralised unions such as in Germany and Holland and federal systems such as operate in France and Italy. In the former case district or regional officials are the local appointees of the national union, and they tend to be numerous. Under the decentralised French and Italian systems the decision whether to employ a full-time representative in a given area is up to the local governing body. What determines the matter is often the availability of funds, and sometimes this can be a prohibitive factor.

The selection of the principal national officers is, for the most part, by election at the periodic conferences. But open and vigorously contested elections are a rarity. Much more common is the arrangement whereby an inner group of leaders, a conference committee or a sub-committee of the general council put forward an official slate of candidates whose acceptance by the conference is usually automatic. Open electioneering is not a recognised part of European union conferences generally. Nowhere did we learn of any recent close election for high office. In cases where periodic re-election is required the process is frequently a mere formality, and in practice office-holding in most unions tends to be permanent. The major exceptions to this are in the French CFDT unions and some levels of Italian CISL unions where rotation of office is practised. Among national officials other than the principal officers the practice is usually for them to be appointed. And at the regional and district level this is also the system used, again with the exception of the decentralised unions in France and Italy where selection is at least formally by means of election.

Finally, in confirmation of the greater relative importance of full-time officials in most continental labour movements, information collected on salaries suggests that in several countries the status of union leaders is higher than that enjoyed by their opposite numbers in Britain. This is certainly the case in Germany and Denmark. In Sweden, Norway and Belgium salaries of officials are also relatively high, though the difference between them and members' pay is not quite so great. Salaries in Italy tend to be on a lower scale, but only in France do unions generally pursue a consciously egalitarian policy of paying officials roughly the amounts earned by their higher-rated members.

7

Collective Bargaining

This chapter considers the question of collective bargaining with a view to describing how the process works and how much direct participation by union members is involved. What we are trying to discover is how responsive the system is to the wishes of the membership.

In the first place it is important to examine the background to the development of the bargaining system and in particular the way this has been affected by government policy and legislation. We need to look at the levels at which bargaining takes place, the nature of the issues dealt with at each level, and the relationship between the different levels of bargaining. The aim here is to see how much centralisation is involved in the process. In bargaining, as in other aspects of union life, there is a tension between the democratic demand for local control and the need to concentrate overall union strength and resources to achieve the maximum effort. It is important that unions should strike a balance between these two.

In so far as the internal decision-making process is concerned it is necessary to investigate how negotiating demands are formulated. Do they genuinely emanate from the rank and file through a process of democratic debate and decision-making at the local level, or are members only allowed to give their approval to demands effectively decided by the leaders? The next step is to consider who is responsible for conducting the negotiations and who supervises the overall bargaining strategy. Is this an area where the members retain control, or is it treated as a specialist matter for 'professionals' only? When agreements are reached, are members allowed to ratify the proposed settlement, and if so, how? And in cases where there is no agreement, how are strike decisions taken and by whom? Finally a capacity for paying strike benefit and maintaining members during a stoppage of work is very important if unions are to be regarded as credible negotiating agencies, and we need to consider what financial resources are available to unions in dispute.

THE COLLECTIVE BARGAINING PROCESS

FRANCE

Of all the countries in Western Europe France has the least developed system of collective bargaining. There are two basic reasons for this. One is the revolutionary element in union ideology which has led them to regard radical political change as the primary means of obtaining real improvements for the workers, and to view institutionalised collective bargaining as a poor substitute for this. The second reason is the organisational weakness of the unions which has prevented them from making gains in bargaining even when these have been sought.

Metalworking and Textiles
It was not until after the Second World War that permanent collective bargaining machinery was established by an Act in 1946. But free wage bargaining was prohibited until 1950. Thereafter the government's intention was to develop a system of national negotiations. Plant bargaining was to be permitted, though only as a means of adapting higher level agreements. This satisfied the unions who felt that in unrestrained negotiations at the plant level they would be no match for the more powerful employers. Indeed in the succeeding eighteen years negotiations at factory level were relatively few and far between, and on the eve of the 1968 strike wave only 750 plant agreements were in effect.

Collective bargaining in textiles has taken place nationally since 1951. However, metalworking employers have steadfastly refused to negotiate at this level and agreements are concluded on a regional basis. In both cases collective agreements cover all sectors of the industry, with the exception that in metalworking there is a separate agreement for the iron and steel sector. Negotiations with individual companies are rare in both industries.

Whether at national or regional level, collective bargaining normally takes place between the particular employers' federation and all the rival unions together, even though they may well have submitted differing demands and are not negotiating as a united team. Indeed there is very often a tactical battle between the unions in the course of negotiations aimed at impressing workers with a given union's greater militancy or responsiveness to the mood of the rank and file. And it is a very common occurrence for one or more unions to refuse to sign the resulting agreement. This need have no practical effect on the negotiations themselves since the terms of the agreement will still be applied to all workers. But in such a case the non-signing organisation may succeed in demonstrating its greater militancy. For practical purposes collective agreements have an indeterminate duration. This is often because employers have either resisted attempts to reopen negotiations or because unions have been too weak to force negotiations to a conclusion. In these circumstances the terms of the existing agreement are understood to continue. Wage increases are negotiated periodically and isolated amendments to other clauses may be made from time to time.

Railways

From the early post-war years separate legislation has regulated industrial relations on the railways and in the public sector generally. For most of this period railway management have not really been free to negotiate with the unions. Wage negotiations only started in the late 1950s and until 1968 unions and management were only free to bargain over the distribution of an increased wage bill arbitrarily fixed by the government.

The 1968 Strikes and the Aftermath

The 1968 eruption in industry can be seen as evidence of widespread frustration among workers over the inadequacy of collective agreement procedures and a resulting mass of unresolved grievances. For practical purposes the significance of the May strikes and the settlement that followed lay not in the immediate concessions granted to the workers but in the changed climate of industrial relations. The prospects for collective bargaining were enhanced and this was largely due to the conclusion of a number of central collective agreements at the national level, including one on job security in 1969 and vocational training in 1970, which called for further adaptation through industry level and local level negotiations. Multi-industry talks also began on the questions of granting salaried status to manual workers, and by the end of 1970 agreements applying this principle had been reached in half a dozen industries. In effect the deadlock had been broken, the mood had changed and by isolating particular pressing social problems and concluding umbrella agreements on them on a multi-industry basis collective bargaining was being stimulated at lower levels where the detailed adaptation had to be made. Bargaining improved in a quantitative as well as a qualitative sense: between 1967 and 1970 the number of national agreements increased by nearly 25 per cent while at plant level the number rose by more than 30 per cent.

In June 1971, a new industrial relations Act was introduced designed to further stimulate bargaining and to formalise some of the practices that had developed spontaneously after 1968. Collective bargaining on a multi-industry basis at the level of the national economy is now formally recognised and encouraged. At industry level national joint bargaining committees are expected to convene and attempt to reach agreement if two of the unions demand it. And on-going bargaining is encouraged by a clause requiring the establishment of procedures for the renegotiation of agreements at regular intervals.

However, it is easy to exaggerate the progress made after 1968. Many of the plant agreements were once and for all affairs which the unions were unable to improve on once the fervour of 1968 had passed. Often there was no real agreement as such, merely a verbal understanding based on consultations with management, or perhaps simply a ruling posted by management in response to some new demand. And while national-level negotiations within the framework of umbrella agreements were successful on a number of limited topics, on-going bargaining in connection with wages and working conditions has not changed much. A reminder that the old pattern of inconclusive bargaining persists was given in 1971 when neither the CGT nor CFDT metalworking unions were prepared to sign the key Paris region collective agreement.

Metalworking

In metalworking the post-1968 period has seen the first moves towards national-level negotiations. Specific agreements on working hours, job security and salaried status have been reached at this level in the iron and steel industry, and an element of continuity is provided by clauses requiring the agreements to be renegotiated in two or three years. The hours of work agreement of 1968 set another precedent in joint industrial government by establishing a permanent joint committee to supervise the adaptation of the agreement at lower levels and to resolve problems arising. However, the national agreements are still limited to isolated topics. Metalworking employers refuse to discuss wages on a national basis and have resisted the unions' pressure for a national wage scale. Actual wage levels are decided in the plant and these bear little relation to the rates set by regional agreement. And since the rates fixed in the plant are often decided unilaterally by management the effect is to leave the unions with little power over earnings. It is possible for strong workshop groups to bargain over piece-rates and job evaluation, though even here the basis of piecework schemes is decided at the provincial level.

Textiles

In textiles the problem is not one of securing national negotiations but of being able to bargain at regional or plant level in a way that enables the terms and conditions at work to reflect local needs. Since 1968 national negotiations have been more frequent, but except in a few strong areas such as Lille, Roubaix-Tourcoing, Vosges and Rhone-Alpes the employers steadfastly refuse to deal with the workers at provincial level. There is only one company-wide agreement in textiles, that with the giant multi-national firm Rhone-Poulenc, and at plant level no systematic bargaining takes place.

... system of incentive payments the unions'
... very limited. Union
... ls or systems of pay-
... erning management.
... complex and union
... or managerial tech-
... system of personal
... r's discretion in most
... collective bargaining.
... iate a national system
... the early 1950s, des-
... ansformed many pro-
... f many jobs.

... ve been more positive.
... dustry as a model for
... nt have been granted
... ations with the unions,
... s bargaining now takes
... gaining process on non-
... o that the local adapta-
... oint union–management

After a generation of Fascist rule during which Mussolini's state-controlled unions had been used as a tool of discipline and indoctrination, collective bargaining was re-established in Italy under the 1948 Constitution. Freedom of organisation and strike action were restored, but the pattern of bureaucratic, centralised industrial relations established under Fascism continued long after the end of the war. In fact the undemocratic union apparatus of pre-war days was not dismantled but merely taken over by the free unions, and this lent itself ideally to the practice of rigid, centralised collective bargaining which held sway unchallenged until the late 1950s.

Bargaining was conducted by the central confederations. The

problem of rival unionism weakened the workers' side, with tactical manoeuvring between unions helping to make the regular re-negotiation of agreements difficult. Bargaining decisions were taken by union leaders, agreements being concluded and strikes called without reference to the membership. While it lasted this system of wage determination was probably more centralised and remote from the rank and file than in any other Western European country.

Inevitably the rigid centralisation began to break down during the 1960s, giving rise to a system of bargaining industry by industry and sector by sector. This entailed a certain amount of local negotiation, but it was closely controlled from above. In the mid-1960s the recession in industry prompted a considerable amount of industrial reorganisation, the introduction of widespread technical changes and the use of more scientific techniques of personnel management. All of this increased the need for genuine, plant-level bargaining. In 1968 a spontaneous movement by workers erupted aimed at forcing negotiations within the factories, and to a large extent this developed in opposition to the official unions. In contravention of national procedures, demands were made for general wage increases at the plant level. And for the first time the introduction of technological changes was made a subject for negotiation.

By early 1969 the unions had largely succeeded in capturing this movement and channelling it in an orderly way. The immediate result was that the metalworking unions made substantial gains in the national negotiations of autumn 1969. And apart from that, the wave of unrest led directly to the passing of the Statute of Rights of Workers in May 1970, in which many of the demands made in connection with the rights of unions in the plant were conceded. In future, plant unionism was to be recognised; discriminatory payments by employers to individual workers were outlawed; their freedom to dismiss workers was curtailed; and the use of television and radio in controlling production was forbidden. The 1970 Act has proved to be a major factor in transforming the system of industrial relations in subsequent years. Almost entirely favourable to the union side, it was, indeed, the result of a process in which unions found themselves negotiating as much with government as with the employers. Since 1969 collective bargaining has taken on a wider perspective, and alongside the standard issues of employment conditions unions are now raising wider social questions such as housing, education, transport and health services as matters for bargaining with government.

Post-1969 Developments

The main result of the 1969 unheaval was the establishment of a union presence in the workshops. The pattern established in metal-working in 1969 was repeated in other industries such as textiles and clothing in 1970–1, and by 1972 there were an estimated 4,500 plant agreements in effect in industry generally. For this the unified factory delegate movement was largely responsible.

The post-1969 years have also seen the collapse of the earlier system under which such negotiations as did take place in the plant were closely controlled by higher level union officials. In the 1969 national negotiations the employers were unable to obtain agreement on the scope of collective bargaining at the various levels, and the 1970 Act made no attempt to deal with the matter. There is now no question of plant negotiations merely rounding off settlements already made above, or even simply confining themselves to questions unresolved nationally. The sudden transition to a more open, democratic form of negotiating, with rank and file workers able to play a full part, has not been compatible with an orderly, structured system of bargaining in which key decisions are taken on high. Collective bargaining now proceeds in a largely unco-ordinated fashion at the level of the industrial sectors and within plants. Sometimes the plant agreements apply the terms negotiated nationally but equally the better plant bargains tend to set a pattern for subsequent national negotiations, and the two forms of bargaining interact.

Agreements at national level last for three years, with wages now geared to the average firm rather than the marginal producer. Meanwhile, during that period there may be more than one round of negotiations in the plant. The subjects of plant agreements are mainly domestic issues ranging from piecework and bonus payments, both of which are less and less tied to output and increasingly constitute a fixed addition to wages, to job enrichment, the regulation of work speeds and the organisation of production generally. However, the unions in the plant also reserve the right to reopen negotiations on matters dealt with at national level, so that a policy of 'permanent conflict' proclaimed by some unions rules out any guarantee of industrial peace during the term of a national agreement.

BELGIUM

Collective bargaining in Belgium is highly institutionalised. Since the early 1960s it has taken place at three levels – at the level of the national economy, individual industry level, and plant level. Most industry-wide negotiations are conducted between unions and federations of employers such as the engineering employers' federation, Fabrimetal. But in metalworking quite a number of firms, some of them multi-nationals like General Motors, do conclude separate company agreements with the unions, while in textiles there are perhaps half a dozen separate company level agreements.

Multi-Industry Bargaining

The present pattern of collective bargaining is the result of a long process of development that has been unfolding since the war. Economy-level negotiations have existed since the 1947 agreement which provided for the establishment of union delegations in plants. In 1952 the National Labour Council was established as a forum for economy-wide discussions between unions and employers. The council acts as an advisory body to the government on social and employment questions, and since 1968 the two sides among its members have been empowered to conclude regular collective agreements. The sort of things covered by recent agreements include such broad questions as guaranteed monthly wages, the disclosure of financial and economic information by employers, pensions, public holidays, leave for union education, and manpower problems. It has sometimes been suggested that the council now acts almost as a social parliament, making rules that apply throughout the private sector.

National Bargaining – Metalworking and Textiles

National-level negotiating machinery for individual industries was re-established and extended at the end of the war, and there are currently joint industrial committees in approximately eighty industrial sectors. These are statutory bodies with a minimum of four members from each side of industry. On the union side the seats are divided in proportion to the strengths of the rival organisations. The committees are responsible for negotiating collective agreements, conciliating and arbitrating disputes arising, and overseeing the activities of works councils in their industry. In post-war years national negotiations have assumed greater and greater importance in most industries although in exceptional cases the key bargains are still struck at plant level. In metalworking there are eight basic national agreements covering the different sectors such as garages, electrical engineering, precious metals, and so on. In textiles there is one general agreement with sub-sections applying to the different sectors.

Railways

In the public sector separate negotiating machinery exists. The railway industry has had a well-established system of national wage bargaining with the publicly owned railways since 1926. There is a national joint committee with a total of twenty union and management representatives. As state funds are involved in all wage discussions, negotiations tend to involve the government closely, and the Minister responsible for railways chairs the joint committee meetings. Apart from wages, conditions of employment for railway workers are laid down in regulations drawn up by the joint committee, but these can only be modified by a two-thirds decision of the committee. Although there is a system of joint consultation at regional and local level on the railways, the highly centralised system of negotiations rules out any collective bargaining at the local level.

Social Programming

The relationships between these different levels of negotiation became highly formalised in 1960. At that time the dictates of economic planning led unions and employers to agree to introduce a long-term perspective into collective bargaining aiming at a planned growth of wages. The system of social programming involves the making of national umbrella agreements on an economy-wide basis in connection with particular social objectives. Such agreements have become very common since 1968. Following these, national industrial agreements are negotiated in conformity with the terms of the multi-industry agreements. And finally the application of the detailed terms, together with anything not covered at higher levels, is subject to negotiation in the plant. The underlying philosophy behind social programming is the idea of 'social partnership', the community of interests between workers and employers. A major feature of the system is that agreements which used to be negotiated for an indefinite period are now for fixed periods which tend to be longer than in the past. At the same time, unions are required to accept the principle of industrial peace during the term of agreements and to enforce the no-strike clause among their members. In metalworking the unions undertake to prevent unofficial strikes and to get members back to work within three days should a stoppage occur. If the strike continues no benefit is supposed to be paid.

To assist the enforcement of these clauses most employers now pay unions or their members a lump sum each year, normally about 0·6 per cent of annual wages but in the textile industry as high as 1 per cent of average salaries, provided that industrial peace is maintained. A proportion of the payment is withheld if the no-strike provision is broken. A contributing reason for the introduction of these payments was the difficulty faced by unions in persuading members to accept long-term agreements. Since the closed shop is illegal in Belgium the unions feared that members dissatisfied with inflexible national negotiations would quit the organisation. Some method of locking them into the union was sought, and the financial incentive was adopted in textiles in 1963 and in metalworking two years later.

Plant Bargaining

The effect of all this has been to shift the focus of collective bargaining from the workshop to the national bargaining table. National agreements cover general wage increases, annual bonuses for union members, cost of living clauses, supplementary unemployment benefits, and so on, leaving matters like shift work, job evaluation, and piecework to be negotiated at plant level.

Without doubt there is tension created by the transfer of major bargaining decisions to the national level. Since the beginning of the 1970s strikes at the plant level, often unofficial, have been on the increase, indicating a willingness on the part of members to forgo the employers' bonus, and reflecting a sense of unease at the distancing of collective bargaining procedures from local control and also at the length of agreements. Union leaders have found themselves in a quandary, supporting the principle of national negotiations, but under rank and file pressure forced to accept more independent plant bargaining than perhaps they would like. They have found it expedient to place a loose interpretation on the goal of industrial peace, and often local strikes that begin unofficially are subsequently recognised by the union. Since 1971 there has been a tendency for the duration of national agreements to be kept down to twelve months. And unions are generally being forced to keep more closely in touch with rank and file feeling, a symptom of this being the growing tendency for them to hold referenda.

However, unions do attempt to keep control over bargaining activities at the plant level. In theory it is the union delegation composed of the elected shop-floor delegates of both unions who conduct talks with plant management. But unions differ in the extent to which they let their delegates set the pace of negotiations. In metalworking the delegation is accompanied by a full-time regional official, but in textiles, where a more paternalistic attitude prevails among union leaders, the emphasis is reversed and it is the shop-floor delegation who accompany the regional negotiator in plant bargaining. Certainly the unions are against delegates concluding agreements by themselves, and sometimes a union official will negotiate alone with the employer. Before industrial action can be taken at factory level the decision has to be approved by the regional body. In the FGTB textile union national committee approval has to be obtained before any local wage demands can be served which might lead to a strike. And as a last resort the national union has the power to terminate local strike action.

HOLLAND

Collective bargaining in post-war Holland has taken place under the supervision of a network of government agencies created to operate a central wages plan. Even before the war Dutch authorities were more interventionist in collective bargaining than most governments, and since the war Holland has been more persistent than any other Western European state in trying to operate a policy of wage restraint.

Central Wage Bargaining

The policy of controlling wages was developed in answer to the massive problem of reconstruction at the end of the war. Wage restraint was meant to enable the emerging export industries to compete in foreign markets. The government reserved the right to lay down wages for all industry, the rates being based on a standard method of job evaluation. A decree of 1945 gave it the power to approve all new agreements. The task was greatly facilitated by the creation of a private joint union–employer agency, the Foundation of Labour, designed as a national forum for co-operation and consultation. From the start the Foundation took on the job of mediating between the government on the one hand and unions and employers on the other, and all collective agreements had to be vetted and approved by it. The apparatus for controlling wages was added to in 1950 with the establishment of the Social and Economic Council on which unions, employers and government are equally represented. This body is responsible for preparing the annual reports on which government policy for the coming year is based. It also supervises the forty or so Industrial Boards which were created in 1950 to foster co-operation in industry and which serve as the forum for negotiations. In some industries the boards have the power to transform collective agreements into statutory regulations.

One of the distinctive features of Dutch industrial relations throughout most of the post-war period has been the dominant position on the union side of the three central confederations. With the Foundation of Labour acting as a broker for both sides of industry before the government, the confederations assumed a major role in collective bargaining. Remote from the rank and file members, they were better able to take unpalatable decisions about wages restraint than their affiliated industrial unions on whom a certain amount of direct membership pressure could be brought to bear. Indeed Dutch union leaders have tended to act more as policy-makers in the 'national interest' than as sectional representatives of their own members.

National Bargaining – Metalworking and Textiles
Within the framework of the wage norms permitted by the Foundation of Labour, most collective bargaining has been at national industrial level between the industrial unions and employers' federation. The larger companies like Philips and Unilever often negotiate their own collective agreements for the entire firm, but in scope and content both types of agreement are much the same. Most agreements last for one year but some company agreements extend for up to three years, with periodic wage increases provided for during their currency. Since the war there has been a tendency for more workers to be covered by fewer agreements. The number of industry-wide agreements fell from 1,500 to less than 300 between 1940 and 1968, while company agreements dropped off by more than half from 1,100 to 400 in the same period. In metalworking there are two main agreements, one dealing with heavy industry and the other covering light metal trades. National negotiations are conducted for the unions by the national officers, whereas bargaining at company level is often a job for district officials.

The bargaining process tends to be represented by both sides as a highly scientific operation. Wages, hours and holidays are usually fixed here and the wage rates agreed are, with few exceptions, the maximum amount that can legally be paid. This means that tight controls on the application of piecework, incentive schemes and job evaluation have to be imposed centrally to prevent unions and employers agreeing to increase wages at the local level. However, since the 1960s piecework and incentive payments have begun to be phased out. Agreements are legally enforceable, and while strikes are not illegal the actual right to strike has not been codified in law. Until quite recently strikes have been few and far between, which is not surprising since in a period of official wage restraint any industrial action has an element of a strike against the government.

Railways
In the state-owned railways collective bargaining takes place within the same legal framework as for industry generally, except that the Dutch penal code prohibits railway workers from taking strike action. There is a joint union–management council at national level responsible for negotiating railway wages, overtime and bonuses within the terms of the national wage policy. Railway rates generally follow the pattern set in the civil service. General conditions such as hours of work and job classifications are negotiated by the council less frequently and then issued as staff regulations. At the local level similarly constituted joint union–management councils exist but with only consultative functions.

Plant Bargaining

In industry generally there is no collective bargaining with the unions at the plant level. The unions themselves have until recently been preoccupied with wider economic problems at the national level, and since 1950 non-union works councils have been responsible for worker–employer relations in the plant. The councils are basically consultative bodies though they sometimes have a say in the implementation of incentive schemes and they have the right to approve plant rules, hours, holidays, and safety regulations. In the case of grievances arising from collective agreements there is usually a procedure involving an approach to the works council and final resort to arbitration. But this is often ignored, and grievances tend to be resolved by informal contacts between the union and management. The works council's role has been expanded since 1971 and it must now be consulted on major questions of company reorganisation. But this extended sphere of activity is viewed as a threat to trade union authority at the plant level, and in the last few years unions in some manufacturing industries have been concentrating on strengthening their own position in the factories by means of the contactmen described in Chapter 3.

GERMANY

In West Germany collective bargaining was reintroduced in 1949 by Act of Parliament after a gap of sixteen years. The Act, later revised in 1952, gave employers and workers the right to organise for purposes of collective bargaining. Indeed, in contrast to France where collective bargaining has traditionally been, at best, just one of a range of union activities, in the German system of industrial relations the negotiation of collective agreements is clearly established as the unions' main reason for existence. And in the post-war period as a whole there have probably been about four times as many collective agreements negotiated at all levels as in France.

The system is very formal and clear guidelines are set down as to the kind of bodies that may engage in bargaining. The workers' side must be represented by a permanent association, meaning that *ad hoc* unofficial groups of shop stewards or workers cannot negotiate with employers in the way that they sometimes do, say, in Italy or Britain. Also excluded from the official bargaining system are organisations which rely on direct action to secure their goals without first attempting to conciliate disputes. The union must include among its immediate aims the negotiation of a collective agreement, thereby excluding the possibility of so-called 'political strikes' and sympathetic industrial action. Agreements are always formal, written documents and they are binding in law. The law relating to collective bargaining does not define the subject matter for bargaining or the procedure for settling disputes, this being left to the two sides to decide. However, a series of important court rulings over the years have tended to elaborate a code of practice in connection with negotiations.

On signing collective agreements unions undertake not to strike during the term of the agreement over matters dealt with in the document, and also to see that their members abide by this commitment. Breaches of the no-strike clause are serious matters, and in one famous case in 1958 arising from a metalworkers' strike in Schleswig-Holstein the union was ordered to pay damages of 100 million marks. On this occasion the amount was not collected and the employers settled instead for an arbitration agreement. However, the industrial peace commitment is not absolute and matters that are not covered by the current collective agreement can be the subject of industrial action. Unlike British industrial relations, but following American practice, the German system makes a clear distinction between conflicts over 'rights' and 'interests', in other words, between disputes which arise over the interpretation of existing agreements and those concerned with the renegotiation of an agreement. Labour courts exist for the settlement of individual employee grievances, an area which is not usually dealt with in formal labour–management agreements. Disputes over the negotiation of agreements are subject to government conciliation and mediation at either regional or national level, but frequently the two sides of industry establish their own private disputes procedure.

National and Regional Bargaining – Metalworking and Textiles

Negotiations can take place at national level as is the case in the clothing industry, but in sectors like metalworking and textiles the normal procedure is to negotiate at regional level. Even here there are occasional national agreements on single topics such as hours of work or automation which have general application throughout the country. The practice of regional bargaining does not involve any devolution of power, and negotiations in each region may well be over a uniform package of demands that has been decided by the union nationally. However, unions prefer to have some flexibility of manoeuvre against the employees and to pick off weaker opponents first. In all cases the national union keeps close control of the conduct of negotiations. Most key bargaining is between the union and the national or regional employers' federation. In both metalworking and textiles the pace-setting agreement is often negotiated in North

Rhine–Westphalia which includes the Ruhr area. Even so about one-third of all agreements are with single firms, generally smaller ones, that do not belong to the employers' federation, but including some large-scale employers like Volkswagen. The metalworkers' union has in the region of 1,000 separate company agreements. The collective agreements themselves tend to be of two kinds. There is usually a master or skeleton agreement which sets out the basic relationship between the two sides and lays down long-term conditions on issues such as hours and holidays. This agreement lasts for approximately three years. Wages themselves are the subject of a separate agreement of shorter duration which tends to be re-negotiated nowadays every year.

Railways
Collective bargaining on the railways is much the same as in private industry except that over one-half of railway employees are civil servants and have their wages and conditions fixed by legislation. Among the civil servant grades are train drivers and guards as well as administrative and managerial staff. All of these employees are forbidden to strike. But for the remaining manual and white collar employees collective bargaining takes place under the same legislation as for private industry and they have the right to take industrial action, though instances are very rare. The one departure from negotiating practice in private industry is that agreements reached between the union and railway management must be referred to the Minister of Transport under the Federal Railway Act of 1951. Settlements in one part of the public sector can have a big influence on other areas and the government tends to keep a close watch over developments. Indeed, in the public services generally the unions present a common front in negotiations, with the railway, postal and public service unions tending to co-ordinate their demands and bargaining strategy.

Plant Bargaining
Collective bargaining in Germany differs from the systems we have seen in some other countries in that the process does not involve the central confederation, the DGB, in economy-level negotiations. But more important still, the system leaves no scope for union involvement in bargaining at the plant level. This is the responsibility of works councils. Terms and conditions agreed between works councils and the employers do not have the status of collective agreements; they are 'works agreements' and as such are secondary to the collective agreements negotiated outside the plant. The Works Constitution Act attempts to limit any overlapping of jurisdiction by

defining in some detail the scope of works agreements. These basically deal with issues such as the scheduling of hours of work, administration of social and welfare services, discipline and plant rules. Wages as such do not come within their scope, but job evaluation, piecework rates and wage structures are subject to agreement with the works council. Otherwise the councils have responsibility for seeing that collective agreements and relevant legislation are applied in the plant.

One of the chief problems at the plant level for unions is the fact that regional collective bargaining only sets minimum wages, often geared to the needs of the marginal firm. This has sometimes merely served to consolidate increases made unilaterally by individual employers. As a result unions have not been in control of the real levels of pay. Employers have traditionally made discretionary payments over and above the negotiated rates and have reserved the right to withdraw these at will. Such payments, combined with the widespread use of incentive payments negotiated with the works council, have had the effect of lifting earnings far above union rates. And the exclusion of unions from domestic negotiations lessens the value of these organisations in the eyes of the workers.

A similar difficulty confronts unions in connection with job evaluation schemes. Those negotiated at regional level have sometimes had very little relevance for individual plants, and employers have introduced their own preferred local arrangements without union agreement. The result is that over a number of years unions like the metalworkers have attempted, though without much success, to negotiate supplementary agreements on wages and job evaluation in plants where ability to offer better conditions exists. The aim has been to up-date job classifications, to link the movement of plant wage levels directly to movements in negotiated wages, to include in formal collective agreements fringe benefits that employers sometimes introduce unilaterally, and to provide for supplemental wage agreements based on the profitability of individual firms and plants.

As in other countries, the German unions have been confronted with a rank and file revolt in recent years. In this case 1969 was the turning point with an unprecedented wave of unofficial strikes. Two years later, 1971 proved to be a record year for industrial action with over 3 million days lost, mostly in metalworking. Once again in 1973 a substantial amount of time was lost through unofficial action, and in a number of cases final settlements completely bypassed the official unions, being concluded between employers and dissident groups of workers. The peaceful image of German industrial relations is beginning to change. In metalworking this is reflected in the fact that total strike benefits paid out in the years 1971-3 were over £12 million compared with only £26,000 in the preceeding three-year period. And failing the creation of a more effective system for processing plant-level demands, the unrest of the late 'sixties and early 'seventies is likely to recur in the future.

DENMARK

As in all Scandinavian countries, the development of industrial relations in Denmark throughout this century has been marked by a continuing debate in the labour movement as to the appropriate degree of centralisation in collective bargaining. Although centralised bargaining is a characteristic of all three Scandinavian countries, this feature is, perhaps, least developed in Denmark.

At an early stage the two sides of industry developed a commitment to voluntary procedures. A Basic Agreement between LO and the Danish Employers' Confederation was negotiated as early as 1899 and this laid down the ground rules for union–employer dealings with respect to rights, recognition and negotiating procedure. The original agreement remained in effect without revision until 1960 and the amended version finally lapsed in 1969. A replacement for this took until 1973 to be negotiated, an indication of the difficulties experienced by labour and employers in accommodating their conflicting aims during a period marked by a growing restiveness on the part of workers.

Although the Basic Agreement of 1899 was concluded between LO and the Danish Employers' Confederation, the detailed process of collective bargaining was for a long time more a matter for individual unions and employers' federations. LO's role in this area was the subject of disagreement among affiliates from the beginning. One school of thought wanted LO to have the right to vet all bargaining demands prior to their submission to the employers, with the payment of dispute benefit from a central strike fund conditional on the observance of this procedure. Moreover it was proposed that when LO funds were used to support a strike it would have responsibility for conducting subsequent negotiations. However, well-established national unions such as the Smiths and Engineers, whose financial resources were already adequate to support their own industrial policy, insisted on maintaining their freedom of action. The resulting compromise arrangement reached favoured the decentralisers.

Central and Industry-level Bargaining
Since the war there has been a tendency for centralisation in negotia-

tions to increase. During the 1950s there emerged a pattern of central negotiation of general demands applicable to the entire labour movement, while issues specific to particular industries were negotiated at that level. The general demands are dealt with by LO and the central employers' confederation and these include general wage increases, hours and holidays. According to a strict timetable the negotiations at industry level take place in the autumn and are expected to be complete soon after Christmas. Thereafter the second phase begins with bargaining over general demands. Collective agreements last for two years.

In the case of metalworking, industry-level negotiations take place between the employers' federation and the sixteen affiliated unions of the Centralorganisation of Metalworkers. The negotiations tend to establish minimum wage rates. These are then supplemented by local bargaining over piecework which, though declining, is still widely used. This is especially so in metalworking where the skilled unions affiliated to the Centralorganisation have long been confident of their ability to bid up the rates of pay locally in line with the profitability and productivity of individual enterprises. In view of this tendency for negotiations to set minimum wages the metalworking unions have been inclined to place greater emphasis on fringe benefits in national bargaining.

Collective agreements are regarded as binding and there is a strict commitment to industrial peace throughout their currency. When disputes arise over the interpretation of an agreement there is an attempt at mediation by national representatives of the two sides within a matter of days. If no settlement is achieved the dispute must be resolved by binding arbitration or, in more serious cases where there has perhaps been a breach of the agreement, by the Labour Court. The court has been in existence since 1910 although its method of operation has recently been revised following an Act of 1973. Whereas in the past the court has tended to be legalistic in its approach, it is now required to be more informal, and is no longer bound by past precedent. Penalties cannot be imposed on workers involved in spontaneous stoppages of less than two days, nor are they subject to fines if it can be shown that the dispute was caused by the employer. The court is only empowered to impose financial penalties and a standard fine for a breach of agreement tends to be of the order of 70p per hour per person involved.

Plant Bargaining

Because industry-level negotiations concentrate on minimum conditions there is room for bargaining at the plant level where shop stewards are a well-entrenched feature of Danish industrial relations.

As we have seen earlier, the shop stewards are as much brokers between the employer and the workers as they are sectional representatives. Nevertheless much of their time is taken up in administering piecework systems and handling grievances, with the result that shop-floor industrial relations tend to be a continuous round of piecework bargaining and agreement interpretation. At plant level it is well-established practice for employers to make discretionary payments to individual workers for skill or trustworthiness. Theoretically these are a matter for negotiation between the worker concerned and the employer, but in practice they are usually determined unilaterally by the employer. The metalworkers' national agreement actually stipulates that this sort of payment must be made without any interference on the part of the union. However, shop stewards do tend to become involved in the process if there is disagreement over the amount offered, even though their intervention may be for the purpose of mediating the dispute rather than in support of the worker concerned.

SWEDEN

The early development of industrial relations in Sweden was much influenced by Danish practice. But it was the particular experience of domestic conflict in Sweden around the turn of the century that led the country to adopt its own rather more centralised system. The central union organisation, LO, was formed in 1898 as a loose confederation of national unions. But the employers already saw in this a powerful opponent, and following a three-day general strike in 1902 over a demand for the extension of the franchise they set about creating their own strong, co-ordinated body, SAF. Strong organisation on both sides of industry favoured a rapid development of collective bargaining with an emphasis on voluntary procedures. And throughout the first quarter of this century Swedish industrial relations were marked by a continuing high level of industrial conflict.

However, with massive unemployment undermining the strength of the unions, the climate began to change in the second half of the 'twenties. In 1928, influenced by the Mond–Turner talks on industrial collaboration between unions and employers in Britain, Swedish unions and employers began to consider ways in which industrial relations might be regulated peacefully. Two pieces of labour legislation were passed in that year. One on collective bargaining required all agreements to be in writing and to last for a fixed period, while at the same time it made it illegal to strike in disputes over the interpretation of agreements. The second Act established the Labour Court which was to make binding awards in these interpretation disputes. The next major step in the process of accommodation between the two sides came with the formation of the first social democratic government in 1932. The government passed an Act in 1935 requiring seven days' notice of any strike action. In the meantime it established a committee of inquiry into the whole area of industrial relations. It was the report of this committee that prompted LO and the employers' confederation to negotiate the very important Basic Agreement of 1938.

This agreement, the bedrock of all subsequent labour–management relations, set out to enhance the role of the two central confederations. The major feature was the establishment of a Labour Market Council made up of representatives of the two sides of industry. This body was given a negotiating and conciliation role in cases of major disputes, especially in essential industries. Apart from this it was the spirit of co-operation engendered by the agreement, and the boost given to voluntary procedures, that made it so important. An attempt was made to separate out contentious from non-contentious issues, and in the following years a series of Co-operation Agreements were concluded on questions such as industrial safety, training and works councils. In the public sector the unions and management negotiated their own Basic Agreement in 1947 modelled on the private sector's 1938 agreement. And following new legislation on collective bargaining for government employees a further agreement was concluded in 1966 revising the procedure for public service negotiations and for the first time giving all government workers the right to take strike action.

The principal effect of the Basic Agreement was to assist further the centralisation of industrial relations. The role that LO was called upon to play by the agreement required sweeping changes in the organisation's rules, and these were made at the 1941 conference. From now on LO was given responsibility for co-ordinating the collective bargaining policies of affiliates and calling sympathetic strike action. It had the right to participate in negotiations and to recommend settlements to affiliates. LO was also to be the final arbiter of jurisdictional disputes. As far as individual unions were concerned, their freedom to take strike action was limited by an obligation to obtain LO's prior permission in cases where more than 3 per cent of the members were involved. Later LO acquired the further right to refuse permission for strike action in cases where vital social interests might be threatened. And finally, as a condition of affiliation to LO, a union's rules had to reserve for its executive committee the right to make all final decisions in matters of collective bargaining without any obligation to consult the membership.

Central and Industry-level Bargaining – Metalworking and Textiles

During the 1950s the present system of collective bargaining came into existence. In 1951 LO created a Wage Policy Council comprising members of its own secretariat with responsibility for deciding general bargaining demands. The following year the first round of central negotiations involving LO and SAF took place. The same procedure was followed in 1956 and every two years ever since. Essentially the negotiations at this level are over frame agreements which determine the average wage increases the central negotiating bodies are prepared to recommend to their affiliates. But so strong is the influence of LO on the unions that there is little likelihood of the recommendations being turned down. Since the 1950s there has been less and less scope for individual industries to deviate from the terms of the central agreement and all that really remains is for the different unions and employers to apply it.

The industry-level agreements based on these central terms cover minimum wages, piecework systems, hours, holidays and overtime. Altogether there are over 300 national agreements in force. In metalworking there are ten national agreements covering each sector, the main ones being in metal manufacturing, steel, cars, and foundries, while the textile union negotiates separate agreements for the clothing and leather industries. The frame agreements allow for higher increases to be paid in low wage industries as part of the 'wage solidarity' policy, and one of the major beneficiaries of this since the 1950s has been the textile union. The general policy here has been to set the minimum wage rates in line with the capabilities of the average firm and to put the marginal producer out of business if necessary.

Railway Bargaining

In the public sector, including the railways, negotiations for a frame agreement take place every two years between the amalgamated public service union and a board representing the government services. Thereafter the railway management concludes individual national agreements with different categories of workers. At national level and below there is a comprehensive network of joint consultative bodies. However, there are no regular supplementary negotiations at regional or local level except where special conditions exist, and then plus payments are negotiated between railway management and a union official from head office.

Plant Bargaining

Separate agreements with companies outside the employers' federation are made in both metalworking and textiles. And below the national level there are opportunities for negotiating at the local plant level. Altogether there are over 27,000 local agreements; 4,000 of these are in metalworking and relate directly to the terms of the national agreement. The existence of so much plant bargaining in what is basically a centralised system is due to the widespread use of piecework, which gives workers a degree of control over earnings. In metalworking the practice has been to use incentive payments wherever possible, though since the mid-sixties there has been a shift away from straight piecework to group incentive schemes. However, there is also a tendency to use job classification schemes which have the effect of increasing the degree of comparability between work while leaving job rates to be negotiated locally. Where piecework still applies the method of calculating rates is determined by national agreement, but job times and work study are subject to plant bargaining. The result of the system is that centrally negotiated rates bear only the slightest relationship to actual earnings.

However, plant union representatives do not have a free hand in negotiations. They are closely integrated into the union and through the local branch are instructed on how to handle grievances and factory negotiations. Plant bargaining can be initiated at the branch level but the national executive is responsible for all decisions relating to settlements. Branches must have their proposed demands approved by the national union before they are submitted and counter-proposals from the employer have to be reported to the executive committee. Unresolved disputes that occur at the plant level over the interpretation of agreements must be referred to national officials within two weeks, and within the next three weeks an effort must be made to negotiate a settlement nationally. Failing that, the matter goes to the Labour Court where, unlike Denmark, the highly legalistic approach means that disputes are settled on the basis of past precedents. Unofficial strikers are liable to be fined by the Labour Court under the 1928 legislation.

NORWAY

Collective bargaining in Norway has much in common with the Danish and Swedish systems, but there are also important differences. Norwegian industrial relations have always been more centralised than elsewhere in Scandinavia. Right up to the Second World War Norway experienced an exceptionally high level of industrial conflict, even by pre-war Scandinavian standards. And while sharing with Swedish and Danish unions a belief in voluntarism in industrial relations, the Norwegians have been prepared to accept rather more legislative intervention in both procedural and substantive issues. From its foundation in 1899 LO was conceived of as a 'general staff 'of the labour movement. Because of the weakness of its affiliated unions it had to co-ordinate their actions while at the same time administering a central strike fund designed to supplement the resources of the individual unions. Most of these were financially unstable, and the extra support provided by LO ensured that it played an important role in the conduct of disputes. In 1903 LO was vested with the formal right to call sympathetic strikes and to lead negotiations where more than óne union was involved.

Intense industrial conflict in the early 1920s followed by massive unemployment took its toll of the labour movement membership. And after the defeat of a general strike in 1921 the unions' supporters in parliament were ready to vote in favour of introducing a system of compulsory arbitration of disputes. By the early 1930s much of the unions' strength had been sapped, and as in Sweden there began a search for conciliatory procedures in the settlement of disputes, a development that also coincided with the election of the first social democratic government in 1935. In that year the first Basic Agreement was signed by LO and the employers' confederation. and thus began the process of codifying voluntary union–employer procedures which incorporated the principle of industrial peace during the term of a collective agreement.

The agreement opened up for LO leaders an ever-widening sphere of influence. The process was furthered by the wartime agreement between the government in exile and the unions to reintroduce a system of compulsory arbitration after the war. Formal arbitration only remained in force until 1952, but in the years following LO and the employers' confederation have effectively taken over the task of the Arbitration Board. The government still has the residual power to call for arbitration of an unresolved dispute, but so close has been the control over industrial relations exercised by LO and the employers' confederation that this procedure has been used sparingly. In the post-war period as a whole LO has regarded its negotiations with the employers' confederation as a means of making broad economic and social adjustments in the 'national interest' and not just in the interests of its members.

Industry-level Bargaining – Metalworking, Textiles and Railways

The actual process of negotiation takes place simultaneously in each industry at national level every two years between individual unions or groups of federated unions and the employers' associations. The agreements have mainly to do with minimum wage rates, hours and holidays traditionally being fixed by legislation. There are over 160 national agreements, though less than a third of these have really extensive coverage. The key agreements are in industries such as metalworking, building, paper and the textile sector. Metalworking has one major agreement covering 50,000 workers in mechanical engineering. There are fourteen agreements for the auto industry and a total of 540 company agreements with non-federated firms, each following the pattern set in the main agreement. The textile union negotiates three separate agreements for its textile, clothing, and shoe and leather sectors. And for purposes of collective bargaining the railway union is part of a federation of civil service unions made up of twenty affiliated organisations with 100,000 members which negotiates general conditions with the government authorities.

Once the national agreement is signed, all strike action is forbidden for the duration of the agreement. Collective agreements are in writing and last for a fixed period and this facilitates a distinction between disputes over rights and interests. Disputes over rights have to be settled by the Labour Court on the basis of past precedent. In the frequent disputes over piecework, workers can refuse to accept the rates offered and revert to time work, but industrial action is not an option officially open to them. Before an official strike can begin an attempt must be made to mediate the dispute. The 1969 Basic Agreement requires the two sides to give two weeks' notice of intended industrial action. The state mediator must be given detailed information on the stage reached in negotiations, and the strike may be delayed for up to fourteen days while mediation takes place. The union also has to gain LO approval for the strike.

Plant Bargaining

The national negotiations are generally over minimum conditions, and a considerable amount of plant bargaining takes place to supplement these. There are over 10,000 collective agreements altogether in Norway and the bulk of them are concluded at the local level between shop stewards and local management. Shop stewards have a well-defined role in the system of industrial relations and their functions have been laid down in the Basic Agreements since 1935. Much of this plant bargaining is over wages, and because of the extensive use of piecework, shop-floor negotiations over rates tend to take place practically every day. Plant bargaining is limited by the framework of national agreements, yet in recent years wage drift has resulted in earnings rising at twice the rate of negotiated increases in wages. Just as LO closely supervises national negotiations in each industry, so also the national unions control bargaining at the local level. In textiles the local body must obtain national union approval before submitting demands. If a settlement is not reached the union will take charge of the negotiations. And no strike action at the local level is permissible without the approval of the national executive.

THE FORMULATION OF COLLECTIVE BARGAINING DEMANDS

FRANCE

All unions set their general bargaining programmes at the three-yearly conferences. These tend to be very general statements of long-term goals which leave room for further refinement prior to the start of negotiations. This latter process is a matter for the general council or its equivalent in most cases. The CFDT metalworkers' general council publishes its bargaining programme in the union newspaper and then invites a general debate on it at local level. There is in fact a growing tendency to involve the rank and file more in the discussion of demands prior to bargaining even if the machinery used has no formal place in the union structure. For example the CGT textile union has co-ordinating committees of delegates for each particular sector of the industry and these bodies hold *ad hoc* conferences to discuss the problems of their sector.

The actual negotiating at national or regional level is usually conducted by committees of up to a dozen representatives from each union, a majority of whom are from the rank and file. The unions' attitude on this point reflects a tendency to treat collective bargaining as an educational process in the class war, and the CFDT textile union, for example, argues that the greater the number of rank and file members at the negotiating table the more confidence the grass roots will have in the union.

ITALY

With the breakdown of the old, manipulative trade unionism in the late 1960s the system of collective bargaining now allows the rank and file membership some say in what takes place. Following the pattern adopted in 1969, mass meetings of workers at factory level tend to initiate demands. This sort of gathering is also used to decide when local industrial action should be called in support of national demands. And in addition, factory assemblies regard it as their responsibility to keep the progress of negotiations and the strategy being pursued under constant review.

BELGIUM

There is no rigid procedure for deciding demands. In metalworking each regional committee makes proposals to the national executive. These are whittled down by the executive and then approved by the general council. At this stage there is usually consultation between the leaders of the various rival unions aimed at producing a mutually agreeable package of demands, and here there is a possibility that demands will be modified further. Socialist and Christian unions then negotiate jointly.

In general, national negotiations are remote from the membership. The economy-level negotiations only involve a handful of the highest union leaders, and there is no way that members can keep close control over what takes place. The process by which demands are arrived at is very indirect, and to try to mitigate this the CSC unions have in the past resorted to a referendum to find out what the members' priorities were. At the industry level there is usually no rank and file representation on union negotiating committees. As the CSC textile union's national secretary puts it, 'If shop delegates are present the bargaining session becomes a parliament.'

HOLLAND

With unions becoming more conscious of rank and file restiveness there has been a move towards giving members a greater voice in collective bargaining decisions. Though democratic in a formal sense, the system of collective bargaining for much of the post-war period left members with little effective control over developments. Often negotiated settlements have had the force of statutory regulations, and in these circumstances ratification by the membership meant very little. Today the process of formulating demands begins with the executive of the union drawing up proposals for bargaining based on the latest action programme of the confederation. These are debated at the local level where rank and file views are solicited. The aim here is basically to obtain from the membership some order of priorities for the items placed before them. The proposals are then referred back to the general council where changes may be incorporated into the final programme. This then forms the basic policy of the union.

In the case of the industrial workers' unions, with members spread across a number of different sectors, each industrial group must refine its own programme from the basic policy. This is done by advisory bargaining committees for each sector. In the NVV industrial union there are fifteen members on the metalworkers' advisory committee, all elected at district conferences every three years. As a common front has to be achieved between the three sets of unions there is close consultation at each stage of the process. In the railway industry the small size of the unions enables them to hold full-scale extraordinary conferences to set demands and ratify agreements. And since 1973 these have been joint conferences of the three co-operating unions.

GERMANY

Over the years bargaining has tended to assume the proportions of a would-be scientific exercise with both sides relying heavily on the statistical arguments produced by their technical staff. This has tended to cut off the rank and file from any close involvement in the negotiations. The bargaining process as it affects textile workers is indicative of the type of approach often followed. Prior to the commencement of negotiations local officials take the pulse of the membership in their area and submit their views to the regional office where they are collated and passed on to the union head-quarters. A committee of sixty members, including full-time officers, but with a majority of rank and file representatives elected by regional congresses, meets to discuss the bargaining programme. But this body is only advisory and the real decision rests with the national executive. Once a draft programme has been decided on, a questionnaire in the union newspaper asks members to rank the demands in order of preference. The regional officials are then instructed to begin negotiations under the close supervision of the national headquarters.

DENMARK

An important factor in the centralisation of collective bargaining has been the work of the Economic Council of the Labour Movement established in 1936 by the unions and the co-operative movement jointly to formulate economic policy for the labour movement as a whole. The council is under LO control and, as the originator of many basic negotiating demands, it gives LO a considerable amount of influence over what is actually discussed at the negotiating table. In the individual unions bargaining policy is decided at their three- or four-yearly conferences and the actual programme is fixed by the general council. The bargaining committee comprises national union officials and there is very little scope for rank and file involvement.

SWEDEN

General negotiating demands are decided by LO, the views of members being solicited by means of questionnaires issued to a random sample of trade unionists. Thereafter they are discussed within each union by special bargaining councils. These are rank and file bodies with mainly advisory functions. In metalworking the full council consists of some 150 members elected by branches grouped into roughly equal constituencies. The textile union council has 180 members in all. And the full bargaining council for the public service union has 225 members, of whom 55 are railwaymen. The councils not only advise the executive committee on the demands to be put forward, they also choose from among themselves two-thirds of the members of the negotiating committees. The size of these negotiating committees varies according to the sector involved. For metal manufacturing there are some fifteen members, ten of them rank and file workers; in steel the committee is a twelve-man body; and in the foundry negotiations the union side has six members.

NORWAY

On the union side LO plays an important part in deciding the main bargaining demands. It reaches broad agreement with the employers on the outline of the overall settlement which then has to be negotiated in detail in each industry. Once the LO general council has drafted the main points of the bargaining programme they are sent to the national unions for discussion and adoption. In metalworking the practice is to convene some fifteen district conferences of shop stewards with approximately 100 people present at each. These meetings are not part of the official machinery and no decisions are taken; the union officials merely note the views expressed. The matter is then referred to an agreement council such as exists in the Swedish unions. In metalworking this is a 135-man body composed of elected lay delegates. It makes the final decision on the demands and elects two-thirds of the negotiating committee from among its own members. In textiles there are three agreement councils, one each for textiles, clothing and leather. And in the civil service negotiations, those demands peculiar to the railway workers are decided by a national conference involving elected lay delegates from the industry's seventeen occupational groups.

All wage demands apart from those submitted at local level have to be approved by LO in advance. If more than one union is involved LO tends to assume responsibility for negotiations. In the event of a dispute of serious proportions LO must give prior approval for strike action to take place. And the resulting settlement must have LO's stamp of approval.

THE RATIFICATION OF SETTLEMENTS AND PAYMENT OF STRIKE BENEFIT

FRANCE

Ratification of negotiated settlements is always left to the local branches. Each one is responsible for arriving at its own decision, and although there is usually no formal system of voting there is a tendency for branches in some unions such as the CGT metalworkers to hold secret ballots. However much negotiation takes place at national or regional level, decisions regarding industrial action tend to be a local matter, even in industries like the railways. More and more the unions give workshop groups their head and then support them in their action, so that strikes are just as likely to be spontaneous acts as the result of a formal union decision. The attitude that collective bargaining is a form of guerrilla warfare runs deep, especially in the CFDT unions who refer to agreements as 'temporary truces' and prefer to talk of 'fighting measures' rather than settlements.[1]

Strike Benefit

While the CFDT's approach to bargaining may be rather more cerebral than the CGT's, it still has its feet planted firmly on the ground with its businesslike, but rather un-French, policy of operating a strike fund. In the CGT the idea of strike benefits is frowned on. Apart from insisting that they are not insurance societies the unions argue that not all workers are organised, and since the object of a strike is to bring out as many people as possible, whether organised or not, strike payments made only to a minority of workers would be a divisive influence. Largely as a consequence of this absence of strike pay, most stoppages in the private sector last for less than two days on average. Often they are not so much concerned with forcing an immediate concession as with staging a demonstration. And since only a minority of workers are organised it is rare for a plant to be closed down entirely by a strike.

Local attempts at establishing strike funds have been made by different groups in the CFDT for over twenty years, but the present scheme operated by the confederation itself on behalf of its affiliates has only been in existence for little over ten years. The amount of money involved is not very large and would probably be inadequate in any large-scale, prolonged strike. Benefits are £1·52 or £1·90 per day depending on the level of contributions.

ITALY

Since 1969 the democratic tendency in collective bargaining has extended to the ratification process. The responsibility for approving settlements belongs to the mass factory assemblies. In the CISL metalworkers the 1973 rules formalised this procedure and stressed that participation by members in such events is the best way of stimulating their critical faculties.

Strike Benefit

Strike pay is unheard of in Italian trade unionism, and the absence of this is a major reason why most strike action is of short duration.

BELGIUM

The formal ratification of agreements is made by the general council after consulting the regional bodies. There is no provision for balloting the membership, though increasingly leaders are being forced to take note of grass roots opinion.

In the textile industry the very close working relationship between the Christian and socialist unions and the fact that most workers are located in a narrow area makes it easier to involve rank and file members more directly in the process of agreement ratification. After negotiations are completed it is a joint conference of the general councils of the two unions that proposes acceptance or rejection of the agreement. And final ratification is at mass assemblies of factory delegates convened at the respective union headquarters at which anywhere between 300 and 500 delegates may be present. If strike action is proposed notice has to be given, during which time conciliation takes place. The minimum notice is seven days and can be as much as fourteen days in textiles.

Strike Benefit

Most FGTB unions pay £17·74 per week in strike benefit to adult males. The railway union, however, only pays £2·50–£2·60 per day. In the CSC the strike fund is administered centrally by the confederation and the payments are somewhat less than in the FGTB.

HOLLAND

Whereas in the past officials have been able to sign agreements without worrying unduly about the views of the membership, some unions such as the NVV and NKV industrial workers' unions now insist on having a vote. Still this is not yet common practice. The recommendation for or against acceptance is made by the advisory bargaining committee. A strike can only be called after a 75 per cent vote in favour. However, even with a vote against a settlement the general council can overrule the wishes of the membership, and this has happened on occasion.

Strike Benefit

When industrial action is taken, strike pay of £5·49 per day is paid by the industrial workers' unions of both the NVV and NKV, and a smaller amount is paid by the confederation itself. This amounts to 38p per day in the NVV while in the NKV the system is that the confederation reimburses the striking union to the extent of £3·05 for every £5·49 it pays out in benefit.

GERMANY

The negotiators present their results to the advisory collective bargaining committee and it is here that the decision is made in principle, though the final seal of approval is given by the general council. Only if there is some doubt as to the amount of support among the rank and file is the settlement put to a secret ballot of the membership. Here the chances of industrial action resulting are limited by the general requirement that 75 per cent must vote in favour of taking strike action. Even this is not a binding directive on the leaders, and in deciding what course of action to take the unions are required under the DGB rules to take into account general considerations such as the state of business and the repercussions that a strike would have on other parts of the economy. Not surprisingly, this acts as a major constraint and is one reason for the low incidence of strikes in post-war Germany.

Strike Benefit

All unions have large strike funds and in some industries the level of strike benefit is as much as 75 per cent of normal wages. In the metalworking unions benefit varies according to the length of membership and number of dependants and can be anything from £5·74 to £61·24, per week though the average payment is around £22·96 weekly. In rare cases where a union finds itself in a costly dispute the DGB can help by contributing to the strike fund, but most unions have no need of this sort of assistance.

DENMARK

A definite time limit is set for the completion of general bargaining, and failing agreement by mid-January unresolved matters are subject to conciliation and mediation. If no voluntary agreement is reached at this stage the conciliation board is empowered to draft a settlement which must be put to a vote of union members and individual employers. The method of voting on settlements varies from union to union. Some have postal ballots, though the procedure in the metalworkers is to hold a secret ballot immediately following mass meetings at the local level.

Strike action is only legally permissible after a breakdown in negotiations for a new collective agreement. Local strikes cannot be called without the prior permission of the national union, and since the national body is the legally contracting party in agreements great efforts are made to see that members do not breach the no-strike provision. Official strikes are invariably preceded by a vote of the membership. If the vote happens to be on a draft settlement proposed by a conciliation board 75 per cent must oppose the settlement before it can be rejected. Even then there is no automatic freedom to strike. A union must first give two weeks' notice and then the government conciliators are entitled to impose a two-week cooling-off period which can be extended for a further two weeks while mediation takes place.

Strike Benefit

Once an official strike has begun members receive strike benefit of £5·15 per day from the union while LO subsidises the union concerned from levies made on non-striking unions. The latter pay LO approximately £2·74 per week per member and the union involved in the dispute receives from LO £5·15 per week for each member on strike. During the 1973 general strike in engineering the metalworkers' strike fund of £1·6 million was exhausted. Consequently, in an effort to rebuild the fund, the union has had to almost double the amount of the membership contribution to the strike fund from 20p per week to 37p per week.

SWEDEN

By union rule the ratification of settlements is a matter for the national executives, and some unions even give their negotiating committees plenary powers to settle at the bargaining table. Balloting of the membership may sometimes take place but the results are never binding. However, the last time this was done in metalworking was in the 1940s. If a vote is taken it must show a two-thirds majority against the settlement before the executive will consider a strike, and even then the decision rests with them.

Strike Benefit

When industrial action does take place strike benefit is paid by the national union and also LO provided that there are at least thirty members involved. Since 1974 strike pay in the metalworkers' and textile unions has been £4·70 per day. LO's contribution begins in the third week of the strike and amounts to £1·22 per day. The incidence of official strikes in the past twenty-five years has been very low and in textiles the last official strike was in 1931. The members of the public service union have been entitled to strike since 1966, but during the first nine years following the introduction of this right there were no railway stoppages.

NORWAY

Unlike Sweden, ratification votes on the final settlement are compulsory, and provided more than two-thirds of those eligible to vote do so the decision is binding. In metalworking and textiles secret ballots are held in the factories, though in other unions there is a tendency to use postal ballots.

Strike Benefit

Once industrial action is in progress strike benefit is paid by the national union and LO. Traditionally the Norwegian unions have aimed at limiting the numbers involved in industrial action while paying substantial benefits to those actually in dispute. On occasions in the past union members have contributed as much as 5 or 6 per cent of their earnings towards strike funds and levies. However, the amounts are now much smaller and benefits paid by LO are of much less importance than formerly. In metalworking strike pay varies according to the length of union membership and the number of dependants a striker has. The highest rate is £13·65 per week payable from the first day. After eight days LO pays 37p per week.

CONCLUSION

THE LEVELS OF BARGAINING

The most common feature of collective bargaining systems in

Europe is that negotiations tend to take place primarily at national industry level. In some countries there is a tendency for the system to be even more centralised with union confederations playing a part in the economic management of the country through economy-level negotiations. Equally, and to some extent as a reaction against this, there are pressures for more bargaining to take place at the workshop level under the direct control of union members, though in some countries this development is still very recent.

THE FORMULATION OF DEMANDS

How responsive is this system generally to the wishes of trade union members? In the formulation of union bargaining demands ordinary union members often only have a minimal amount of control. In many unions national-level demands originate with the union leaders and subsequent discussions at the local level may or may not afford the rank and file a real opportunity to influence the subject matter for negotiations. The use of delegate conferences to discuss collective bargaining objectives for particular sectors does provide more scope for membership involvement, especially in Scandinavia, though in Sweden these conferences are still only advisory. In some countries the use of opinion surveys among union members has tended to restrict grass roots participation to attaching an order of priorities to a predetermined programme of demands. And however professional the unions' market research techniques may be, the opinion poll approach to collective bargaining can never be a substitute for a vigorous democratic debate working its way up from the base to the national level.

THE NEGOTIATING PROCESS

The extent of lay participation at the bargaining table itself varies considerably. Professional union negotiators often object to negotiating 'in a goldfish bowl', under the close scrutiny of rank and file members. In France, however, where organisational weakness can make it difficult for the union to carry the workers with it, rank and file participation in negotiations is welcomed as a means of increasing the credibility of the negotiators among the workers. The system in Sweden and Norway whereby the rank and file bargaining conferences elect a majority of the negotiating committee from among their own members provides a useful guarantee that the membership's views will be represented. And at times some Italian unions have tended to go a stage further by attempting to have mass meetings of workers decide the strategy of negotiations as they progress. Against this must be mentioned the tendency in countries such as the Netherlands, Sweden, Denmark and Germany for bargaining to be conducted as a scientific operation with technicians playing a prominent part. Undoubtedly technical assistance is invaluable to unions in negotiation, but the notion that economic arithmetic can lead to 'scientific' solutions to negotiating problems is insupportable, and to the extent that the view prevails then the influence of lay members at the bargaining table is likely to be reduced.

THE RATIFICATION OF SETTLEMENTS

Where ratification of agreements is concerned Italian unions have probably made the biggest strides in moving from a situation where workers had no control over the decisions taken to one where the rank and file are now deeply involved. Acceptance or rejection of settlements is also a matter for the local membership in France and Denmark. Where bargaining conferences are held the procedure tends to enable the views of the base to be heard, even if no general ballot is held. But in some countries the reference back to the membership, however democratic the procedure may seem, is largely academic since the effective decision is taken at a higher level. In Sweden, for example, ratification votes, when they are held, mean very little since they are only advisory.

STRIKE BENEFITS

When official industrial action takes place varying levels of financial support are available to the strikers. The Italian unions and the CGT in France, of course, make no strike payments at all and in both cases the non-payment of benefit is elevated to the level of a principle. Elsewhere unions tend to have substantial strike funds although, as recent major strikes in the Netherlands and Denmark have shown, what at first sight may seem to be vast reserves can soon be depleted. In most cases the main funds are maintained by the industrial unions. In the Christian unions of Belgium and the Netherlands and in the French CFDT the central confederation administers the strike fund. And in the Scandinavian countries benefits are paid by both the industrial union and the central confederation. The Scandinavian unions have traditionally made a point of holding large strike funds while attempting to confine industrial action to a limited number of workers so that high benefits can be paid. The same principle applies on an international basis as between Nordic countries. Unions in each country subscribe to the strike funds of counterpart organisations over the border, and the Norwegian metalworkers alone paid some 5 million kroner to the Danish trade unions on strike in 1973.

LEGAL CONSTRAINTS ON INDUSTRIAL ACTION

The possibility of taking industrial action is limited in a number of unions by the requirement that a strike vote must show a 75 per cent majority. And often compulsory mediation schemes lessen the availability of a strike weapon. However, a more important factor in restricting the use of industrial action is the distinction between disputes of rights and disputes of interests, and this clearly has a major bearing on the nature of plant bargaining. The largest strike funds are of little value if the strike weapon is denied to workers over a wide range of issues. In countries like Germany and the Netherlands the lack of a real union presence on the shop floor inhibits bona fide plant bargaining, but even over issues on which the non-union works councils can negotiate there is no right to strike. This situation does not apply in France and Italy where, for all practical purposes, only the organisational weakness of the unions themselves limits the development of plant bargaining. In Belgium, strong trade unionism and plant bargaining go together and although the national unions have accepted no-strike clauses there are no legal penalties for the breach of these. However, in Scandinavia the limitation on the right to strike in support of plant grievances is absolute during the term of the agreement. Once national settlements are reached, as they are every two years, all local disputes must be resolved without recourse to economic sanctions and this clearly limits the unions' scope for encroaching on managerial rights. Whether the system will always be able to block industrial action over plant disputes is an interesting question in view of the significant number of unofficial strikes in Scandinavia since 1970. Denmark has already been forced to adopt a more tolerant attitude towards unofficial strikes. Unofficial strikers in stoppages which are of brief duration or which have been provoked by employers are no longer subject to financial penalties. And in 1975 a joint union–management committee recommended a similar change for Sweden which, if accepted, will come into effect in 1977.

NATIONAL AND LOCAL BARGAINING: THE CORRECT BALANCE

Finally, there is the question of the correct relationship between industry-level and plant bargaining. Industry-level negotiations have obvious limitations, remote as they are from the rank and file, even in compact countries like the Netherlands and Denmark. Yet bargaining over national conditions can be an important unifying force among the union membership. On the other hand, a system with too much decentralisation may have important weaknesses. In the United

States, for example, where collective bargaining is primarily at enterprise level, and where the average number of union members covered by an agreement is in the region of 100, situations can easily arise in which strong groups are unable to give support to weak local unions in dispute because of the fragmentation of bargaining. In Europe industry-wide bargaining can be democratised and made more relevant to the needs of the workers. Recent experience in Sweden and Italy shows that the industry-level negotiations need not deal only in minimum rates geared to the marginal producer. Indeed the latter approach can have the effect of perpetuating low wages in weak areas.

At the same time much progress in levelling up wages and conditions can be made at plant level where local comparisons across industrial boundaries often tend to increase expectations among different groups of workers. Indeed plant bargaining is probably the best method of encroaching on managerial rights, and gains made at this level need to be made general by means of industry-wide negotiations. But such bargaining should not be conducted in isolation, since there are definite limits on the value of highly localised or privatised militancy.

In any event the threat of rising unemployment in most Western European countries means that trade unionists will have to look to wider industrial strategies if they are not to suffer defeat in small, unco-ordinated actions. However, trade unions are not disciplined armies, and ultimately such co-ordination as does take place between plant and national level will have to be based on a voluntary recognition by workshop groups that they can never be entirely self-sufficient and that the wider needs of the labour movement must be constantly borne in mind.

8

Conclusion

We began this study with the aim of gathering some comparative information which is not always readily available about the operation of Western European trade unions. The reason for doing this at the present time is obvious: the interdependence of Western economies becomes more apparent day by day, while the influence of multi-national companies on conditions of employment and the livelihood of workers is increasingly being felt by the European labour force. The expansion of the Common Market in 1973 has added to this tendency and has increased the need for greater co-ordination of activities on the part of both sides of industry. The trade union movement has a long-standing commitment to internationalism, but for much of its history this has been little more than a decorative adornment, for quite understandably its primary interest has been in domestic bread-and-butter issues. But now day-to-day trade union activities are being directly conditioned by international forces, and the traditional commitment to international brotherhood among organised workers, so far largely restricted to conference resolutions, is having to be translated into practice. If unions are now to work together internationally it is important for members to understand how organisations in other countries arrive at the policy positions they themselves may be asked to support.

Beyond describing various facets of union structure we have attempted to compare aspects of internal government in a number of organisations. This is a subject which is frequently ignored. It is often forgotten that the process by which unions reach decisions is quite different from the system employed in authoritarian organisations, even if in practice unions do not always operate as they theoretically should. When union government is dealt with it tends to be treated in isolation as a specialist field unrelated to the organisation's aims and activities. Yet the system of internal government, and the element of democracy therein, is closely connected to the underlying ideology of the organisation, reflecting the way it sees its role in society and at the same time affecting its capacity to achieve its goals. Consequently internal union democracy ought not to be seen simply as a goal in itself. It is not enough for a union to be a model democracy on paper, it must also represent its members effectively before employers and government. In other words, the union must find a balance between the decentralisation of control which leaves decision-making in the hands of ordinary members and thereby serves as a force for education in the democratic process, and the centralisation necessary for effective operation. The very principle of trade unionism involves the subordination of the individual member to the collective, of the parts to the whole. The system of internal government must reflect this while leaving as much power in the hands of lay members as possible. The task of balancing the two is not an easy one, and has been approached by unions in different ways with different results. The starting point of this analysis was that formally democratic structures, while not enough to guarantee the success of democracy, are a necessary precondition for it, and without them the likelihood of minority control is greatly increased.

In many of the European unions conference, theoretically the hub of internal union government, is so organised as to make effective lay control of proceedings a very unlikely possibility. In most cases conferences are too infrequent and too short-lasting for them to lay down much more than the vaguest policy guidelines. From the point of view of internal democracy, two years is long enough for any organisation to go without providing a broadly-based conference of rank and file delegates with the opportunity to pass judgement on the leadership's record and to engage in a thorough reappraisal of policies. However, most of the European unions considered have full-blown policy-making assemblies at three-yearly intervals and sometimes even longer; too long, one would think, to enable members to keep a tight rein on policy through this medium.

Again many unions have a large number of full-time officers in attendance at conference and these constitute at least a substantial minority of those present. Whether or not they are entitled to speak and vote it is reasonable to conclude that their presence often provides the leadership with a solid corps of support for its policies, both inside and outside the conference chamber. Conference procedure itself in unions in France, Italy, Belgium and Holland is quite unlike that practised in Britain and some Northern European countries, and tends to leave most of the initiative for introducing policy proposals with the leadership while granting the delegates little opportunity to do more than agree or disagree with these. We suggested that this system results from the divisions in the labour movement. Workers join the union with whose policies they identify. The narrow range of membership views results in a low level of open internal conflict and makes conference much less a battlefield of competing ideologies and policy proposals. Consequently the control of conference committees, the procedure for handling conference business, and the precise wording of policy proposals, factors which can make all the difference at conferences elsewhere, tend not to be regarded as very important. In this situation the distinction we posed between representative democracy and delegatory democracy in internal government seems to be irrelevant. Conference delegates are, in fact, often mandated in France, Italy and Belgium, but the significance of this is not very great. In other countries, where close voting on conference business is perhaps a greater possibility, the practice of mandating delegates is disapproved of by the leadership and tends to be formally or informally discouraged.

The insubstantial nature of conference in many unions means that the task of detailed policy-making is often passed on to another body, the general council, which combines its legislative functions with the role of supervising the executive committee and the national officers in the secretariat. The result is that most European unions have four tiers of government – conference, general council, national executive and secretariat. General councils themselves frequently have significant numbers of full-time officials present at their deliberations, and the numerical strength of the latter is often proportionately greater than it is at union conference. Indeed, few of the general councils examined, and none of the executive committees that the general councils are expected to supervise, are purely lay bodies. Full-time officers account for one-quarter or more of the membership of general councils in about half of the unions considered, and in most of the unions full-time officials account for at least one-third of the national executive. Moreover, in the midst of these full-time officials is usually a solid corps of national officers from the secretariat, as a rule more numerous than their counterparts in Britain and America, who, by their strategic membership of the general council and the national executive, tend to be the repository of executive power and enjoy considerable freedom to make and interpret policy.

In general it seems fair to characterise the continental unions studied as being more dominated by officialdom than is usually the case in Britain. Certainly the numbers of full-time officials at all levels and their status in the unions tend to be higher than in British unions. Only in France, Denmark and Norway are unions to be found in which the number of members per official is greater than in the British labour movement generally. And with the exception of France and possibly Italy, union salaries are usually sufficiently high as to make the officials' style of living distinct from that of their members. Among the full-time officials national officers are formally elected, usually at conference and sometimes in the general council. However, openly and vigorously contested elections are rare. Electioneering is not normally practised, and union secretariats are usually elected on a slate prepared officially or unofficially by an inner group of the executive or general council. At regional level field officers tend to be appointed in most organisations, with only French, Italian and sometimes Belgian unions employing a system of formal election. This relatively heavy staffing of most European unions also extends to the administrative area where the number of administrative staff under the supervision of the national officers is often proportionately greater than in Britain.

Of course, the other side of the coin in so far as staffing is concerned is that European unions are far less dependent on unpaid lay officers. In particular, the pattern of organisation at the all-important plant level involves fewer accredited shop representatives exercising far less power than is the case with the British shop steward system. With the exception of the Scandinavian countries the traditional form of in-plant worker representation on the continent is by means of works councils which are essentially non-union, even anti-union, bodies based on an assumed community of interests between employers and workers, and providing little scope for the pursuit of workers' sectional interests. However, in recent years a growing restiveness on the part of rank and file members has convinced many unions of the need for strong work-place organisation under official control.

The trust men of Germany and Holland and the shop union delegates of France and Italy are a reflection of this development. In a number of countries the ratio of in-plant union representatives to members is now about the same as in Britain where the $1:35$ ratio of shop stewards to members provides reasonably dense representation of trade unionists on the shop floor. But internal union democracy requires these representatives to be elected by the union membership, and yet, as we have seen, unions from a number of countries, notably Belgium, Holland and Germany, often dispense with the system of elections and have their plant spokesmen appointed from on high. Moreover, in most countries studied there are severe limitations on the ability of shop representatives to represent union members effectively. This may be because only the works council has the right to engage in plant bargaining or to handle grievances. It may be because the union's organisational strength at the shop level is insufficient to compel management to deal with it, as often appears to be the case in France. Or it may be, as in Scandinavian countries, that legal restrictions on the right to take strike action during the course of a fixed term agreement prevent workshop groups from bringing their full strength to bear in plant disputes. All things considered, only the Italian workshop delegates in certain industries appear to combine the numerical strength of British shop stewards and the ability freely to call industrial action in support of local disputes.

The ability to negotiate and conclude settlements with employers at the work place is of fundamental importance for union democracy since bargaining at this level offers rank and file members the best chance of controlling the demands presented and also the course of negotiations. But it also raises the thorny question of what is the correct overall balance between centralisation and decentralisation in collective bargaining. As was suggested earlier, unions have to steer a course between abstract notions of democracy which leave all power at the local level but may impede the effective mobilisation of the whole union, and the top-heavy centralisation which denies the ordinary member any role in the negotiating process and as a result tends to deaden rank and file interest. As Edelstein and Warner note, democracy thrives on interest, controversy and hope, and excessive centralisation in collective bargaining can lead union members to believe that participation in union activities is ineffective as a means of influencing policy.[1]

There is no universal formula for establishing the correct balance between local and national bargaining, but in the case of most of the unions considered here there would appear to be considerable scope for decentralising the existing system and granting more local autonomy. In the German and Belgian unions major collective bargaining rarely involves the rank and file directly; and in Scandinavia and Holland, with the central confederations rather than the individual unions making the key bargain, negotiations are even further removed from the rank and file. In a number of unions delegate conferences are held to decide demands, ratify agreements and sometimes even to elect the negotiating committee from among their members. But equally some of these conferences are only advisory, the final decision being left to the leadership. And a majority of union leaders prefer not to have rank and file members present at negotiations.

In most cases there would seem to be a need for collective bargaining structures to be made more flexible, with increased scope for direct rank and file participation at all levels, and a significant devolution of decision-making to plant bargaining under genuine rank and file control. It is not enough for plant bargaining to be regarded merely as a means of applying terms and conditions negotiated above. Indeed it is quite reasonable and perhaps more productive for unions in certain situations to let local negotiations set the pace and to seek to make general the local gains made through national bargaining. The orderly nature of collective bargaining in some countries might have to be sacrificed as a consequence of increasing rank and file participation, but this is perhaps the price of democracy. In any event the demand for decentralised bargaining structures is likely to grow with the development of multi-national corporations, partly as a reaction against remote management, but also because the multi-national firms have been among the pioneers of industrial engineering and personnel management techniques that generate a need for union resistance on the spot. In this area the internationalisation of industrial relations runs parallel with the need for greater internal union democracy.

Throughout the analysis there has been a tendency for unions to fall into broad groupings. The Scandinavian unions, though by no means uniform in their structure and approach to internal government, form one obvious group. The French and Italian unions are often referred to in the same breath, and indeed there are great similarities in the overall structure of the labour movements, the way unions are organised at different levels, and the styles of internal government and external activities. Between these two types come the German and Benelux unions. No doubt because of the language connection, Belgian unions have many characteristics in common with the French labour movement. But Belgian unions are altogether much better organised and more businesslike bodies, and in this respect they differ from their Gallic counterparts. German unions are similar to their opposite numbers in Scandinavia in terms of their unitary structure, strength of organisation and financial resources. However, German unions are perhaps more subject to central control than is the case in Scandinavia in that there is less scope for rank and file autonomy at the local level. In this respect they come closer to the bureaucratic organisations of the Dutch labour movement. Cutting across these national differences are certain similarities between unions in the same industry, reflecting the history of the industry's development, its structure and its present state of buoyancy or decline. Of course, to group unions together in this way is rather crude, and quite possibly there are significant differences between them which offset the similarities mentioned. But the exercise is useful if it helps to highlight characteristics that seem to be relevant from the perspective of someone viewing the continental scene from outside.

The analysis may seem to have concentrated on unfavourable aspects of European unions while ignoring the strengths. In fact there are a number of features that British unions could profitably borrow from their continental counterparts. For example, the rational structure of several of the movements based on a few unions is preferable to the British system of numerous, often competing organisations. Divorced from the system of election by slates, the practice of collective leadership employed by many unions has much to commend it, and is potentially more democratic than leadership by a single top officer in the form of the general secretary. To this might be added the French union practice of paying union officials the same level of pay as the workers they represent. And the financial strength of unions in Germany and Scandinavia based on a system of high contributions is something that unions in Britain would do well to try and emulate, provided that the increased resources were used to provide better services for the membership and to supplement strike funds.

As in many other areas, the trade union practices of one country are not always exportable to another. Cultural factors largely determine the way organisations operate, and we may be told that we have not made sufficient allowance for the different cultural environments in which unions have to work. It is quite possible that we have misunderstood the significance of the practices of different unions; this is perhaps unavoidable. However it does seem to us that our analysis has pointed to one or two areas in several labour movements, where there are obvious restrictions on union democracy which are built into the formal system.

In the final analysis, the only way for ordinary trade unionists to discover in detail how different national unions operate is for them to forge direct links with their counterparts abroad and to insist on being given an opportunity to participate in international co-ordinating bodies. And when widespread international co-ordination among trade unionists at the rank and file as opposed to the leadership level begins to take place, that in itself will reflect a major advance along the road to internal trade union democracy.

Selected Bibliography

GENERAL

Balfour, C., *Industrial Relations in the Common Market* (Routledge, 1972).

Berry, A. P. (ed.), *Worker Participation: The European Experience* (Coventry and District Engineering Employers Association, 1974).

Bouvard, M., *The Labour Movement and the Common Market Countries* (New York: Praeger, 1972).

CIR, *Worker Participation and Collective Bargaining in Europe* (HMSO, 1974).

Coventry and District Engineering Employers Association, *Labour Relations and Employment Conditions in the European Economic Community* (CDEEA, 1972).

European Economic Community, *The Trade Union Movement in the European Community* (EEC, 1972).

Galenson, W., *Trade Union Democracy in Western Europe* (University of California Press, 1961).

Gorz, A., *Strategy for Labour* (Boston: Beacon Press, 1967).

ICFTU, *Labour–Management Relations in Western Europe* (Brussels, 1966).

ILO, *Basic Agreements and Joint Statements on Labour–Management Relations* (Geneva, 1971).

ILO, *Rights of Trade Union Representatives at the Level of the Undertaking* (Geneva, 1969).

ILO, *Methods of Collective Bargaining and Settlement of Disputes in Rail Transport* (Geneva, 1966).

Jacobs, E., *European Trade Unionism* (Croom Helm, 1973).

Jones, D. D., *Wages and Employment in the EEC* (Kogan Page, 1973).

Kamin, A. (ed.), *Western European Labour and the American Corporation* (Washington, D.C.: Bureau of National Affairs, 1970).

Kassalow, E., *Trade Unions and Industrial Relations: An International Comparison* (New York: Random House, 1969).

Kendall, W., *The Labour Movement in Europe* (Allen Lane, 1975).

Malles, P., *The Institutions of Industrial Relations in Continental Europe* (Ottawa: Labour Canada, 1972).

Management Counsellors International, *European Labour Relations in the 1970's: An Overview* (Brussels, 1972).

Marx, E. and Kendall, W., *Unions in Europe* (University of Sussex, 1971).

Myers, F., *European Coal Mining Unions* (University of California Press, 1961).

Spitaels, G. (ed.), *Crisis in the Industrial Relations in Europe* (Bruges, 1972).

Sturmthal, A. (ed.), *Contemporary Collective Bargaining in Seven Countries* (New York: Ithaca, 1957).

Sturmthal, A., *Workers' Councils* (Cambridge, Mass: Harvard University Press, 1964).

Western European Metal Trades, *Aspects of Industrial Democracy* (Brussels, 1972).

Wool Textile Economic Development Committee, *Employment Practices in EEC Textile Industries* (NEDO, 1973).

Articles

Carew, A., 'Shop Floor Trade Unionism in Western Europe', *European Studies*, no. 18 (London, 1974).

Carew, A., 'EEC Trade Union Groupings', *Public Affairs* (Dublin, March 1973).

Schregle, J., 'Labour Relations in Western Europe: Some Topical Issues', *International Labour Review*, vol. 109 (Geneva, January 1974), pp. 1–22.

Weber, A., 'The Structure of Collective Bargaining and Bargaining Power: Foreign Experiences', *Journal of Law and Economics* (Chicago, October 1963), pp. 79–151.

BRITAIN

Allen, V. L., *Power in Trade Unions* (Longmans, 1954).

Banks, J. A., *Trade Unionism* (Collier Macmillan, 1974).

Clegg, H. A., *The System of Industrial Relations in Britain* (Oxford: Blackwell, 1970).

Clegg, H. A., Killick, A. J., and Adams, R., *Trade Union Officers* (Oxford: Blackwell, 1961).

Cole, G. D. H., *The World of Labour* (Harvester Press, 1973).

Commission on Industrial Relations, *Industrial Relations at Establishment Level: A Statistical Survey* (HMSO, 1973).

Edelstein, J. D., and Warner, M., *Comparative Union Democracy* (George Allen & Unwin, 1975).

Hughes, J., *Trade Union Structure and Government*, Research Paper no. 5., part 2 (Royal Commission on Trade Unions, 1968).

Lane, T., *The Union Makes Us Strong* (Arrow, 1974).

Marsh, A., *Industrial Relations in the Engineering Industry* (Oxford: Pergamon, 1965).

McCarthy, W. E. J., *The Role of Shop Stewards in British Industrial Relations*, Research Paper no. 1 (Royal Commission on Trade Unions, 1968).

Ministry of Labour, *Evidence to the Royal Commission on Trade Unions* (1965).

Pelling, H., *A History of British Trade Unionism* (Macmillan, 1969).
Roberts, B. C., *Trade Union Government and Administration in Great Britain* (G. Bell and Sons, 1956).
Royal Commission on Trade Unions and Employers' Associations (HMSO, 1968).
Trades Union Congress, *Trades Unionism* (London, 1966).
Trades Union Congress, *Training Full-time Officers* (London, 1972).
Turner, H. A., *Trade Union Growth, Structure and Policy* (George Allen & Unwin, 1962).
Unofficial Reform Committee, *The Miners' Next Step* (1912).
Webb, B. and S., *Industrial Democracy* (Longmans, 1913).

Articles
Marsh, A., and Coker, E., 'Shop Steward Organisation in the Engineering Industry', *British Journal of Industrial Relations* (June 1963).
Fletcher, R., 'Trade Union Democracy: The Case of the AUEW Rule Book,' *Trade Union Register 3*, eds K. Coates and T. Topham (Spokesman Books, 1973).

FRANCE

Adam, G., *La CFTC 1940–1958* (Paris, 1964).
Adam, G., *La CGT–FO* (Paris, 1965).
Adam, G., *et al.*, *La Négotiation Collective en France* (Paris, 1972).
Barjonet, A., *La CGT* (Paris, 1968).
Caire, G., *Les Syndicats Ouvriers* (Paris, 1971).
Capdevielle, J., and Mouriaux, R., *Les Syndicats Ouvriers en France* (Paris, 1970).
Erbes-Seguin, S., *Démocratie dans les Syndicats* (Paris, 1971).
Lefranc, G., *Le Mouvement Syndical de la Libération aux Événements de Mai-Juin, 1968* (Paris, 1969).
Lesire-Ogrel, H., *Le Syndicat dans l'Entreprise* (Paris, 1967).
Lorwin, V. R., *The French Labour Movement* (Cambridge, Mass: Harvard University Press, 1954).
Mothé, D., *Le Metier de Militant* (Paris, 1973).
Schifres, M., *La CFDT des Militants* (Paris, 1972).
Seyfarth, Shaw, Fairweather and Geraldson, *Labour Relations and the Law in France and the United States* (University of Michigan Bureau of Business Research, 1972).

Articles
Delamotte, Y., 'Recent Collective Bargaining Trends in France', *International Labour Review*, vol. 103 (Geneva, April 1971), pp. 351–77.
Verdier, J-M., 'Labour Relations in the Public Sector in France', *International Labour Review*, vol. 109 (Geneva, 1974), pp. 105–18.

ITALY

Aglieta R., *et al.*, *Revolution dans l'Entreprise: le Mouvement des Délégués Ouvriers en Italie* (Paris, 1972).

Coker, E., and Kendall, W. (eds), *Report of Motor Industry Study Tour* (Oxford: WEA Industrial Branch, 1975).
Guigni, G., 'Articulated Bargaining in Italy', in Allen Flanders (ed.), *Collective Bargaining* (Penguin, 1969).
Horowitz, D., *The Italian Labour Movement* (Cambridge, Mass: Harvard University Press, 1963).
Kendall, W., 'Labour Relations in IRI', in Stuart Holland (ed.), *The State as Entrepreneur* (Weidenfeld and Nicolson, 1972).
Lapalombara, J., *The Italian Labour Movement* (Cornell University Press, 1958).
Neufeld, M. F., *Italy, School for Developing Countries* (Cornell University Press, 1961).
Raffaele, J. A., *Labour Leadership in Italy and Denmark* (Madison: University of Wisconsin Press, 1962).
Seyfarth, Shaw, Fairweather and Geraldson, *Labour Relations and the Law in Italy and the United States* (University of Michigan Bureau of Business Studies, 1970).

Articles
Guigni, G., 'Recent Trends in Collective Bargaining in Italy', *International Labour Review*, vol. 104 (Geneva, 1971), pp. 307–28.
Ross, A. M., 'Prosperity and Labour Relations in Western Europe: Italy and France', *Industrial and Labour Relations Review* (October 1962), pp. 63–85.
Sellier, F., 'Les Transformations de la Négotiation Collective et de l' Organisation Syndicale en Italie', *Sociologie du Travail* (April–June 1971), pp. 141–58.
Valcavi, D., 'Recent Trends and Future Prospects of Collective Bargaining in Italy', OECD Trade Union Seminar on New Perspectives in Collective Bargaining (November 1969).

BELGIUM

Blanpain, R., *Public Employee Unionism in Belgium* (Ann Arbor, 1971).
Chlepner, B. S., *Cent Ans d'Histoire Sociale en Belgique* (Brussels, 1956).
Coates, K. (ed.), *A Trade Union Strategy in the Common Market: The Programme of the Belgian Trade Unions* (Spokesman Books, 1971).
Confédération des Syndicats Chrétiens, *Responsable de l'Avenir* (Brussels, 1969).
Ebertzheim, R., *Les Syndicats Ouvriers en Belgique* (Liège, 1959).
European Economic Community, *Monographies Syndicales – Belgique* (Brussels, 1966).
Seyfarth, Shaw, Fairweather and Geraldson, *Labour Relations and the Law in Belgium and the United States* (University of Michigan Bureau of Business Research, 1969).
Spitaels, G., *Le Mouvement Syndicale en Belgique* (Brussels, 1969).

Articles

Blanpain, R., 'Recent Trends in Collective Bargaining in Belgium', *International Labour Review*, vol. 104 (Geneva, July–August 1971), pp. 111–29.

HOLLAND

NVV/NKV/CNC, *Programme of Action* (Amsterdam, 1967).
NVV/NKV/CNV, *Programme of Action, 1971–1975* (Amsterdam, 1970).
Ryder, M. S., *Managing Industrial Conflict in Holland at the Plant Level* (Ann Arbor, 1970).
Windmuller, J. P., *Labour Relations in the Netherlands* (Cornell University Press, 1969).

Articles

Albeda, W., 'Recent Trends in Collective Bargaining in the Netherlands', *International Labour Review*, vol. 103 (Geneva, March 1971), pp. 247–68.

GERMANY

Bye, B., *The Struggle for Workers' Participation in Germany* (Chichester: St Richard's Press, 1973).
DGB, *Co-determination: A Contemporary Demand* (Dusseldorf, 1970).
DGB, *The Basic Programme of the German Trade Unions' Federation* (Dusseldorf, 1964).
Grebing, H., *History of the German Labour Movement* (Wolff, 1969).
Seyfarth, Shaw, Fairweather and Geraldson, *Labour Relations and the Law in West Germany and the United States* (University of Michigan Bureau of Business Research, 1969).

Articles

Leminsky, G., 'Central Union Organisation and the Individual Union in Federal Germany', a paper given to the 3rd World Congress of the International Industrial Relations Association, September 1973.
Lepinski, F., 'The German Trade Union Movement', *International Labour Review* (Geneva, January 1959).
Reichel, H., 'Recent Trends in Collective Bargaining in the Federal Republic of Germany', *International Labour Review*, vol. 104 (Geneva).
Ross, A. M., 'Prosperity and Labour Relations in Europe: The Case of West Germany', *Quarterly Journal of Economics* (August 1962), pp. 331–59.

DENMARK

Galenson, W., *The Danish System of Labour Relations* (New York, 1969).

Landsorganisation i Danmark, *The Danish Trade Union Movement* (Copenhagen, 1967).
Raffaele, J., *Labour Leadership in Italy and Denmark* (Madison: University of Wisconsin Press, 1962).

Articles

Carlsen, P., 'Improved Industrial Relations System in Denmark', *Free Labour World* (Brussels, February 1974).
Lund, R., 'Some Aspects of the Danish Shop Steward System', *British Journal of Industrial Relations*, vol. 1 (1963), pp. 371–9.
Lund, R., and Milhoj, P., 'Social Research on Labour in Denmark', *International Labour Review* (Geneva, March 1963).

SWEDEN

Carlson, B., *Trade Unions in Sweden* (Stockholm: Tiden, 1969).
Geijer, A., *Industrial Democracy* (Stockholm: LO, 1971).
Ingham, G. K., *Strikes and Industrial Conflict: Britain and Scandinavia* (Macmillan, 1974).
ILO, *The Trade Union Situation in Sweden* (Geneva, 1961).
Johnston, T. L., *Collective Bargaining in Sweden* (George Allen & Unwin, 1962).
Landsorganisationen i Sverige, *Swedish Trade Union Confederation* (Stockholm, 1970).
Meidner, R., and Ohman, B., *Fifteen Years of Wage Policy* (Stockholm: LO, 1972).

Articles

Ahlvarsson, L., 'New Developments in Collective Bargaining', OECD Trade Union Seminar on New Perspectives in Collective Bargaining, November 1969.
Faxen, K. O., and Pettersson, E., 'Labour Management Co-operation at the Level of the Undertaking in Sweden', *International Labour Review* (Geneva, August 1967).
Hoberg, G., 'Recent Trends in Collective Bargaining in Sweden', *International Labour Review*, vol. 107 (Geneva, 1973), pp. 223–38.
Peterson, R. B., 'Management Rights and the Swedish Collective Bargaining Agreements at the Federation and Plant Levels', *Labour Law Journal* (Chicago, June 1968), pp. 364–79.

NORWAY

Bull, E., *The Norwegian Trade Union Movement* (Brussels: ICFTU Monographs, 1956).
Galenson, W., *Labour in Norway* (Cambridge, Mass: Harvard University Press, 1949).

Goss, J., *Industrial Relations and Employee Participation in Management in Norway*, Research Paper no. 5 (Centre for Contemporary European Studies, University of Sussex, 1973).

Lansdsorganisasjonen i Norge, *Norwegian Federation of Trade Unions* (Oslo, 1970).

Appendix 1
Trade Union Membership

ITALY

CISL

Food workers	45,280
Chemical workers	118,970
Construction workers	115,180
Electricians	47,430
Miners	8,120
Gas and oil workers	17,250
Metalworkers	278,730
Printers	36,560
Textile and clothing workers	182,360
Agricultural workers	213,310
Peasants	83,040
Local government workers	106,850
Hospital workers	106,030
Civil servants	68,020
State employees	75,160
Elementary school teachers	97,510
Secondary school teachers	30,630
University lecturers	1,070
Scientists	1,570
Railwaymen	38,810
Postal and telegraph workers	81,770
Telephone workers	6,660
State monopolies	5,660
Commercial workers	74,300
News vendors	7,780
Bank employees	32,230
Insurance workers	5,030
Telephone workers (IRI)	16,390
Tramwaymen	35,960
Seamen	12,240
Traffic wardens	38,320
Airline workers	4,030
Self-employed fishermen	12,610
Port workers	5,940

Theatre and cinema workers	7,780
Pensioners	158,610
Others	6,910
Total CISL	2,184,100

Note CISL is the only union confederation in Italy or France to issue membership figures by industry. These figures are for 1972.

BELGIUM

FGTB

Building workers	199,000
Metalworkers	180,000
Public service workers	208,000
Textile workers	60,000
Transport workers	32,000
White collar and technical workers	82,000
Mine workers	21,000
Food workers	37,000
Clothing workers	21,000
Printing workers	14,000
Diamond workers	4,500
Journalists	160

CSC

Building and wood workers	182,078
Food workers	80,438
Railway, postal, radio, aviation and marine workers	45,188
Diamond workers	6,934
White collar workers	164,477
Energy, chemical and leather workers	50,550
Technical teachers	30,261
Printing and paper workers	19,146
School teachers	50,632
Metalworkers	213,605
Mine workers	30,708
Stone, cement, pottery and glass workers	29,894
Public service workers	70,720
Textile and clothing workers	128,345
Transport	14,713
Others	18,486
Total	1,136,175

Note FGTB figures are for 1973. CSC figures are for 1975.

HOLLAND

NVV

Industrial workers	195,085
Civil servants	155,485
Construction workers	99,034
Transport workers	48,060
Shop assistants and clerical workers	50,816
Food and agricultural workers	33,533
Printing workers	32,662
Teachers	29,244
Police	12,431
Seamen	6,923
Hotel and restaurant workers	6,973
Performing artists	2,513
Chemists' assistants	2,194
Professional footballers	700
Football coaches	1,480
Total	677,133

NKV

Industrial workers	136,697
Construction workers	86,428
Civil servants	50,367
Food and agricultural workers	26,030
Transport workers	24,428
Printing workers	16,659
Others	14,561
Total	355,170

CNV

Industrial workers	56,958
Construction workers	43,744
Civil servants	58,721
Food workers	18,022
Transport workers	13,103
Police	8,423
Printing workers	6,316
Chemists' assistants	701
Journalists	169
Others	21,723
Total	227,880

Note Figures for January 1975.

GERMANY

DGB

Building workers	517,902
Mining workers	374,082
Chemical workers	655,703
Printing and paper workers	164,465
Railwaymen	455,380
Education and scientific workers	132,106
Agricultural workers	39,859
Bank, insurance and commercial workers	236,642
Wood workers	135,205
Musicians and artists	36,150
Leather workers	57,600
Metalworkers	2,593,480
Food, tobacco and catering workers	248,481
Public service, transport and communications workers	1,051,098
Postal workers	419,966
Textile and clothing workers	287,641
Total	7,405,760

Note Figures are for December 1974.

DENMARK

LO

Bakery workers	5,774
Clothing workers	18,649
Plumbers	7,175
Bookbinders	9,500
Electricians	15,585
Hairdressers	3,126
White collar workers	11,998
Food workers	5,358
Jewellers	1,565
Shop and clerical workers	155,661
Hospital workers	2,580
Hotel and restaurant workers	1,666
Domestic workers	24,700
Railwaymen (state)	8,780
Iron and metalworkers	994
Coach builders	1,192
Pottery workers	3,197
Local government workers	58,224
Women workers	68,678

Lithographic workers	2,955
Train drivers	125
Engine drivers	1,655
Painters	13,299
Dairy workers	1,970
Metalworkers	108,574
Bricklayers	14,305
Paper workers	2,199
Postal workers	13,140
Railwaymen (private)	280
Upholstery workers	5,572
Ships' carpenters	1,791
Boot and shoe workers	3,068
Slaughterhouse workers	20,845
Joiners and carpenters	40,112
General workers	258,429
Confectionary workers	1,755
Marine stokers	1,400
Seamen	5,480
Dental workers	362
Textile workers	14,306
Waiters	5,823
Tobacco workers	3,409
Wood workers	15,840
Typographical workers	12,222
Total	953,318

Note Figures are for December 1974.

SWEDEN

LO

Textile and clothing workers	56,382
Sheet metal workers	4,824
Building workers	162,563
Electricians	26,686
Factory workers	99,944
Building maintenance workers	33,649
Hairdressers	3,986
Insurance workers	17,021
Printing industry workers	38,941
Commercial workers	133,310
Hotel and restaurant workers	26,779
Local government workers	309,121
Agricultural workers	11,796
Food workers	53,917

Metalworkers	443,700
Musicians	9,025
Painters	23,154
Pulp and paper workers	49,641
Seamen	15,200
Forestry workers	24,242
Chimney sweeps	1,289
Public service workers	174,788
Transport workers	50,231
Wood workers	79,630
Mine workers	13,662
Total	1,863,481

Note Figures are for December 1974.

NORWAY

LO

Journalists	557
Supervisors and technical employees	10,562
General workers	30,144
General officers	2,981
Clothing, textile and footwear workers	19,435
Building workers	48,407
Electricians and power station workers	17,162
Printing industry workers	14,145
Prison officers	1,182
Goldsmiths	1,037
Commercial and office workers	44,270
Hotel and restaurant workers	9,631
Iron and metal workers	105,363
Railwaymen	15,087
Chemical workers	39,133
Local government workers	100,823
Policemen (country)	840
Train drivers	1,809
Bricklayers	3,343
Air force officers	1,501
Musicians	1,394
Food, drink and tobacco workers	29,983
Paper industry workers	17,062
Postal workers	7,213
Postmen	5,808
Sub-postmasters	2,443
Seamen	27,712
Forestry and agricultural workers	11,960

Policemen	2,450
Telegraph and telephone workers	9,072
Telegraphmen	2,743
Civil servants	30,329
Customs officers	829
Transport workers	18,446
Wood workers	5,808
Watchmakers	25
Total	642,396

Note Figures are for June 1975.

Appendix 2
Major Centres of Employment in Metalworking and Textiles

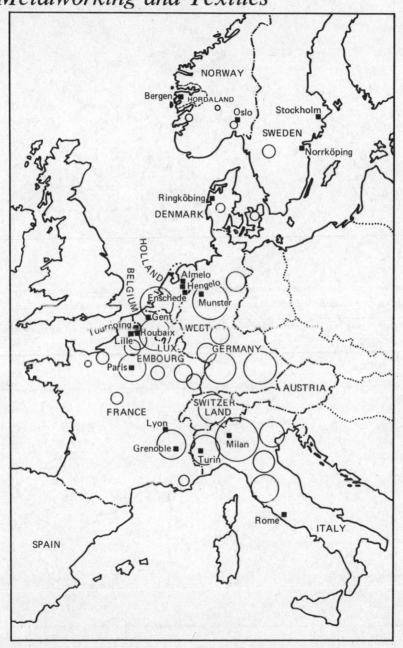

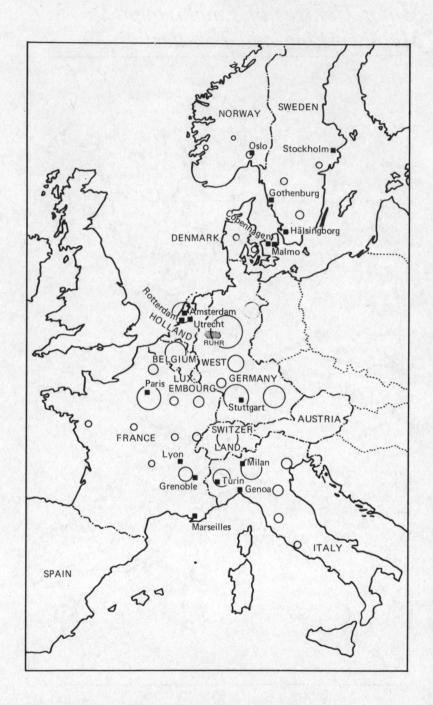

Appendix 3
Major Trade Union Organisations in Europe

INTERNATIONAL ORGANISATIONS

European Trade Union Confederation (ETUC), 37–41 rue Montagne aux Herbes Potagères, Brussels 1000

European Metalworkers' Federation (EMF), 37–41 rue Montagne aux Herbes Potagères, Brussels 1000

European Textile Workers' Federation, Rue Joseph Stevens 8, Brussels, 1000

European Regional Organisation, International Union of Food and Allied Workers' Associations, Rampe du Pont-Rouge 8, CH 1213 Petit-Lancy, Geneva

European Co-ordinating Committee for Transport Unions, 37–41 rue Montagne aux Herbes Potagères, Brussels, 1000

European Co-ordinating Committee for Chemical Unions, 3 Hannover, Konigsworther Platz 6

European Co-ordinating Committee for Building and Woodworkers' Unions, 6 rue Watteeu, Brussels, 1000

European Co-ordinating Committee for Postal and Telegraph Workers' Unions, Galerie Agora, 105 rue Marché aux Herbes, Brussels, 1000

FRANCE

Central Confederations

CGT Confédération Générale du Travail, 213 rue Lafayette, Paris 10

CFDT Confédération Française Démocratique du Travail, 26 rue de Montholon, Paris 9

CGT-FO Confédération Générale du Travail (Force Ouvrière), 198 Avenue du Maine, Paris 14

Agricultural Workers

CGT Fédération Nationale (Agriculture), 59 rue de Chateau d'Eau, Paris 10

CFDT Fédération Générale (Agriculture), 26 rue de Montholon, Paris 9

CGT–FO Fédération Nationale (Agriculture), 198 avenue du Maine, Paris 14

Food Workers
CGT Fédération Nationale (Alimentation), 213 rue Lafayette, Paris 10
CFDT Fédération Générale (Alimentation), 26 rue de Montholon, Paris 9
CGT–FO Fédération Générale (Alimentation), 198 avenue du Maine, Paris 14

Railway Workers
CGT Fédération Nationale (Cheminots), 19 rue Pierre Semard, Paris 9
CFDT Fédération Générale (Cheminots), 26 rue de Montholon, Paris 9
CGT–FO Fédération Nationale (Cheminots), 9 rue Cadet, Paris 9

Building Workers
CGT Fédération Nationale (Bâtiment), 213 rue Lafayette, Paris 10
CFDT Fédération Générale (Bâtiment), 26 rue de Montholon, Paris 9
CGT–FO Fédération Nationale (Bâtiment) 198 avenue du Maine, Paris 14

Gas and Electricity Workers
CGT Fédération National (Gaz et Électricité), 213 rue Lafayette, Paris 10
CFDT Fédération Générale (Gaz et Électricité), 5 rue Mayran, Paris 9
CGT–FO Fédération National (Gaz et Électricité), 13–15 rue des Petites Ecuries, Paris 10

Textile, Clothing and Leather Workers
CGT Fédération Nationale (Textile/Habillement/Cuirs et Peaux), 213 rue Lafayette, Paris 10
CFDT Fédération Générale (Ha-Cui-Tex), 26 rue de Montholon, Paris 9
CGT–FO Fédération Nationale (Textile/Vêtement/Cuirs et Peaux), 198 avenue du Maine, Paris 15

Chemical Workers
CGT Fédération Nationale (Industries Chimiques), 33 rue de la Grange aux Belles, Paris 10
CFDT Fédération Générale (Industries Chimiques), 26 rue de Montholon, Paris 9
CGT–FO Fédération Nationale (Industries Chimiques), 9 rue Cadet, Paris 9

Metalworkers
CGT Fédération Nationale (Métaux), 10 rue Vézelay, Paris 8
CFDT Fédération Générale (Métallurgie), 5 rue Mayran, Paris 9
CGT–FO Fédération Nationale (Métaux), 83 rue de la Victoire, Paris

Port and Dock Workers
CGT Fédération Nationale (Ports et Docks), 213 rue Lafayette, Paris 10
CGT–FO Fédération Nationale (Ports et Docks), 198 avenue du Maine, Paris 14

Transport Workers
CGT Fédération Nationale (Transports), 213 rue Lafayette, Paris 10

CFDT Fédération Générale (Transports), 26 rue de Montholon, Paris 9
CGT–FO Fédération Nationale (Transports), 198 avenue du Maine, Paris 14

Mine Workers
CGT Fédération Nationale (Mineurs), 213 rue Lafayette, Paris 10
CFDT Fédération Générale (Mineurs), 35 rue des Ferroniers, 59 Douai
CGT–FO Fédération Nationale (Mineurs), 169 avenue de Choissy, Paris 13.

Post and Telecommunication Workers
CGT Fédération Nationale (Postale), 213 rue Lafayette, Paris 10
CFDT Fédération Générale (Postes et Télécommunications), 26 rue de Montholon, Paris 9
CGT–FO Fédération Nationale (Postes et Télécommunications), 78 rue de l'Université, Paris 7

Seamen
CGT Syndicat Marins, 213 rue Lafayette, Paris 10
CGT–FO Fédération Marine Merchande, 198 avenue du Maine, Paris 14

ITALY

Central Confederations
CGIL Confederazione Generale Italiana del Lavoro, 25 Corso d'Italia, 00198 Roma
CISL Confederazione Italiana Sindacati Lavoratori, 21 via PO, 00198, Roma
UIL Unione Italiana de Lavoro, 6 via Lucullo, 00187 Roma

Metalworkers
FLM Corso Trieste 36, 00198 Roma

Textile and Clothing Workers
CGIL Federazione Italiana Lavoratori Tessili e Abbigliamento, 25 Corso d'Italia, 00198 Roma
CISL Federazione Italiana dei Lavoratori Tessili e Abbigliamento, Viale Lungigiana 5, 20125 Milano
UIL Unione Italiana Lavoratori Tessili, Via Gherardini 2, 20145 Milano

Food and Agricultural Workers
CGIL Federazione Italiana Lavoratori Zuccherieri Industrie Alimentari Tabacchine, Via Viminale 43, 00198 Roma
CISL Federazione Unitaria Lavoratori Prodotti Industrie Alimentari, Via Romagna 17, 00187 Roma
UIL Unione Italiana Lavoratori Industrie Alimentari, via Sicilia 154, 00187 Roma

Railway Workers
CGIL Sindacato Ferrovieri Italiani, Via Vicenza 5A, Roma
CISL Sindacato Italiano Unitario Ferrovieri, Piazza Sallustio 9, Roma
UIL Sindacato Autonomo Unificato Ferrovieri Italiani, Via Degli Ana-
mari n 20, Roma 3.

Chemical Workers
CGIL FILCEA, Corso d'Italia 25, 00198 Roma
CISL Federchimici, Via Isonzo 42, 00198 Roma
UIL UILCID, Viale Piave 21, 20129 Milano

Construction and Wood Workers
CGIL FILLEA, Via Boncompagni 9, 00187 Roma
CISL FILCA, Via PO 22, 00198 Roma
UIL FENEAL, Via Savoia 82, 00198 Roma

Port and Transport Workers
CISL Federazione Italiana Lavoratori dei Porti, via Piave 61, Roma
UIL Unione Italiana Lavoratori Transporti, via Palestro 78, Roma

Seamen
CISL Federazione Italiana Lavoratori del Mare, via Cassiodoro 19,
Roma
UIL Unione Italiana Marittimi, via Lucullo 6, 00187 Roma

Printing Workers
CGIL FILPC, Via Piemonte 39, 00187 Roma
CISL Federlibro, Via Volturno 42, 00185 Roma
UIL FILAGC, Via Sicilia 154, 00187 Roma

Agricultural Workers
CGIL FNMC, Via Boncompagni 19, 00187 Roma
CISL Federcoltivatori, Via Tevere 22, 00198 Roma
UIL UIMEC, Via XX Settembre 18, 10122 Torino

Local Government Workers
CGIL FNDEL, Via Boncompagni 19, 00187 Roma
CISL FIDEL, Via Tevere 44, 00198 Roma
UIL UNDEL, Piazza Statuto 18, 10122, Torino

Civil Servants
CGIL FNDS, Via Boncompagni 19, 00187 Roma
CISL FILS, Via Livenza 7, 00198 Roma
UIL UILDEP, Via Lucullo 6, 00187 Roma

Electricians
CGIL FILCEA, Corso d'Italia 25, 00198 Roma
CISL FLAEI, Via Salaria 83, 00198 Roma
UIL UILCID, Viale Piave 21, 20129 Milano

Urban Transport Workers
CGIL FIAI, Via Amendola 5, 00185 Roma
CISI FILTAT, Via Nizza 45, 00198 Roma
UIL UILSP, Via Bormida 1, 00198 Roma

BELGIUM

Central Confederations
FGTB Fédération Générale du Travail de Belgique, rue Haute 42, Brussels 1000
CSC Confédération des Syndicats Chrétiens de Belgique, rue de la Loi 135, Brussels 1040

Food Workers
FGTB Centrale des Travailleurs de l'Alimentation et de l'Hotellerie, rue de la Loi 110, Brussels 1040
CSC Centrale Chrétienne des Travailleurs de l'Alimentation, rue de l'Association 27, Brussels 1000

Textile Workers
FGTB Centrale des Ouvriers Textiles de Belgique, Keizer Karelstraat 98, Gent 9000
CSC Centrale Chrétienne des Travailleurs du Textile et du Vêtement de Belgique, Koning Albertlaan 27, Gent 9000 (includes clothing workers)

Clothing Workers
FGTB Centrale du Vêtement et Parties Similaires de Belgique, Ommeganckstraat 32, Antwerp 2000

Metalworkers
FGTB Centrale des Métallurgistes de Belgique, rue Jacques Jordaens 17, Brussels 1050
CSC Centrale Chrétienne des Métallurgistes de Belgique, rue de Heembeek 127, Brussels 1120

Miners
FGTB Centrale Syndicale des Travailleurs des Mines de Belgique, rue Joseph Stevens 8, Brussels 1000
CSC Centrale des Francs Mineurs, avenue d'Auderghem 26–32, Brussels 1040

Transport Workers
FGTB Union Belge des Ouvriers du Transport, Paardenmarkt 66, Antwerp 2000
CSC Centrale Chrétienne des Ouvriers du Transport, Entrepotplaats 12–14, Antwerp 2000

Public Service Workers
FGTB Centrale Générale des Services Publics, Place Fontainas 9–11,

Brussels 1000 (including railway, gas, electricity, postal, telecommunications and bus transport workers)
csc Centrale Chrétienne des Services Publics, avenue d'Auderghem 26, Brussels 1040

Building Workers
csc Centrale Chrétienne des Travailleurs du Bois et du Bâtiment, rue de Trèves 33, Brussels 1040

Chemical Workers
csc Centrale Chrétienne de l'Energie, de la Chimi et du Cuir, avenue d'Auderghem 26–32, Brussels 1040

Railway Workers
FGTB as for public service workers
csc Syndicat Chrétien du Personnel des Chemins de Fer, avenue d'Auderghem 26–32, Brussels 1040 (includes postal and telecommunications workers)

General Workers
FGTB La Centrale Générale, rue Watteeu 6, Brussels 1000

HOLLAND

Central Confederation
NVV Nederlands Verbond van Vakvereningingen, Plein 40–45, No. 1, Amsterdam W
NKV Nederlands Katholiek Vakverbond, 12 Oudenoord, Utrecht
CNV Christelijk Nationaal Vakverbond, 1 Ravellaan, Utrecht

Civil Servants
NVV Algemene Bond van Ambtenaren, Stadhouderslaan 9, Den Haag
NKV Katholiek Bond van Overheidspersoneel, Mesdagstraat 118, Den Haag
CNV Nederlands Christelijk Bond van Overheidspersoneel, Postbus 1804, 's Gravenhage

Agriculture and Food Workers
NVV Agrarische en Voedingsbedryfsbond, Goeman Borgesuislan 77, Utrecht
NKV Katholiek Bond van Personeel in Agrarische, Voedings- en Genotmiddelen, Zaanenstraat 18, Haarlem
CNV Christelijke Bond van Werknemers in de Voedings – Agrarische, Mauritsstraat 45–47, Utrecht

Industrial Workers
NVV Industriebond NVV, Plein 40–45 No. 1, Amsterdam W
NKV Industriebond NKV, Maliebaan 34, Utrecht
CNV Industriebond CNV, Nijenoord 2, Utrecht

Building and Wood Workers
NVV Algemene Nederlandse Bond voor de Bouw- en Houtnijverheld, Plein 40–45, No. 1, Amsterdam W
NKV Nederlands Katholiek Bond voor de Bouw- en Houtnijverheld, Drift 8, Utrecht
CNV Hout- en Bouwbond, Kromme Nieuwegracht 22, Utrecht

Transport Workers
NVV Nederlandse Bond van Vervoerspersoneel, Goeman Borgesiuslaan 77, Utrecht
NKV Nederlandse Katholiek Bond van Vervoerspersoneel, Drift 10–12, Utrecht
CNV Algemene Christelijke Bond van Vervoerspersoneel, Kromme Nieuwegracht 50, Utrecht

Printing Workers
NVV Algemene Nederlandse Grafische Bond, Koninginneweg 20, Amsterdam
NKV Nederlandse Katholiek Grafische Bond, PC Hoofstraat, 170–172, Amsterdam
CNV Nederlandse Christelijke Grafische Bedrijfsbond, Valeriusplein 30, Amsterdam 2

Teachers
NVV Algemene Bond van Onderwijzend Personeel, Herengracht 56, Amsterdam
CNV Vereniging van Christelijke Leranen en Leraressen, Beneluxlaan 14, Utrecht

Shop, Clerical and Managerial Staffs
NVV Algemene Bond Mercurius, Plein 40–45, no. 1, Amsterdam W
NKV Unie van Beamten, Leideinggevend en Hoger Personeel, Maliestraat 5, Utrecht
NKV Katholiek Bond van Personeel in de Handel, Oudenoord 12, Utrecht
CNV Nederlandse Christelijke Vereniging van Hoger Personeel, Maantensdijklaan 344, 's-Gravenhage

Miners
NKV Nederlandse Katholiek Mijnwerkersbond, Schinkelstraat 13, Heerlen

Seamen
NVV Federatie van Werknemerorganisaties m de Zeevaart, Heemraadssingel 323, Rotterdam 6

GERMANY

Central Confederation
DGB Deutscher Gewerkschaftsbund, 4, Dusseldorf 30, Hans-Bockler Strasse 39, Postfach 2601

Building Workers
I.G. Bau, Steine, Erden, 6, Frankfurt/Maine, Bockenheimer Landstrasse 73–77, Postfach 3049

Mining Workers
I.G. Bergbau und Energie, 463, Bochum, alte Hatlinger Strasse 19, Postfach 1229

Printing and Paper Workers
I.G. Druck und Papier, 7, Stuttgart 1, Friedrichstrasse 15, Postfach 1282

Railway Workers
Gewerkschaft der Eisenbahner Deutschlands, 6, Frankfurt/Maine, Beethovenstrasse 12–16

Education and Scientific Workers
Gewerkschaft Erziehung und Wissenschaft, 6, Frankfurt/Maine, Unterlindan 58, Postfach 180109

Agricultural Workers
Gewerkschaft Gartenbau, Land und Forstwirtschaft, 35, Kassel, Wilhelmshohe 1, Druseltalstrasse 51

Bank, Insurance and Commercial Workers
Gewerkschaft Handel, Banken und Versicherungen, 4, Dusseldorf 30, Tersteegenstrasse, 30, Postfach 729

Woodworkers
Gewerkschaft Holz und Kunstoff, 4, Dusseldorf 1, Sonnenstrasse 14

Leather Workers
Gewerkschaft Leder, 7, Stuttgart 1, Theodor-Heuss Strasse 2A

Metalworkers
I.G. Metall, 6, Frankfurt/Maine, Wilhelm-Leuschner Strasse 79–85, Postfach 3069

Food, Tobacco and Catering Workers
Gewerkschaft Nahrung, Genuss, Gaststatten, 2, Hamburg 1, Gertrudenstrasse 9

Public Service, Transport and Communications Workers
Gewerkschaft Offentliche, Dienste, Transport und Verkehr, 7, Stuttgart 1, Theodor-Heuss Strasse 2

Postal Workers
Deutsche Postgewerkschaft, 6, Frankfurt/Maine 71, Rhonestrasse 2

Textile and Clothing Workers
Gewerkschaft Textil-Bekleidung, 4, Dusseldorf 30, Rossstrasse 94, Postfach 3509

Musicians and Artists
Gewerkschaft Kunst, 4, Dusseldorf 1, Hans-Bockler-Haus, Hans-Bockler Strasse, 39, Postfach 2601

Chemical Workers
I.G. Chemie, Papier, Keramik, 3, Hannover, Konigsworther Platz 6

DENMARK

Central Confederation
LO Landsorganisationen i Danmark, Rosenørns Alle, 1970, Copenhagen V

General Workers
Arbejdsmands og Specialiarbejder Forbund Dansk, Nyropsgade 25, DK-1602, Copenhagen V

Clothing Workers
Beklaedingsarbejderforbund Dansk, Vendersgade 29, DK-1363, Copenhagen K

Electrical Workers
Elektrikerforbund Dansk, Hauchsvej 17, DK-1825, Copenhagen V

Shop and Clerical Workers
Handels og Kontordunktimaerenes Forbund i Dankmark, Hans Christian Andersens Boulevard 43, DK-1553, Copenhagen V

Railway Workers
General – Jernbaneforbund Dansk, Tjenestemaendenes Hus, Bredgade 21, DK-1260, Copenhagen K
Train drivers – Lokomotivmands Forening Dansk, Hellerupvej 44, DK-2900, Hellerup

Textile Workers
Textilarbejderforbund Dansk, Nyropsgade 14, DK-1602, Copenhagen V

Metalworkers
Metalarbejderforbund Dansk, Nyropsgade 38, DK-1602, Copenhagen V

Printers
Typograf-Forbund Dansk, Martinswej 8, DK-1926, Copenhagen V

Plumbers
Blikkenslager Sanitet og Rorarbejderforbundet i Danmark, Mimersgade 47, DK-2200, Copenhagen

Public Employees
Kommunalerbejderforbund, Thorvaldsenvej 2, DK-1871, Copenhagen V

Women Workers
Kvindeligt Arbejderforbund i Danmark, Ewaldsgade 3, DK-2200, Copenhagen N

Seamen
Sømaendenes Forbund i Danmark, Herluf Trollesgade 5, 1052, Copenhagen K

Painters
Malerforbundet i Danmark, Tomsgardvej 23 C, DK-2400, Copenhagen-NV

Bricklayers
Murerforbundet i Danmark, Mimersgade 47, DK-2200, Copenhagen N

Postal Workers
Postforbund Dansk, Vodroffvej 13, DK-1900, Copenhagen V

Boot and Shoe Workers
Skotojsarbejderforbund Dansk, Niels Ebbesens Vej 27, DK-1911, Copenhagen V

Slaughterhouse Workers
Slagteriarbejderforbund Dansk, Lundsgade 9, DK-2100, Copenhagen Ø

Joiners and Cabinet Makers
Sneder og Tomrerforbundet i Danmark, Mimersgade 47, DK-2200, Copenhagen N

Wood Workers
Traeindustriarbejderforbundet i Danmark, Mimersgade 47, 2, DK-2200, Copenhagen N

SWEDEN

Central Confederation
LO Landsorganisationen i Sverige, Barnhusgaten 18, PA 105 53, Stockholm

Textile and Clothing Workers
Bekladnadsarbetarnas Forbund, Box 1129, S 111 81, Stockholm 1

Sheet Metal Workers
Svenska Blech- och Platslagareforbundet, Horngaten 120, S 117 21, Stockholm

Building Workers
Svenska Byggnadsarbetareforbundet, Box 19013, S 104 32, Stockholm 19

Electricians
Svenska Elektrikerforbundet, Box 1123, S 111 81, Stockholm 1

Factory Workers
Svenska Fabriksarbetareforbundet, Box 1114, S 111 81, Stockholm

Building Maintenance Workers
Fastighetsanstalldas Forbund, Kungsholms Strand 125, S 112 34, Stockholm

Hairdressers
Svenska Frisorarbetareforbundet, Box 1146, S 111 81, Stockholm 1

Insurance Workers
Forsakringsanstalldas Forbund, Box 1119, S 111 81, Stockholm 1

Graphic Industry Workers
Grafiska Fackforbundet, Box 1101, S 111 81, Stockholm 1

Miners
Svenska Gruvindustriarbetareforbundet, Box 19, S 772 01, Grangesberg 1

Commercial Workers
Handelsanstalldas Forbund, Fack S 200 70, Malmo

Hotel and Restaurant Workers
Hotell- och Restauranganstalldas Forbund, Box 1143, S 111 81, Stockholm 1

Municipal Workers
Svenska Kommunalarbetareforbundet, Box 19039, S 104 32, Stockholm 19

Agricultural Workers
Svenska Lantarbetareforbundet, Box 1104, S 111 81, Stockholm 1

Food Workers
Svenska Livsmedelsarbetareforbundet, Box 1156, S 111 81, Stockholm 1

Metalworkers
Svenska Metallindustriarbetareforbundet, Torsgatan 10, 6tr., S 105 52, Stockholm

Musicians
Svenska Musikerforbundet, Box 43, S 101 20, Stockholm 1

Painters
Svenska Malareforbundet, Box 1113, S 111 81, Stockholm 1

Pulp and Paper Workers
Svenska Pappersindustriarbetareforbundet, Box 1127, S 111 81, Stockholm

Seamen
Svenska Sjofolksforbundet, Jarntorget 1, 7tr. Folkets Hus, S 413 04, Goteborg

Forestry Workers
Svenska Skogsarbetareforbundet, Box 903, S 801 32, Gavle 1

Chimney Sweeps
Svenska Skorstensfejeriarbetareforbundet, Saltmatargatan 14, 2 tr., S 113 59, Stockholm

Civil Servants
Statsanstalldas Forbund, Box 1105, S 111 81, Stockholm 1

Transport Workers
Svenska Transportarbetareforbundet, Box 158, S 101 22, Stockholm 1

Woodworkers
Svenska Traindustriarbetareforbundet, Box 1152, S 111 81, Stockholm

NORWAY

Central Confederation
LO Landsorganisasjonen i Norge, Folkets Hus, Youngsgate 11, Oslo

Metalworkers
Nors Jern- og Metallarbeiderforbund, Folket Hus, Youngsgate 11, Oslo

Textile and Clothing Workers
Bekledningsarbeiderforbundet, Folkets Hus, Youngsgate 11, Oslo

Railway Workers
General – Norsk Jernbaneforbund, Storgaten 23 c, Oslo
Train drivers — Norsk Lokomotivmandsforbund, Storgaten 23 d, Oslo

Food Workers
Norsk Naerings- og Nytelsemiddlelarbelderforbund, Arbeidersamfunnetsplass 1, Oslo

Transport Workers
Norsk Transportarbeiderforbund, Folkets Hus, Youngsgate 11, Oslo

Seamen
Norsk Sjømannsforbund, Sjømennenes Hus, Grev Wedelsplass 7, Oslo

General Workers
Norsk Arbeidsmandsforbund, Møllergt. 3, Oslo 1

Building Workers
Norsk Bygningsindustriarbeiderforbund, Henrik Ibsensgt 7, Oslo 1

Electricians and Power Station Workers
Norsk Elektriker og Kraftstasjonforbund, Folkets Hus, Youngsgate 11, Oslo

Commercial and Office Workers
Norges Handels og Kontorfunksjonaerers Forbund, Folkets Hus, Youngsgate 11, Oslo

Printing Industry Workers
Norsk Grafisk Forbund, Arbeidersamfunnets Pl 1, Oslo 1

Chemical Workers
Norsk Kjemisk Industriarbeiderforbund, Folkets Hus, Youngsgate 11, Oslo

Bricklayers
Norsk Murerforbund, Storgt. 23c, Oslo 1

Paper Industry Workers
Norsk Papirindustriarbeiderforbund, Arbeidersamfunnets Pl, 1 Oslo 1

Postal Workers
Norsk Postforbund, Storgt. 23c, Oslo 1

Telegraph and Telephone Workers
Norsk Tele Tjeneste Forbund, Torgt, 17 vll, Oslo 1

Forestry and Agricultural Workers
Norsk Skog og Landsarbeiderforbund, Arbeidersamfunnets Pl 1, Oslo 1

Civil Servants
Norsk Tjenestemannslag, Hammarborg torg. 1, Oslo 1

Wood Workers
Norsk Treindustriarbeiderforbund, Storgt. 23v, Oslo 1

Notes

Chapter 1
1 Walter Kendall's recent book *The Labour Movement in Europe* (Allen Lane, 1975) is the first work to come to grips with this European dimension of continental trade unionism.
2 Walter Kendall, 'Some Problems of Methodology Encountered in a Study of European Labour Movements' (mimeographed, 1973).
3 E. J. Hobsbawn, *Industry and Empire* (Penguin, 1969), p. 289.
4 Robert Michels, *Political Parties* (Jarrold, 1915).
5 S. M. Lipset, M. A. Trow and J. S. Coleman, *Union Democracy* (Glencoe, Illinois: The Free Press, 1956).
6 The point is argued most forcefully by Richard Fletcher, 'Trade Union Democracy, Structural Factors', in *Trade Union Register*, ed. K. Coates and T. Topham (Merlin Press, 1970), and 'Trade Union Democracy: The Case of the AUEW Rule Book', *Trade Union Register* 3, ed. K. Coates and T. Topham (Spokesman Books, 1973).
7 John Hughes, *Trade Union Structure and Government*, Research Paper No. 5, part 2 (Royal Commission on Trade Unions and Employers' Associations, 1968), p. 8.
8 J. David Edelstein, 'An Organisational Theory of Union Democracy', *American Sociological Review*, vol. 32 (February 1967), pp. 19–31. Indeed Edelstein recognises the importance for union democracy of such factors as: an independent appeal system; frequent conferences; the accountability of top officers to the executive; and the political culture of the country, while regarding the closeness of elections for high office as the acid test of the degree to which these other elements influence particular situations. See J. David Edelstein and Malcolm Warner, *Comparative Union Democracy* (George Allen & Unwin, 1975).
9 Roderick Martin, 'Union Democracy: An Explanatory Framework', *Sociology* (May 1968), pp. 209–20.
10 V. L. Allen, *Power in Trade Unions* (Longmans, 1954).
11 Walter Galenson, *Trade Union Democracy in Western Europe* (University of California Press, 1961).
12 Sabine Erbes-Seguin, *Democratie dans les Syndicats* (Paris: Mouton, 1971).
13 'The Miners' Next Step' (Unofficial Reform Committee, 1912).
14 G. D. H. Cole, *The World of Labour* (Harvester Press, 1973), p. 259.
15 B. and S. Webb, *Industrial Democracy* (Longmans, 1913).
16 H. A. Turner, *Trade Union Growth, Structure and Policy* (George Allen & Unwin, 1962), p. 89.
17 J. A. Banks, *Trade Unionism* (Collier Macmillan, 1974), p. 89.
18 Edelstein, op. cit., p. vii.

Chapter 2
1 For the sake of conciseness and because FO represents only a minority of

trade unionists, most references to the French trade unions will be limited to the CGT and CFDT.

2 For a detailed discussion of the style of leadership at the confederal level, *see* Kendall, op. cit., pp. 70–2.

3 Dues figures quoted here and in subsequent sections were those in force in late 1973 and early 1974. They have been converted to sterling at January 1974 exchange rates.

4 Seyfarth, Shaw, Fairweather and Geraldson, *Labour Relations and the Law in Italy and the United States* (University of Michigan, 1970), p. 5.

5 Maurice Neufeld, 'The Italian Labour Movement in 1956', *The Annals of the American Academy*, vol. 310 (March 1957), p. 75.

6 On this *see* Kendall, op. cit., p. 159.

7 For the sake of conciseness most examples of Dutch trade union practices will be drawn from the NVV and NKV.

8 Seyforth, Shaw, Fairweather and Geraldson, *Labour Relations and the Law in West Germany and the United States* (University of Michigan, 1969), p. 13.

9 *The Trade Union Situation in Sweden* (International Labour Office, 1961), p. 13.

Chapter 3
1 Seyforth, Shaw, Fairweather and Geraldson, *Labour Relations and the Law in West Germany and the United States* (University of Michigan, Bureau of Business Research), p. 92.

2 Ordnance of February 1945.

3 Italian works councils were not required by law. They first appeared in 1943 and their role was subsequently formalised in collective agreements in 1953 and 1956.

4 Works Council Act, 1950. Amended in September 1970.

5 Works Constitution Act, October 1952. Amended in 1972.

6 Law of 20 September 1948. Amended 27 November 1973.

7 CIR, *Industrial Relations at Establishment Level: A Statistical Survey* (HMSO, 1973), p. 4.

8 'Worker Participation and Collective Bargaining in Europe', Commission on Industrial Relations, Study no. 4 (1974), p. 89.

Chapter 4
1 Banks, op. cit., p. 88.

2 *Engineering Voice* (August 1974).

3 B. C. Roberts, *Trade Union Government and Administration in Great Britain* (Bell, 1956), p. 168.

4 V. L. Allen, *Power in Trade Unions* (Longmans, 1954), p. 101.

Chapter 5
1 In the following discussion the term 'general council' is used to describe bodies that come between the executive and conference and usually act as the highest authority between conferences. In different unions these are given different names. Similarly, the term 'executive committee' is used to describe the union body directly responsible for supervising the national officers. Again different unions call this body by different names.

Chapter 6
1 Edelstein and Warner, op. cit., p. 351.

2 V. L. Allen, *Trade Union Leadership* (Longmans, 1957), p. 216.

3 Ibid., p. 249.
4 H. A. Clegg, A. J. Killick and R. Adams, *Trade Union Officers* (Blackwell, 1961), p. 40.
5 *Donovan Report*, p. 188.
6 V. L. Allen, *Power in Trade Unions* (Longmans, 1954), pp. 203–4.
7 The salaries referred to in this section were those in force in late 1973 and early 1974.
8 Computed from *ILO Yearbook of Labour Statistics* (Geneva, 1974).
9 ibid.
10 1973 earnings figures for industry generally are not available. Latest statistics indicate that for a five-day week workers in the non-agricultural sector earned £42·70 in 1971. (*ILO Yearbook of Labour Statistics*, 1974.)
11 *ILO Yearbook of Labour Statistics* (Geneva, 1974).
12 Ibid.
13 Ibid.
14 Ibid.
15 Clegg, Killick and Adams, op. cit., p. 103.

Chapter 7
1 Y. Delamotte, 'Recent Trends in Collective Bargaining in France', *ILO Review* (1971), p. 375.

Chapter 8
1 Edelstein and Warner, op. cit., p. 19–20.

Index of Union Organisations

101; conference, full-time officials at 92; conference, mandating of delegates to 103; conference procedure 99; dues of
44; executive committee, election of 122; final appeals 106;
full-time officials, ratio to members 146, 155; full-time officials,
salaries of 150; general council,
composition of 119; general
council, election of 113; membership of 43; national officials,
age of 138; national officials,
number of 138; regional and
local officials 145; strike pay of
187; trust men 67; union journal
127
Railway workers (Gewerkschaft
der Eisenbahner Deutschlands):
administrative and professional
staff of 153–4; conference,
chairmanship of 101; con-
ference, full-time officials at 92;
conference, mandating of
delegates to 103; dues of 44;
executive committee, election of
122; final appeals 106; full-time
officials, ratio to members 146;
general council, composition of
119; general council, election of
113; membership of 44; national
officials, age of 138; national
officials, number of 138; regional
and local officials, number of
145; trust men 67; union journal
127
Textile workers (Gewerkschaft
Textil-Bekleidung): administrative and professional staff of
153–4; collective bargaining,
formulation of demands 183;
conference, chairmanship of
101; conference, full-time officials at 92; conference, management of 99; conference, mandating of delegates to 103; dues
of 44; executive committee,
election of 122; full-time officials, ratio to members 146;
full-time officials, salaries of
150; general council, election of
113; membership of 43–4;
national officials, age of 138;
national officials, number of

138; regional and local officials,
number of 145–6; trust men 67;
trust men, selection of 72; union
journal 127

European Trade Union Confederation (ETUC) 17

Fédération Générale du Travail de
Belgique (FGTB): affiliates,
number of 34; dues, income of
37; membership of 34; political
base of 33; structure of 34–5
FGTB metalworkers' (Centrale des
Métallurgistes de Belgique):
administrative and professional
staff of 153; collective bargaining, formulation of demands
182; combine organisation 76–7;
conference, chairmanship of
100; conference, full-time officials at 91; conference, mandating of delegates to 102–3; conference procedure 97; dues of
37; executive committee, election of 122; executive committee, frequency of meetings
124; final appeals 105; full-time
officials, ratio to members 144;
full-time officials, salaries of
149; general council, composition of 118; general council,
election of 113; membership of
35–6; national officials, election
of 136; plant delegates 64; plant
delegates, election of 71;
regional officials, election of
144; regional officials, number
of 143
FGTB public service workers', *see*
railway workers
FGTB railway workers (Centrale
Générale des Services Publics):
conference, chairmanship of
100; dues of 37; executive committee, election of 122; final
appeals 105; full-time officials,
salaries of 149; general council,
composition of 118; general
council, election of 113; membership of 35–6; national officials, election of 136; regional
officials 143; shop delegates,
election of 71; strike pay of 186

cials, age of 139; shop stewards of 67–8; shop stewards, election of 72

Landsorganisasjonen i Norge (LO): collective bargaining 179–80, 184–5; dues, income of 53; membership of 51; political base of 51; shop stewards 68; strike pay of 189; structure of 51–2

Locomotive engineers 53

Metalworkers' (Jern-og Metal-larbeiderforbund): collective bargaining, formulation of demands 184; conference committees 100; conference, full-time officials at 92; conference, mandating of delegate to 104; dues of 53; executive committee, election of 122; final appeals 106–7; full-time officials, ratio to members 147, 155; full-time officials, salaries of 151; general council, composition of 120; general council, election of 112; membership of 52; national officials, election of 140; national officials, number of 140; regional officials, number of 147; shop stewards 69; shop stewards, election of 73–4; strike pay of 189, 191

Railway workers (Jernbanefor-bund): collective bargaining 180; collective bargaining, formulation of demands 184; conference committees 100; executive committee, election of 122; full-time officials, ratio to members 147; general council 115; membership of 53; national officials, number of 140; shop stewards 69; shop stewards, election of 73

Textile Workers' (Beklednings-arbeiderforbundet): collective bargaining 180–1; collective bargaining, formulation of demands 184; collective bargaining, ratification of settlements 189; conference committees 100; conference, full-time officials at 92; conference, mandating of delegates to 104; dues of 53; execu-

tive committee, election of 122; full-time officials, ratio to members 147; full-time officials, salaries of 151; general council, composition of 120; general council, election of 113; membership of 52–3; national officials, election of 140; national officials, number of 140; shop stewards 69; shop stewards, election of 73

Landsorganisationen i Sverige (LO): affiliates, number of 48; collective bargaining 175–77; collective bargaining, formulation of demands 184; dues, income of 50–1; membership of 48; political base of 48; strike pay of 189; structure of 48–9

Metalworkers' (Metallindustri-arbetareforbundet): administrative and professional staff of 154; collective bargaining, formulation of demands 184; collective bargaining, ratification of settlements 188–9; combine organisation 80; conference, chairmanship of 101; conference, full-time officials at 92; conference procedure 100; dues of 51; executive committee, election of 122; final appeals 106; full-time branch officials 146–7; full-time officials, ratio to members 147; full-time officials, salaries of 151; general council, composition of 120; general council, election of 113; membership of 49; and nationalisation 50; national officials, number of 139; shop stewards 68, 79–80; shop stewards, election of 73; strike pay of 189; union journal 127

Public Service workers, *see* Railway workers

Railway workers (Statsanstalldas Forbund): collective bargaining 177, 189; collective bargaining, formulation of demands 184; conference, chairmanship of 101; conference, full-time officials at 92; dues of 50–1; full-

Index of Subjects